NOTHING IS WASTED

A Spiritual Journey from Fear and Judgment to Grace and Mystery

MARILYN J. BENSON

Edited by Kerry Stapley

"Tell the Truth But Tell It Slant" was previously published as "The Power of a Third Thing: A Process for Peer Supervision" in *Presence: An International Journal of Spiritual Direction + Companionship*, Vol. 28, No. 01, March 2022

ISBN 13: 978-1-64343-506-0
Library of Congress Catalog Number: Applied for
Printed in the United States of America
First Printing: 2025
29 28 27 26 25 5 4 3 2 1

Book design and typesetting by Dan Pitts

Beaver's Pond Press
526 Seventh Street West
Saint Paul, MN 55102
(952) 829-8818
www.BeaversPondPress.com

Contact Marilyn J. Benson at marilynjbenson.com for speaking engagements, book club discussions, and interviews.

To Tim, with love and gratitude

Advance Praise

"I deeply admire this book, and the human journey it chronicles candor—a journey from fear and guilt to grace and mystery. Mari son writes wonderfully well about difficult topics, including her qu liberation from the distortions of fundamentalism. That quest took a more reliable form of faith, one rooted in both the natural world anc human world of friendship and family. Like all of us, she made mista along the way, but as her title suggests, nothing is wasted: experiencing th darkness can open us to the light. If you're looking for light in the dark, I believe you will find it here, as I did."

—Parker J. Palmer, author of *Let Your Life Speak*,
A Hidden Wholeness, and *Healing the Heart of Democracy*

"Penning a spiritual memoir is an act of courage, especially if one leaves room for unknowing rather than easy certitude. Forthright, yet lyrical, the author narrates a journey from fundamentalist constriction . . . to a faithful stance of wondering in the face of mystery. Rich in acquaintance with deep spiritual traditions and poetic imagination, this skilled practitioner of spiritual direction and pastoral counseling shines light on the pathway toward human wholeness. Reading this memoir has both deepened my faith and my questions."

—Rev. Molly T. Marshall, PhD, president,
United Theological Seminary of the Twin Cities

"As readers we walk with Marilyn through vivid and vulnerable accounts of her life as she shows us, in an unassuming way, what it's like to tend to the inner life. She narrates how she has lived into important questions, the same ones that so many of us wrestle with: How might one heal from spiritual abuse and heartbreak? How do we overcome guilt and shame and move toward forgiveness? How do we integrate faith language into our own lives so that we can also live authentically, courageously, and with gratitude? I highly recommend this engaging and wise book to everyone, especially to those o both give and receive pastoral counseling and spiritual direction."

—Peter Watkins, MDiv, spiritual director and faculty member at Sacred Ground Center for Spirituality and School for Formation

"The journey from a childhood haunted by fear of the Rapture and its abandonment of the unsaved takes the reader through many shifts of worldviews and experiences to arrive at an adult mind. Benson manages these expansions without discarding the protective 'ropes' of her childhood faith. College, participation in the wider world, the examination of philosophers Martin Buber and Richard Rohr are a few of the markers of her ever-expanding world into maturity and critical thinking . . . *Nothing Is Wasted* is an apt title for this book and this attitude. The following poses the questions of her search:

> *I come back again and again to the image of a rope stretched between two places, a rope that allows safe passage. I wonder about the rope that was put in place for me in my childhood. . . . How did I grow not to trust it? Why didn't I believe it could keep me safe?*

With those questions, we readers are in the poetic hands of an experienced writer and thinker."

—Mary Moore Easter, author of poetry book *The Body of the World* and the memoir *The Way She Wants to Get There: Telling on Myself*

"By exposing her painful life experiences with vulnerability, Benson does more than share her story, she invites the reader to uncover their own narratives, encouraging them to read themselves as living texts in need of compassion and interpretation. While it is her story . . . it is also a celebration of the universal journey of liberation and sovereignty."

—Dr. Suzanne M. Begin, executive director, ARC Retreat Community

"She speaks in a comfortable voice, becoming for readers a mentor, companion, and beloved friend. Sensual detail—*Wet mittens rest on the shelf above the kitchen range,/ winter smell filling the room,/ Warm wet wool and farm animals*—grounds the telling in immediacy. Each story unfolds the way a life unfolds. Readers, especially those on their own spiritual journeys, will find themselves in these pages."

—Ranae Lenor Hanson, author of
Watershed: Attending to Body and Earth in Distress

"A story of the consequences of a strict fundamentalist Christian formation on a young girl and . . . [her] decades-long struggle to move beyond restrictive teachings and male-dominated theology to a transforming theology of goodness, love, and self-trust."

—Ruth Halvorson, founding director,
ARC Retreat Community

Contents

Prologue

I first read W. H. Auden's poem "For the Time Being: A Christmas Oratorio" in graduate school. I was twenty-three. Ten years later—after a marriage, my daughter's birth, and a divorce—I typed the following lines from the poem on an index card and pinned it to the bulletin board above my desk:

> For the garden is the only place there is, but you will not find it
> Until you have looked for it everywhere and found nowhere that
>   is not a desert;
> The miracle is the only thing that happens, but to you it will not
>   be apparent,
> Until all events have been studied and nothing happens that you
>   cannot explain;
> And life is the destiny you are bound to refuse until you have
>   consented to die.[1]

The card is there still, yellow and stained. I am now eighty-four. Auden reminds me of the myriad ways I have tried to understand and control my life, until yet one more time, I surrender to not knowing, not controlling. Even in the writing of this memoir, I am trying to understand who I am and how it is that I have come to be who I am.

What I do know is that two entwined forces shaped me and my trajectory into the world: conservative Christianity and being a girl (and then a woman) in a male-dominated world. That these forces shaped me is not unique, although my life, like all lives, is. The chapters that follow are windows into a lifelong story of coming to awareness of what shaped me, of trying to disregard it, resenting its power, and reclaiming what can be redeemed. I will tell you some of what I know about being born into a farming family in 1940, the third daughter of white immigrant parents. I will tell you about growing

---

1 W. H. Auden, "For the Time Being: A Christmas Oratorio," in *Collected Poems*, ed. Edward Mendelson (New York: Vintage Books, 1991), 353.

up immersed in fundamentalist, evangelical Christianity. I will tell you about eschewing the religion of my upbringing, finding my own identity, and asking questions that opened the doors that led me inward and onward.

I tell this story as a psychotherapist, a seminary graduate, a spiritual director, a mother, and a grandmother. I write as a woman who has come to claim progressive Christianity, recognizing it is one well among many that reach deep into what theologian Matthew Fox calls the great underground river that links all faiths.[2]

My story is one of searching and having been invited, of choosing and having been chosen. And it is also a story of coming to realize that nothing is wasted. To paraphrase the philosopher Martin Buber, everything that happens in your life is an occasion to listen to God.[3]

---

2 Matthew Fox, *One River, Many Wells* (New York: Jeremy P. Tarcher/Putnam, 2000).
3 Katharine Whiteside Taylor, personal conversation with author about Taylor's conversation with Martin Buber.

PART I:
DISORIENTED

The Rope

In high summer, decades after we had each moved away, my brother and I walked on the farm where we grew up. Over the years he has restored much of the land to prairie. The big bluestem grass and the Maximilian sunflowers are taller than he is. We recalled a story we heard as children: how in the fall, a farmer had stretched a rope from house to barn in advance of the winter blizzards. Because the tall prairie grass had been plowed under and replaced with crops, there was nothing to stop the driven snow from creating disorienting whiteouts. In a snowstorm, a farmer could follow the rope to get to the barn and back safely. But one farmer had let go and lost his way, freezing to death only yards from the safe harbor of house and barn. Like our father, the man was a Swedish immigrant. I heard that story of warning many times as a child.

I come back again and again to the image of a rope stretched between two places, a rope that allows safe passage. I wonder about the rope that was put in place for me in my childhood. How did I grow not to trust it? Why didn't I believe it could keep me safe?

My rope was braided with strands of the farming culture of the Midwest in the middle of the twentieth century, my immigrant parents, and fundamentalist Christianity. As a child, the rope was invisible to me, but I learned early its dominant strand: we were sinners, Jesus had died for our sins, and not getting saved was tantamount to going to hell. I needed to accept Jesus Christ as my Lord and Savior because he might return at any moment to take the saved to be with him forever in heaven. Everyone else would be left behind, doomed to terrible suffering.

I had no choice but to take hold of the rope I was given.

My Mother's Faith

My story begins with my mother's faith.

My mother, Bertha, told her children many times the story of why she left the small village of Voikka, Finland. In large part, it was because her family was hungry before, during, and long after the Finnish Civil War. Lasting several months in 1918, the war was fought for the country's leadership during its transition from a Grand Duchy of the Russian Empire to an independent state. Bertha was nine when troops of "Whites," non-socialists supported by German troops, swept into her village and took all the men and boys—including her father and brother—to the schoolyard. With her mother and two younger sisters, Bertha hid in the root cellar. Many of the village men did not return home that day. They were shot and buried in a mass grave. It is not entirely clear why my grandfather Elias Niilo-Rama and my uncle Einar were allowed to return home. When the Whites asked them when they had joined the resistance, Elias reportedly replied, "I was not the first, but I wasn't the last."

Hunger, in this family of nine children, drove three of Bertha's older sisters to emigrate to Sweden to work as domestic servants. All three of them married Swedish men. One of them, Maija, eventually emigrated with her husband to the United States. When Maija needed help with her children, Bertha was ready to go, and her parents were willing to send her. She waited three years for a visa.

After arriving at Ellis Island in 1926 as a seventeen-year-old who didn't know English, Bertha got on a train with a note pinned to her coat indicating her destination in rural Nebraska. She told of going to sleep on the long train ride, almost missing her stop. On the first night in her sister and brother-in-law's home, several local farmhands were playing cards in the kitchen. One of them was Gustaf, a tall, lean Swede with lots of red-blond hair and a straight nose. She remembered liking the look of him. They married three years later at the beginning of the Great Depression. Their wedding picture shows Gustaf in a dark suit and Bertha in a black dress, choices made for practicality, as dark clothing would be appropriate for funerals and other occasions as well. Bertha's dark hair is marcelled, and around her neck she appears to wear a string of pearls. The two look young and solemn.

Both Bertha in Finland and Gustaf in Sweden were baptized Lutheran as infants, as Lutheranism was the state church of both countries. But Bertha's older sister, Saima, broke from tradition to become a part of the Pentecostal movement in Finland. Pentecostalism emphasized personal experience of God and the baptism of the Holy Spirit. Perhaps knowing that Saima had joined a Pentecostal church explains why newly married Bertha and Gustaf became friends with the Penhallows, a neighboring Nebraska farm family who participated fully in Pentecostal revival culture. In meeting the Penhallows, Bertha found connection, relationship, and community—so much of what she had left on the other side of the Atlantic with her parents, seven siblings, and her best friend, Siiri.

Bertha and Gus began to attend revival meetings with the Penhallows. Soon, my mother had a conversion experience, a classic "walk down the aisle." Bertha responded when the preacher invited attendees to accept Jesus as their personal Lord and Savior. What was it that stirred in her, that drew her to get up and walk forward, to leave the wood bench where she sat with her husband, Gus, and little daughter, Gladys? What did the preacher say that touched her? What was happening within her? Were they singing, "Just as I Am, Without One Plea?" What scripture had been read? She did not remember, but she told how part way down the aisle she looked back and saw Gus following her.

She told the story of her conversion again and again with satisfaction, and I did not doubt it.

In July, in my childhood, when the corn was cultivated and the oats were not yet ready for harvesting, our family drove to Lake Okoboji in Iowa for weeklong revival meetings. The big gray revival tent with its sawdust floor and wood benches was pitched adjacent to the lake and not far from a small amusement park. The raucous merry-go-round music mixed with the sound of our voices singing hymns. The smell of frying food drifted through the tent. Small children dozed in their mothers' arms. The popular R. R. Brown preached every night. I remember the pleading of the preacher, the intense emotion, and people walking down the aisle to get saved.

My mother spoke often of how thankful she was that she and my father had left the dry hills of Nebraska in 1939 for southern Minnesota. They not only found a farm, they found a church as well. Nils Moberg, the land agent who arranged the farm purchase, was a longtime member of the Indian Lake Baptist Church, a historically Swedish congregation. Though ten miles was a long way to drive in those days, the connections my parents made through the Moberg family resulted in our family's full participation in the church and its community for the rest of their lives.

Getting saved worked for my mother, perhaps as well as any preacher could have hoped. It did not work for me. From an early age, my doubts and questions were always with me.

My Place in the Family

As a newly married couple, my parents survived the Great Depression in rural Nebraska, renting land owned by a relative who was willing to install running water for the cattle tanks but not for the house. When they explored moving north to Minnesota to buy a farm in 1939, the uncle told them they would fail and soon return with their tails between their legs. They persisted, moving household, machinery, cattle, and their hopes to 160 acres of fertile land in southwest Minnesota.

While they lived in Nebraska, my mother had given birth to my older sisters, Gladys and Shirley. When they moved, Gladys was nine, Shirley was two, and my mother was pregnant for the third time. Now living on their own land, having been married eleven years, my parents hoped for a son to whom they would someday give their hard-won land.

Throughout the last months of 1939, they waited in anticipation. The birth of a boy would be the culmination of years of dreaming and hard work. They chose a name, David Gustaf, David after my mother's favorite Bible character and Gustaf after my father and the Swedish king.

But I was the child born in January 1940. And as I grew up, I came to know too well the details of the son who wasn't born.

Only one photo exists of just my father and me in childhood. It's black and white. He is in profile, standing slim and tall in dress trousers and a white long-sleeved shirt. It must have been a Sunday morning. All other days of the week he would have been wearing overalls. He is thirty-eight. I am eight months old with a bit of wispy blond hair, wearing a dress that covers my legs. My father is holding me the way I have seen him hold other infants: the child, facing forward, sitting on one of his large hands.

Many times in my childhood, my parents told the story of how they had picked out a boy's name when my mother was pregnant with me. The conversation between my mother and her good friend Violet was not the first time I heard it. Violet went to our church and taught third and fourth grade at the Bigelow elementary school my sisters and I attended. She would drive her Ford Model T to the farm to have afternoon coffee with my mother. I liked listening to their conversations, especially if they were talking about "the girls"—my sisters and me. If they sat in the kitchen, I found something to do in the dining room. And if they went to the dining room, I could easily slip into a corner of the living room where they could not see me. One day, I overheard that my first-grade teacher was pleased I already knew how to read so well, but that she thought I was a bit bossy. Violet wondered if I would grow up to be a teacher like her. Speaking very quietly, my mother said something about how they had really wanted a boy, and they had the name David picked out for a long time. Violet replied, "But you're so glad she's healthy and doing so well." I wanted to keep listening, though I knew I shouldn't eavesdrop.

In 1947, during the early months of my mother's fourth pregnancy, her sister Maija died of uterine cancer. Our family got up early to drive ninety miles to Stanton, Nebraska, for the funeral. It rained and rained all day. At the cemetery, under a dark sky, we stood at the side of the open grave for the prayers. Everyone was quiet. My mother was crying. We could not stay long because we needed to get home to take care of the cattle and hogs. I wanted to sit in the front seat of the car next to my mother, but I crawled in the back. Soon, I began to feel sick. When we were on the bridge over the Elkhorn River, I knew I was going to throw up. My mother pulled me out of the car just in time. I vomited right on the bridge. A few months after Maija's death, my mother's best friend, Margaret, died in childbirth. A month later, my mother gave birth to my brother David. I was seven.

When I was nine and David was two, two cousins from Sweden came to live with us for several years. My parents sponsored their emigration. They were educated adults and were able to find jobs in Worthington. I especially liked Arne. He was in his early twenties and always ready to play softball or race around the house. Arne's older sister, Valborg, looked like a sophisticated French woman with her black hair done in a chignon. She worked in a women's clothing store in Worthington where women were pleased to get her advice. She loved spending time with David. She liked to say that David was teaching her English. I felt left out.

The cousins were living with us when our family had the car accident. That sunny summer Sunday morning Valborg stayed at the farm with David. The rest of us went to church. On the way home, my father stopped at a stop sign at Highway 59. A field of tall corn hid the car coming from the north. It hit us broadside. I must have passed out, because the next thing I remember I was standing in the grassy ditch looking at the upside-down car, watching its wheels spinning slowly. Several men were looking at the car and talking. I realized that my mother was badly hurt. A farmer had come to help us and called an ambulance. A man from the ambulance looked at me and said, "This girl looks all right." Then, frightened and confused, I watched as they loaded my mother, Arne, and my sister Shirley into the ambulance.

The farmer brought me home. Someone else must have given my father a ride to the hospital. Later that day, after my father came home, the hospital called to tell us that my mother had a broken pelvis and would be in the hospital for a long time. Shirley had several cuts and bruises and would probably come home the next day. Arne had a badly bruised leg and some cuts.

That evening, Valborg fed David, put him to bed, and made dinner for the three of us. My father said he wasn't hungry and went outside. I tried to read, but I kept thinking about my mother. When it started to get dark, my father still had not come back into the house. I went outside to see if I could find where he might be. Finally, I saw him in the distance pacing slowly back and forth between the corncrib and the chicken house. I watched him for a long time. The way he walked frightened me. I went back to the house and crawled into bed with my clothes on, the bed I should have been sharing with Shirley. I couldn't stop thinking about my mother in the hospital, and my father, just walking slowly back and forth in the dark. He was alone. I was alone. In the dark.

My mother was hospitalized for six weeks. Only grown-ups and children over twelve were allowed to visit her. Shirley was twelve, so she could go inside. David and I visited her each week, standing outside her hospital window. Valborg held David up so Mother could see him and talk to him. I tried to see her, but the screen blurred everything.

Months later, on a weekly Saturday shopping day in Worthington with our mother, we had an encounter with a neighbor. David was in the stroller, smiling his sweet smile, his blond hair shining in the sunlight. Shirley was pushing the carriage, and I came along behind. Passersby looked at David and smiled. Then Mrs. Rust came down the street wearing her high heels and white gloves. She and her husband lived on the farm across the road from us. Stopping, she greeted Mother and then looked at David and said, "Well, you and Mr. Benson finally got your boy." Looking at Shirley and me, my mother proudly replied in her accented English, "The girls just love him so."

A wave of guilt swept over me. Much of the time I did not "love him so."

Indian Lake Baptist Church

Life for my family revolved around the Indian Lake Baptist Church. Sitting amidst the farmland of Nobles County in southwest Minnesota, its white clapboard building was the center of our social and spiritual life. We were full participants, driving ten miles each way, twice on Sunday and again on Thursday evening for prayer meeting and choir practice. My siblings and I had perfect Sunday school attendance. My older sister Shirley and I sang duets. She sang alto and I sang soprano. When others said to Mother how proud she must be that we sang so well, she would reply, "I just give God the glory."

At every church gathering I heard the language of getting saved. I heard it Sunday morning in worship. I sang it: "What can wash away my sin? Nothing but the blood of Jesus." Most Sunday evening worship services ended with the congregation singing all the verses of "Just as I Am" while the pastor invited us to come forward to be saved or to rededicate our lives to Jesus. As a curious child, often lurking just out of sight, I overheard conversations about whether Catholics, Lutherans, neighbors, and acquaintances were "in" or "out," saved or not saved. It became clear to me that a specific conversion experience was required to be born again. Although these comments did not so much come from my parents as from other adults, they became part of my worldview.

In summer, I attended Daily Vacation Bible School, a weeklong event for children every June. My mother drove us to church daily, stopping to pick up three neighbor girls. If we were early, we ran to play in the cemetery. We were not supposed to step on the graves or climb on the gravestones. I found the graves of lots of babies and two children who were my age when they died. Sometimes we ran down the paths and called out the names on the big stones: Larson, Norberg, Nystrom, Saxon, Swedberg, Anderson, Blixt, Swanson. There were no graves with my family's name yet.

When the bell rang, we entered the church by marching up the wide wooden steps, singing "Onward, Christian Soldiers." The boys, carrying the American and Christian flags, went first, and the girls followed. I especially liked the class where we did "sword drills," an exercise to prove we could find Bible verses. We sat with our Bibles on our laps and our hands at our sides, our starting position. The teacher called out the Bible book, chapter, and verse. I could page through the slippery onion-skin pages of my Bible very fast. When I found the verse, I would stand and begin reading, "Micah 5:7. Then the remnant of Jacob, surrounded by many people, shall be like dew from the Lord . . ." You had to begin reading to prove you had found it and weren't just standing up to be first. I often won.

My Gideon New Testament is inscribed with the words, "Marilyn Joyce Benson accepted Jesus Christ as her Savior on June 7, 1947." I was seven. A teacher must have asked me if I wanted to be saved and then knelt with me on the linoleum floor of the church basement and prayed. She likely told me to ask Jesus to come into my heart. But later, I had no memory of it. And I did not feel saved, not like those adults who stood up and gave their testimonies on Sunday nights with such assurance. Could those words in my New Testament be trusted? By the time I was nine, I did not know with certainty whether I was "in."

Of all the yearly evangelistic meetings I attended, there is one I can still see on the inside of my eyelids. The preacher was tall, with thick black hair and a very loud voice. He used a long black stick to point to a paper chart that stretched across the end wall of the church basement. A diagram of the End Times, it showed people dying amid orange and red flames and black smoke. Their eyes were huge, and their mouths gaped with screams. Some were kneeling, some had thrown themselves face down on the ground, and others were trying to run away. This was the horror that awaited everyone who would be left on Earth at the time of the Rapture—the time Jesus would return to take the saved with him. For years afterward, I was haunted by the terror and despair of those images.

One November afternoon when I was nine, I came home from school on the bus without my sister Shirley, who had stayed at school for an activity. My mother had left a note saying that she and Dad and my two-year-old brother David had gone to town. I knew the routine of feeding the chickens and gathering the eggs; Shirley and I did it every afternoon. I set out to take care of those chores, planning to surprise and please my mother. It was windy and cold with a smell of snow in the air. I pumped the water at the windmill and carried the pails to the chicken house, slopping the cold water down my legs. I opened the big sliding doors of the corncrib, filled the feed buckets with ground feed, carried the buckets to the chicken house, and spread the feed evenly in the troughs. After watering and feeding, I walked back to the house to get the wire egg baskets from the basement. I hated the dark basement, even in daylight. My shins were bruised from the times I stumbled while hurrying up the wooden stairs.

By now it was dusk, and a few dim lights at neighboring farms began to show. I watched the gravel road to the east, waiting to see the lights of our black Oldsmobile. I began to wonder why they were not home yet. I tried singing. Singing was often some protection from my fears, but it did not help this time, not even hymns. I gathered the eggs slowly, telling myself that when I came out of the chicken house, my mother and father would be driving into the yard. But when I emerged, the yard was still empty.

Now it was almost dark. What could be taking them so long? Maybe the Rapture had happened. I latched onto those words from scripture, "One shall be taken, the other left behind." Many nights when I lay in bed with Shirley next to me, I fully expected that she would be taken, and I would be left behind. Perhaps in the last hour, Jesus really had returned to claim the saved. Perhaps the worst had already happened, and our black Oldsmobile was in a ditch, engine still running, Mother, Dad and baby David taken up to heaven.

In the time it took me to walk to the house, a car drove past. I saw more lights in the east, but then I despaired when the second car did not slow down and turn into the driveway. I looked south and saw the lights of the Kramer's farm a mile away, and then north to the Rust's farm across the road. But I was not comforted. The Kramers and Rusts didn't go to our church. They probably weren't saved. I was alone.

I sat on the back steps, the egg basket to one side, my forehead on my knees, my eyes tightly closed. I did not hear the car drive into the yard. I looked up suddenly to see my little brother tumble out of the back seat and run toward me. My body flooded with relief. "Are you just sitting there in the dark?" my mother asked. "Come, help carry in the groceries." I did not tell her how frightened I had been. It did not even occur to me that I could tell her.

I carried these images of terror through childhood. Much of the time I suppressed them. Other times, they hijacked my consciousness. Only in later years did I begin to understand my convoluted childhood logic. For me to confess that I was afraid somehow meant that I must not be saved. If I were saved, I should feel safe and secure. I should be looking forward to Jesus's return. I was afraid, and I did not feel saved—and both confirmed my unredeemed state.

Age of Accountability

I gave my granddaughter what was left of my doll house furniture,
    the grand piano, the green sofa,
    the bathroom sink, the toilet minus the cover.
I could not find the red dustpan and the yellow trash can.

In that farmhouse on the prairie, my doll house stayed upstairs.
Most times I loaded up my furniture and migrated
    to the warm space under the oak buffet,
Perhaps trying out what it would mean to leave.

My father asked,
    "Do the girls have to have all this stuff on the floor?"

My mother was talking to the clerk in Ben Franklin
    when I stole them,
    the red dustpan and the yellow trash can two inches high.
I tried the tiny foot pedal again and again
    before my hand slipped them quietly into my coat pocket.

Home in the farmhouse I burrowed into the bed covers,
    listening to voices coming up through the heat register.
Call her for supper said my mother's voice.
I could not eat.
They thought I must be sick.
I was.

I knew no way to cross the space between my bed
    and the warm kitchen,
No way to run down the stairs and find my place at the table.

What might have happened had I run crying to her?
But I had learned so young that a deed done could not be undone,
    that grace was just a word.

1985

The Farm

One of my earliest memories is my mother telling the story of the little calf who wanted to go to the pasture. It is simple in plot and consists mostly of dialogue.

"Moo, moo, Mama Cow," said Little Calf, "when can we go to the pasture?"
"When the snow melts, Little Calf, then we will go to the pasture."
"Moo, moo, Mama Cow," said Little Calf, "when can we go to the pasture?"
"When the grass gets green, Little Calf, then we will go to the pasture."
"Moo, moo, Mama Cow," said Little Calf, "when can we go to the pasture?"

Little Calf's voice gets more plaintive. Mama Cow's voice is patient. The dialogue continues; Mama Cow's answers vary. Sometimes they must wait for the sun to shine or the grass to get taller or the farmer to open the gate. But finally comes the answer:

"Tomorrow, Little Calf, we will go to the pasture."

And clearly, Little Calf trusts that it will be tomorrow. My mother told this story to me and my three siblings in the farmhouse during the bitter cold of a Minnesota January, feeding the kitchen stove more wood. I believe the story underlying the story was my mother's love for the land and her longing for spring, for warmth, for green growth, for new life. And as well, it expressed the nurture of a mother for her child, and a trust in the seasons, the cycle of life.

My mother also told us many stories about her childhood in the small Finnish village of Voikka in eastern Finland, stories about swimming almost every summer day with her friends and walking two miles to and from a nearby dairy farm for milk. My favorite was the Christmas Eve story. My mother and her two younger sisters were disappointed every Christmas Eve because their older brother Nestor always "went to get the mail" on Christmas Eve and therefore wasn't home when Saint Nicholas knocked on the door. We wanted to know how old she was when she understood that Nestor, all bundled up, scarf over his face, *was* Saint Nicholas. She also told us less happy stories about living through the Finnish Civil War, being hungry, and hiding in the root cellar on more than one occasion.

I loved listening to radio stories, especially "Let's Pretend" on Saturday mornings. The program sponsor was the cereal Cream of Wheat. I can still sing the jingle: "Cream of wheat is so good to eat that we have it every day. It makes us strong. . . . and makes us shout 'Hurray.'" Sometimes I would stand on a kitchen chair with my head near the radio, which sat atop the refrigerator, so I could hear more clearly.

And then there were the Bible stories. On Saturday nights after supper and baths, we sat at the kitchen table to read the Bible stories in our Sunday school lessons. I especially liked the Old Testament stories about Abraham and Sarah, Isaac and Rebekah, and their twin sons Esau and Jacob. I identified most with Jacob. His cleverness intrigued me. But I also noted nervously how he tricked his brother and manipulated his father, Isaac, into giving him the blessing. And I felt it unfair that Jacob had to work an extra seven years for Rachel. I suspected that it was not much fun for Leah, his first wife, to be the consolation prize. When Jacob returned home many years later and asked for forgiveness, I felt relief and completion.

The intricacies of the lives of the Hebrew people fascinated me. The characters seemed to be real people who tried to love God, made many mistakes, but tried to do good most of the time. The characters in New Testament stories seemed less real to me, perhaps because the Jesus I heard about in childhood seemed to be much more God than human being. Against the backdrop of stories kindling my imagination was the reality of life on a working farm.

My parents' strong work ethic was intensified by their experiences farming during the Great Depression. They worked very hard to save for a down payment on the 160 acres of fertile land in southwest Minnesota. After paying off the farm in the 1950s they were never in debt again, not even for a car or farm implements. The farm always came first, especially at planting and harvest times. Everything else was secondary—even church.

When I was needed for chores, I was often in the grove, orchard, or pasture, the settings for my daydreaming and imaginative play. Once I learned to read, I stashed books under the dining room buffet, the sofa, and various beds so I could read when I was supposed to be dusting. I remember my father stepping into the dining room, noting my paper dolls strewn about the floor, and saying with irritation, "Does she have to?"

It was our mother who greeted us every day when we came in from the school bus, acknowledged our achievements, and attended choral and band concerts and school plays. My father rarely joined her. I did not ask him to come; it did not occur to me to ask. I must have been in my early teens when I yelled at my mother, "He hates me!"

My mother answered gently, "No, no, he doesn't." But it was hard to believe her.

Whenever my father called my name, I expected I would be told to do something. For the most part, his expectations were not beyond my capabilities. Carrying water and feed to the chickens, gathering eggs, and washing the dishes and the cream separator were daily tasks I shared with Shirley. We children planted potatoes every spring and harvested them in fall. We planted and weeded the vegetable garden, picked raspberries and strawberries, and helped in canning vegetables and fruit.

One chore I truly hated began with Dad saying at breakfast on a random Saturday morning that he was going to grind feed. I could not escape his coming into the farmhouse later, asking "Where's Marilyn? Marilyn, come out now, and hold a half dozen sacks for me." I was irritated because I did not want to do the chore he had in mind and because he could not pronounce my name easily. His Swedish accent was strong. Marilyn sounded like Merlin. And I hated holding sacks. No matter how I turned my head and tried not to breathe, clouds of feed dust choked me. I had to just stand there holding the gunny sacks open, wide enough for the shovels of ground feed. There were always more than a half dozen sacks.

I did not gracefully accept the priority of farm work. One summer joy was the annual Fourth of July picnic at our church. I looked forward to it for days. I could spend the whole day with my friends. There were games and races, softball, fried chicken, Jell-O, and ice cream cones. One Fourth when I was about ten, I spent most of the morning pacing back and forth under the clothesline, watching my father on the John Deere Model A tractor a half mile to the south. Back and forth he drove, east to west and back again, cultivating corn. The longer he drove, the more frustrated I became. As noon approached and Dad was still in the field, I could hardly hold in my anger. I wanted to go to my mother and beg her to do something. But I was powerless. The cultivating needed to be done. The corn was almost too tall to slip easily under the axles of the John Deere. We would wait. No one in my family would have considered the possibility of Mother driving us children to the picnic and returning later for Dad. Pleasure and fellowship were not good enough reasons to make more than one trip to church that day.

Often farm tasks involved everyone, adults and children. By the time I was eleven, I had learned to drive the tractor for haying. Haying involved mowing and raking and bringing the hay into the barn. Most important was Dad's assessment of when to mow, when to rake, and when to bring the hay in. Was the alfalfa still too damp? Would the rain hold off another day? Once he decided it was the day to bring in the hay, my father's urgency motivated all of us.

Before hay balers came into being, loose hay was taken from windrows in the fields by a hay loader, a sort of elevator, which brought the hay up from the ground and dumped it into a hayrack. The arrangement was pulled by a tractor. My father stood in the rack, leveled the hay as it came from the loader, and spread it in the rack over a rope sling, stretched out flat. A sling consisted of three ropes, with metal rings on their ends. Three slings of hay, each one on top of the other, made a full load.

I felt a sense of power and agency in being able to drive the tractor, and I had the satisfaction of doing a good job. Yet, it was tricky to maneuver tractor, rack, and loader. Driving straight along a windrow, I could readily keep the hay between the tractor's tires so that the hay was not crushed. Reaching the end of a row was when my anxiety began to rise.

I knew enough never to take the immediate next row. The whole rig could not be turned that sharply. Should I try the third one to the east or the fourth? Could I manage the turn so that the hay loader picked up the last of the windrow and the first of the next? As I was turning, would Dad on the hayrack yell over the sound of the tractor, "Too long, too long," or "Too short"? Would I have to stop the tractor, jump off, and grab a fork to pick up the hay that the loader had missed? What a relief it was when the rack was full, all three slings, and I could climb into the rack and sink into the sweet-smelling hay for the ride back to the barn.

Getting the hay into the hayrack was only the first part of harvesting hay. When Dad parked the rack below the big barn door, it was time for all hands to show up to get the hay into the barn. We hoped the three sets of ropes, the slings, had been laid carefully in the rack so that their rise to the hayloft would go smoothly. With my father up in the hayloft waiting, my mother, sister, and I fastened the metal rings of the sling to two hooks on a large rope in the pulley system that would hoist the slings of hay, one at a time, up the front of the barn, through the big door, and along the track into the interior of the hayloft. This large rope extended to the far end of the barn, around a pulley, then down to ground level, around another pulley, returning through a small door in the front of the barn where it was attached to the tractor. When the sling of hay was up in the haymow, Dad, using a pole, could swing the sling of hay back and forth. When it was positioned exactly where he wanted it, in one fluid motion, he would pull the trip rope and release one side of the sling so the hay dropped into the haymow just where he wanted it.

My part in all this maneuvering was to drive the tractor that pulled the large rope, lifting the sling of hay up the front of the barn to the loft and into the interior. If all went well, I stopped when Dad yelled to. Then I needed to release the large rope from the tractor hitch. This allowed Dad to be in full control of what went on in the hayloft.

One time all did not go smoothly. Dad yelled at me to stop. Although I stopped, I forgot to pull the pin to release the large rope from the tractor. I drove off, pulling the sling of hay to a crashing halt at the end of the track at the far end of the hayloft, tearing the top pulley loose from its moorings. This last movement of the pulley system could only have taken six seconds, but the shouts of Dad, Mom, and Shirley seemed endless. I finally stopped, frozen in disbelief and fear.

Haying was over for the day. Dad would have to repair the pulley system and maybe take the time to go into town to buy a part. The hay would stay in the field, risking ruin by rain. I knew my mistake meant more work and maybe the loss of part of the hay crop.

I was sure my father would yell at me. I waited and waited. When the scolding did not come, I felt confused. He never mentioned my mistake—not then, and not later. Never.

Applesauce

East of the farmhouse, a string of evergreens
    marks end of lawn and beginning of orchard.
East of the evergreens, the plum trees, too small to climb,
    fragrant in spring.

East of the plums are the McIntosh, the Winesap
    and the small, hard crab apples
Whose name I never knew, only their pale wrinkled shapes
    in mason jars,
Just their vinegary taste.

In late summer we make applesauce.
Washing, peeling, slicing, and cooking down,
Or cooking the whole apple, core and peel,
    dumping it, steaming, into the sieve.

We gather windfalls for the pigs, my sister and I,
    five-gallon buckets of them,
Dumping them over the wood fence onto the concrete floor.
The spring piglets are hogs now: huge, snorting, hungry,
    pushing each other aside,
Pushing against the wood fence that sways and trembles.

We climb from the fence to the hog house roof,
    hauling our half-full buckets with us.
Rotten apples smack and squish against broad hog bodies.
They squeal and snort and slip on the wet concrete.

We remember that farmer, that old man, from our church,
    Whose heart attack left him flat in the hog yard.
They ate his face, those animals he had fed with his hands.

Breathless, our buckets empty,
    we climb down, quick, before Dad sees us.

1980

Much to Love, Much to Fear

For me as a child, there was so much to love on the farm.

The orchard of apple and plum trees, fragrant with blossoms in late spring and heavy with fruit in late summer.

The lilac bushes, old even then, their hollow centers making perfect hiding places.

The four tall spruce trees north of the house, their branches spaced just right for climbing up and up. The fire ring below where on summer nights we roasted hot dogs and marshmallows.

The two tall maples at the south of the house where Dad put our rope swing.

The kitchen garden where I picked strawberries by the dishpan-full, and raspberries, dropping them directly into my cereal bowl on summer mornings, watching for the hard-shelled black bugs that would float to the surface of the milk.

The creek, where in spring we took our homemade wooden boats, imagining they sailed the creek of melted snow the two miles to Iowa and further.

My favorite pink rock next to the creek, just long enough for my body, where I lay in the sun, looking at the sky, listening to bees buzz and meadowlarks sing. The gentle hills of the south pasture, where in winter we took our sleds.

I liked being in the barn when my dad milked the cows. Sitting on a low wood stool, he could turn the direction of the cow's teat and shoot a stream of milk into the cats' pan, and sometimes into their mouths. When my dad harnessed up the two big workhorses, Bud and King, I watched their muscles ripple under their red-brown coats. I was so sad when Bud died. Then King wasn't any use without Bud, so the truck came to get him too.

I delighted in knowing that when I went to the cow yard and sang "Oh, What A Beautiful Mornin'," the cows would come over to the fence. All I had to do was begin with "There's a bright golden haze on the meadow," and they would raise their heads, stir and stomp, and saunter toward me.

Many chores I liked, especially if I could be outside during the day. Late mornings and midafternoons in the summer, I hoped that Mother would tell me to take lunch to Dad in the field. Lunch was not our noon meal. Dinner was the noon meal, a full menu of meat and potatoes, a vegetable, bread, and dessert. Lunch was sustenance for men working in the fields—meat sandwiches and a sweet in midmorning and midafternoon. Supper, the evening meal, was often meat and potatoes again. On days I delivered lunch, I walked to where Dad might be cutting or raking alfalfa, cultivating corn, or, later in the summer, harvesting oats. I carried his lunch and a quart-jar of hot coffee with cream, wrapped in a dish towel. I liked going alone. The best part of this chore was the slow walk in the warm sun, a slight breeze, birds circling, the sound of the tractor in the distance, the dog nosing at good smells along the way. Maybe saying hello to some cattle. And knowing that Dad would be glad to see me coming with his lunch. I looked forward to whatever treat Mother had sent for me. Dad would motion to me to show where he would stop. He would sit in the shade of the tractor and lean against its big tire. I sat beside him, just resting, no expectations.

Free until chicken-chore time in the late afternoon, I could roam the farm. In the south pasture, I could find a depression in the grass and make myself a nest. Lying on my back, I would watch the clouds drift across the vast prairie sky. I could rest in my nest and daydream. During the day, I loved the west ash grove where my sister and I created villages, situating fallen branches and raking leaves to form paths and buildings. In our tin-can kettles we stirred mixtures of dirt, grain, and seeds, held together by the two or three eggs we sneaked from the henhouse. When we tired of the grove, we played on the rock pile, hundreds of boulders stacked at the edge of the grove by Dad and the farmer before him.

Late on a summer afternoon, Mother might say, "Will you go see if you can find some asparagus for supper?" Shirley, David, and I would head out to the roadsides, remembering where we had found asparagus last time or last season. Sometimes the spears were hard to find in the thick grass along the fences. Other times the wispy fronds of asparagus gone to seed signaled we were too late. Often, coming back to the farmhouse, one of us would enter the kitchen with a sad face and a small bundle of asparagus, while the others would wait outside the screen door. And then, just as Mother was saying,

"Well, that's not a lot, but we can still make a bit of creamed asparagus," the others would burst in with a huge bundle. She always acted surprised.

Most summer afternoons, unless my dad was in the field, we had coffee time under the maple tree to the east of the house. Many summer evenings we picnicked on the lawn to the north of the house, roasting hot dogs and marshmallows over a fire set in the space among the four big spruces. We raced one another around the house. I was proud that Arne, our older Swedish cousin, noted how fast I could run. I am certain that he paced himself so that occasionally I could win.

Caring for animals was the only work that needed to be done on Sundays. (I remember overhearing critical comments about a neighbor woman who had hung her washing out on Sunday.) I especially enjoyed Sunday afternoons when the grown-ups, satiated by a roast beef dinner, would take naps, my father on the grass beneath the maple trees and my mother in the darkened bedroom.

Flocks of white leghorn chickens were ever present in my childhood—two hundred and fifty full-grown chickens in the henhouse south of the corncrib, and every spring another two hundred and fifty baby chicks in the brooder house. Cardboard boxes of chicks came by train from Lincoln, Nebraska, to Bigelow, Minnesota, three miles from the farm. In those first few weeks of their lives in the warm brooder house, I found compassion for these tiny, vulnerable creatures. It was peaceful being with my mother, sterilizing the glass containers and filling them with fresh water, carefully spreading the feed in the narrow troughs. Our movements were slow, and we spoke softly so that the chicks would not startle, pile up in a corner, and suffocate. I was pleased to help them get a good start. I held them, my hands a circle of safety, brushing their soft yellow fluff against my cheek. Then, as the baby chicks grew into adults, my tender feelings for them began to diminish.

The well-being of full-grown chickens was a seven-days-a week responsibility for Shirley and me. Weekdays, we came home from school on the bus, ate our snack, changed into our chore clothes, and ran to do the chicken chores between our favorite radio programs, "Judy and Jane" and "Ma Perkins." Shirley carried the ground feed from the corncrib down the slope to the chicken house. I pumped two five-gallon pails of water at the windmill and dragged them across the yard. If I could manage two almost-full pails, I might have to make only one trip, and then I could race back to the house to find out what was happening to Ma Perkins.

After feeding and watering, we gathered the eggs, hundreds of them. Sometimes it took both of us to do the job, especially when the hens were ready to peck the hands that took their eggs. We almost perfected a process, using an old board from a stash kept near the henhouse door. One of us would lift the hen off her egg by putting the board under her, and then we'd carefully smoosh her up and back against the back boards of the nest. The other would grab the warm egg. She squawked as if she were about to have her head chopped off—which she would, once my mother determined she was no longer a layer, destined to become Sunday dinner.

These were not the only confrontations we had with chickens. Spring, summer, and fall, the roosters chased us, and we chased the roosters. Their advantage was surprise, coming up behind us, attacking the backs of our bare calves with their claws and taking a quick bite that could take out a bit of flesh. We fought back. Our advantage was that we could almost always find an ally to run down an aggressive rooster. When I got tired, Shirley or David would take over. We chased that rooster until he collapsed in a panting heap while we stood righteously over him, benignly allowing him to recover and stagger away. Revenge of a sort came at butchering time in the summer when Mother determined that the roosters had reached fryer stage.

In the summer the chickens became major—though passive—characters in the fear-filled drama enacted most summer evenings. When the weather warmed, Dad would pull the brooder house with its several hundred young chickens out to a nearby field where they could graze in a clean area. Closing the brooder house doors at dusk was a task for one of us kids, done alone in the gathering dark. It was then that my fears about not being saved, about God's judgment of my evil ways, about the Rapture leaving me behind, coalesced into a swirl of generalized terror. Who knew what dark figures might reach out of the ash grove to snatch me? Who knew what lurked around the other side of the brooder house? Or lay in wait, silently, in the oats field? Late summer afternoons were shaped by the anticipation of this chore. Sometimes I would try to be unavailable when Dad yelled, "Go shut the chicken house doors." But hiding was not an option. If I stalled, it would be darker when I left. The task was heavy with significance. Doors left open in the dark meant the foxes, raccoons, and weasels would have a feast.

The way to the brooder house was an overgrown lane that went straight west and then south along the ash grove into the open fields where the brooder house perched on a rise. In the daylight, Shirley and I spent hours playing Laura Ingalls Wilder, knights and ladies, explorers, and spies beneath the ash trees and on the rock piles. But at dusk things changed.

Every evening, I steeled myself for the ordeal, forcing myself to walk slowly west from the circle of farm buildings along the north grove and the rock pile. When I turned south along the grove I would begin to sing loudly, "Blessed assurance, Jesus is mine. . . . What a friend we have in Jesus. . . . Amazing grace, how sweet. . . ." I was safe as long as I walked slowly, sang, and looked straight ahead. Doing it just right seemed to give me limited protection. At the end of the grove, I would struggle to open the cattle gate, leaving a small space to slip through when I returned.

Out in the wide-open field at the south side of the brooder house, I would quietly close the big double door with care. First, the lower half, hooking it on the inside, then the upper half, making sure the latch held. My final task was closing the small chicken-sized door to the right of the big door. I would position myself carefully, so that crouching, in one fluid motion I could fling the small door closed and take off to the north at a full run.

No singing then, just running, running across the field toward the dark grove, through the gate, along the west grove, my heart pounding, gasping, my eyes straight ahead. Then, round the curve and along the north grove and the rock piles, past the looming threshing machine, its giant maw open, along the north side of the barn, and finally, into the open yard between the barn and the house. Panting and puffing, I'd slow down abruptly when I reached the open space, not wanting to invite comments. Safe.

I did not tell my parents how frightened I was. The inevitability of the chore and the fear it evoked evening after evening laid something deep down in my psyche. I dreamed of the dark grove repeatedly. Sometimes in my dreams a Hereford bull came out of the trees, like the one that stomped and bellowed in the barnyard, the one my father had held off with a pitchfork.

I Never Thanked Him

Winter evenings in the farmhouse,
    sitting close to the kerosene lamp,
    our mother knits our mittens.
We each have three pairs handed down,
    from Sunday, to school, to chores.

Wet mittens rest on the shelf above the kitchen range,
    winter smell filling the room,
Warm wet wool and farm animals.

Late afternoons, we drag our sled to the wood pile,
    loading it almost too high,
Hoping one trip will fill that dark space
    beneath the bulkhead doors.

Next, clean corncobs for the kitchen stove,
Two-bushel baskets on the sled from the cob house.

The worst is left till last,
    kindling for the stock tank heater.
In the half-frozen hog yard,
    we pry loose the dirty cobs.

How many winter mornings did my father start fires,
    his hands cold and cracked?
How many trees did he fell for the cook stove, the furnace?
How many shovels of ear corn into the sheller,
    dust rising and choking?

I never thanked him.
I did not think to, not even that last winter visit
    when he wheeled himself down the hall

To show me the warm corner where he could sit
    and look out the window.

2005

Departures

By the time I was thirteen, the farm I loved at age nine was not large enough for the life I wanted. The shift began with reading. In our house, there was the Bible, Bible story books, *The Farm Journal, Successful Farming*, the *Reader's Digest*, the Finnish *Kalevala* in translation, lots of Nancy Drew and Hardy Boys books, and by the time I was nine, my sister Gladys's medical books from her nurses' training program. I read it all. I would sit on the living room floor in front of the bookcase, a medical book open in front of me, looking at the drawings of human bodies, aware that my mother might appear at any moment. Sunday afternoons at the Baptist pastor's home, I headed for the corner bookcase, where I read *Sapphira and the Slave Girl* while the adults visited over coffee.

Bigelow's grade school was three miles from the farm and housed eight grades, two grades per teacher. When I was in seventh and eighth grade, I was frequently sent to the library when I finished my lessons. The school building had previously included high school grades, and shelves of books had been left behind. They were my oasis in a desert. I brought stacks of books home on the school bus. Adults did not monitor my reading, except my mother, who sometimes paged through what I brought home.

Reading was a vicarious reality into which I gladly stepped. I left books open to the page I was reading wherever my indoor chores took me. And when I was not reading, I was imagining myself into the story. I loved the Nancy Drew mysteries. Here was a young heroine who was smart, competent, and adventurous. I can remember the book covers with a silhouette of Nancy peering through a magnifying glass. Historical fiction was my favorite, and I soon learned the full line of the British monarchy. My reading gave me a window to worlds where some young women went to college, traveled, and had jobs. I began to daydream that I might, although I could not see how. No one in my family had gone to college.

I read every free moment. At eleven, I secretly read *Gone with the Wind* on Thursday evenings when my mother, who would have disapproved of the book's sexual tension, left with Shirley for two hours of prayer meeting and choir practice. Sitting at the kitchen table, my father and David already in bed, I could read undisturbed until I saw car lights; it was likely that car lights in the east at 9:15 p.m. belonged to our Oldsmobile. I had to wait to find out whether Ashley was really going to marry Melanie. I imagined a series of alternate endings where Rhett and Scarlett would come back together.

When I was fourteen, I began high school, riding the school bus to Worthington ten miles from the farm. I found myself on the edge of a world I wanted to join—a world of teens whose parents were doctors, businessmen, the junior college president, and the high school band director. Most of these classmates played instruments in the high school band and sang in the choirs. Their futures certainly included college. Although they were active in the local Lutheran church, they did not seem to live with the same expectations I felt, nor did they seem to experience the judgment and shame that I did. I felt pushed and pulled among my loyalties to three distinct subcultures: the farm kids; the Baptist church kids; and this newly found world of town kids from educated and professional families.

I was ashamed of my parents for their lack of formal education and their accents. I could not imagine that the town girls whom I wanted to befriend would ever consider riding the school bus an hour to stay overnight in my home, where I shared a room and a double bed with my sister. I did have an active social life connected to our church and 4-H. My sister Shirley and I created various activities for our church friends, sledding in the winter and swimming in the summer. We went to summer Bible camp, which entailed a week of swimming and softball during the day and Bible study and campfires in the evening. Every campfire included the invitation to rededicate our lives to Jesus. But I was not content to stay in those worlds of farm and church. I wanted what I saw and what I imagined in the lives of kids from town.

In my sophomore year, Gladys and her husband, Ray, provided a way. They had married when I was twelve and lived in Worthington. I began to stay with them several days a week so I could participate in after-school activities. This meant I didn't have to spend two hours on the school bus every weekday. I could babysit their two boys. In their house on Clary Street, I listened to big band and jazz and read mysteries and westerns that belonged to Ray. I got jobs for two summers doing childcare, and a third summer I worked as a carhop at the local A&W root-beer stand. I did not consider how my parents, especially my mother, might have felt about my choice to live so much of my three years of high school in my sister's home.

I was more of a peer than a friend to the town teens I so admired; I'd lined up a list of achievements, including salutatorian of my class. I had parts in the school plays and took bass clarinet lessons from my favorite teacher and voice lessons from the choir director. I loved singing Bach and other classical composers. One year I sang "My Heart at Thy Sweet Voice" from Camille Saint-Saëns's *Samson and Delilah* at the vocal solo contest. When our choir took an extended tour to sing at various colleges, including St Olaf College in Northfield, I continued to imagine that maybe I would go to college.

Near the end of my sophomore year of high school, having taken German for two years and having done well in all my classes, I was chosen to be one of two exchange students to spend our junior year in Crailsheim, West Germany, Worthington's sister city. I was so pleased. But I knew that my mother did not want me to go so far away nor to be gone for such a long time. She was thinking, I was certain, of leaving her family when she was seventeen and never seeing her father again. I was direly conflicted. Although I was anxious, unsure of managing so long a time in a new place, I was excited about the possibility. I really wanted to go and have this adventure. Yet, I was distressed about hurting my mother. Making a decision was exhausting. I talked with the pastor of our church. I made lists of reasons to go and reasons to stay home. Finally, I had to decide. I did not go. I felt deep disappointment. But I also felt some relief because my mother was relieved.

My inner life felt conflicted and compartmentalized. I was pushed and pulled between wanting to please God and my parents and wanting my own life. I felt guilt, fear, and resentment. Pushing against the Baptist "Don't" list (don't go to movies, don't dance, don't drink or smoke, don't play cards), I began to go to movies at age fifteen. The first film I saw was *Rebel Without a Cause* (1955). A couple of years later, watching Hemingway's *The Sun Also Rises* on a double date, my friend whispered, "What does impotent mean?"

I whispered back, "He can't get an erection."

All that reading had become a social, as well as an academic, asset. I went to the junior prom wearing a strapless pink formal. I knew my choices disappointed my mother. She had not said no, but neither had she said yes.

On Friday nights, I went to high school sports events to watch my boyfriend play football and baseball. I never spoke of having played second base on the Bigelow elementary school softball team as a seventh and eighth grader (and as the only girl on the team). Rather, I stepped readily into the role of the girlfriend who sits on the bleachers. On Saturday evenings, I went to the movies and necked with my boyfriend in his car. I struggled, knowing I was not living up to the expectations of my Baptist upbringing.

Beginning in my early teen years, the question loomed: What is God's will for my life? I asked it in a variety of settings: sitting at campfires at summer Bible camp, during sermons on Sunday morning, at evening evangelistic services, and in musings in my diary. I believed that God had planned something very specific for me to do and be. My job was to find out what this plan was. Sometimes, I felt a low-level anxiety, and at other times, resentment. How was I to know whether I was really in God's will? Yet, I also secretly feared that whatever God's will would be, it would not be what I wanted.

There were few variations for fulfilling God's will if you were a woman. If I were to marry, and this was expected, the best possibility would be to marry a missionary; marrying a pastor would be the next best. And if I did not marry, I should train to become a nurse. In fact, being an unmarried missionary nurse would be almost as good as marrying a missionary. Most of the time, the missionaries I saw, heard, or read about in Sunday school pamphlets were married couples, but occasionally, a single woman was featured, and she was highly admired. Here was a woman who had forgone not only a comfortable life in the United States but also marriage and children to answer God's call to the mission field.

Periodically, missionaries came home on furlough. These visits were special opportunities to hear how God's saving grace was working in places like Burma. We would all pile into the car and go to hear them speak, and even better, to see their slides. Sitting next to my parents, listening to the missionaries' stories of saving souls for Jesus, I struggled with my guilt. I wanted my own life. I wanted to go to college, do some kind of work, get married, and have children. In Baptist language, I was "convicted," meaning I was aware that I was sinning.

Those gospel texts about losing one's life to gain it were especially distressing. I did not want to give up my life. Yet, it seemed that God demanded everything from me and of me. More imminently, this was the God that might, any day now, send Jesus to take the saved to heaven—a disadvantage, however I considered it. On the one hand, I might not actually be saved, and on the other, if I were saved and the Rapture happened soon, I would miss most of my life. I lived my early teen years with frequent anxiety, pushed and pulled between my search for a life that felt like mine and the life presented to me by fundamentalist Christianity. Intermittently, I thought of those questions that had been with me since I was twelve. Questions like: How does this getting saved *work*? I had tried to imagine how it was possible for every single person to even hear about Jesus, to have even a small chance to accept him. And what about all those people who had lived before Jesus lived and died? I tried to be content with the answer I had gotten, which was, "Leave that to God. God will take of that." So, I juggled my doubts and questions. On Sundays, I went to Sunday school and worship both morning and evening, often responding to the pleas to rededicate my life to Jesus.

When I was a high school sophomore, Shirley went off to St. Paul to enroll in a nursing program, following in the footsteps of our sister Gladys. A couple years later, she and her fiancé, Ken, were making tentative plans to become missionaries. She was living the life expected of a young woman in our world.

Although both my sisters became nurses, having completed three-year diploma programs, they had not gone to college. I knew female teachers at my school. I knew the man in our church who taught at the local junior college. It was college that I wanted. I don't know whether I knew what a liberal arts education was, but by the time I was a high school student, I had read novels about women who went to college, some to the women's colleges known as the "Seven Sisters."

When the pastor's daughter, a year older than me, began a prenursing program at Bethel College, a Baptist-affiliated school in St. Paul, I thought maybe I could do the same. When I began my senior year of high school, I brought the possibility to my parents. I told them that I wanted to do what our pastor's daughter was doing. I wanted to pursue nursing at a four-year Baptist college. It wasn't that I had consciously assessed my interests and abilities. I simply hoped that my plan would appeal to my father. His favorite sister, who had died young, had been a nurse. Even so, he said that college would probably be a waste, that I would just get married. In the end, it was my mother who persuaded my father to let me go, she who had learned English by sitting in the back of a one-room schoolhouse in rural Nebraska the year after she immigrated.

Neither my mother nor I could know that my college experience would fray the rope that was meant to keep me safe—the one that anchored me to the belief system I'd been raised with.

Arrival

In September 1958, I left the farm to begin my freshman year at Bethel College in St. Paul, Minnesota. At that time, Bethel College and Seminary were located across Snelling Avenue from the Minnesota State Fairgrounds. Supported by an association of evangelical churches called the *Baptist General Conference*, the campus was growing, and new buildings were under construction. During the four years I was in college, the campus included three dormitories (Edgren, Bodien, and Hagstrom), an administration and college classroom building, a field house, a library, and a separate building housing the seminary. Sidewalks crisscrossed the large central green. Although the campus was almost 200 miles from the farm, the area near the campus was familiar to me. I had come to St. Paul several times to visit my sisters when they were in nurses' training, and Shirley, recently married, lived five blocks south of the campus with Ken. I had been to the fairgrounds several times with 4-H activities, staying overnight in the big several-storied building on Snelling Avenue.

My freshman year was organized around clear academic expectations and a curfew for the girls' dorm. I liked my classes: freshman composition, zoology, history of western civilization, survey of sociology, and study of Biblical literature. The academic work was not difficult, and I was excited to learn. I excelled in zoology, which seemed to indicate that my nursing plan might be a good one. I went to chapel every weekday morning and to special convocation programs. I wrote letters to my mother and detailed accounts of how much I liked my classes. I received more scholarship money for the second semester, which pleased both my parents and me.

My roommate, the daughter of a Baptist pastor, wasn't a complete stranger, which relieved me. (She was the sister of someone Shirley knew.) I befriended other girls on the floor of my dorm. We made popcorn many evenings while we studied. We shared one phone at the end of each hall and worked out a system that limited phone time for each of us. On weekend nights, I often walked with friends several blocks north to Larpenteur

Avenue to the Lido Cafe or the Flame Burger. In the winter, we went sledding at the Como Park golf course on stealthily gathered dining hall trays. Early each morning my freshman year, I worked in the dining hall, sending hundreds of slices of bread through a revolving toaster, slapping butter on them as they slipped out, and stacking them on large stainless-steel trays. I often heard complaints about the soggy toast, but I never told anyone that I had made it.

Most students at Bethel had grown up in churches and a religious culture like mine and spoke of dedicating their lives to Jesus and entering some kind of Christian ministry. Many of the young men were considering seminary. On Sundays, I traveled with a student gospel team to nearby rural churches. We girls sang hymns; the boys preached and led worship. The sexism of this arrangement did not occur to me, nor, as far as I was aware, to my peers. Many Sunday mornings I sang soprano to the words of a missionary hymn:

> So send I you to labor unrewarded,
> To serve unpaid, unloved, unsought, unknown,
> To bear rebuke, to suffer scorn and scoffing,
> So send I you to toil for Me alone.

The words epitomized the attitude expected of me, and I worked to accept those expectations and the role that accompanied them. I was somewhat relieved. Perhaps, finally, I might find myself "in God's will."

There was one person that year who stood apart from the crowd—the young woman in the dorm room next to mine. Her name was Gina, and she had come all the way from southern California on the Greyhound bus, in fact, to attend Bethel. I wanted to know her. Maybe it was her love of avocados. I had never seen an avocado and certainly had never eaten one. Her mother sent them by mail. Intrigued, I watched her smash them onto saltine crackers. Maybe it was that she was from California, a place I had only been to once when I was fourteen. Maybe I sensed somehow that she was not as embedded in the culture of fundamentalism and evangelicalism as most of the students around me. Several times I invited her to come home with me for holidays. She sent a letter to her family describing in detail a Christmas morning with my family: "Then Marilyn,

David, and I went out to the barn and swung on a swing in the hayloft . . . . Everything is safe as long as we don't let go of the rope at the wrong time." She included illustrations, trying to show how the rope swing in the barn worked.

Finland

As if leaving the farm and going to college were not enough of a change in perspective, the summer after my freshman year, my parents took my twelve-year-old brother and me to Sweden and Finland to visit the families they had left when they emigrated. It was 1959. I was nineteen, two years older than my mother had been when she left Finland. For many days, we stayed with my mother's sister Saima and her husband, Suulo, in Voikka, my mother's birthplace in eastern Finland. They lived in the house Grandfather Elias had built in the late nineteenth century. Birch and tall pine surrounded the house and nearby sauna. Often built before the house, the sauna was the spiritual center of Finnish life and always the cleanest place; it was where my grandmother Amanda had given birth to my mother and her nine siblings.

We swam in Lake Sompanen, where my mother had swum every summer day with her sisters and childhood friends. We took saunas. Sitting in the shade, we drank strong coffee and ate homemade *pulla*, a traditional Finnish cardamom bread. We picked and ate blueberries. We reluctantly tolerated a yogurt-like drink that Mother loved and Aunt Saima insisted we pour over cornflakes, and a fermented fruit juice that I furtively poured into a large house plant. With Saima, we went to a Pentecostal revival meeting where David and I sang readily in Finnish—not difficult if you just pronounce everything: double consonants and double vowels. We visited Uncle Nestor and Uncle Einar and their families. We listened to Finnish for hours, often wondering what Mother and Aunt Saima were talking about, watching them alternately laughing and wiping away tears.

It was midsummer, and at latitude 61°, the nights were never completely dark. After the adults had gone to bed, David and I crept out at 2:00 a.m., careful not to wake anyone. We ventured away from the house, down village paths, through groves of birch trees, marveling at the faint glow in the sky, listening to the subtle sounds of small, unfamiliar animals. Minnesota was too far south for such midsummer-night explorations. This small village in rural Finland was fresh geography—and filled with mystery.

The trees and water of Finland helped me understand why my mother loved our rare family vacations in northern Minnesota, where so many Finns had settled. Southwestern Minnesota, on the other hand, was tree-barren prairie with rich topsoil, exactly what my parents had looked for when they moved from Nebraska to Minnesota before my birth. My parents eventually nurtured countless trees to protect against blowing snow and the expanse of open prairie, but it was the birch trees of her homeland that my mother longed for. Though she planted them, the birch were short lived, their thin branches inevitably shattered by the ice storms of harsh Minnesota winters.

Nor was our farm in southern Minnesota near any bodies of water. One small creek flowed through our farm but only in the spring snowmelt. Like northern Minnesota, Finland is lake-dappled and flowing with whitewater rivers. A few miles from Voikka, the Kymijoki River wound its way through southeastern Finland, providing power for villages and the paper mills where my uncles and cousins worked. When our farm finally got electricity in 1949, my mother proudly reminded us that her Finnish home had water-powered electricity when she was a young child.

After many days in Voikka, my mother began to talk of traveling farther east to see the Olavinlinna Castle at Savonlinna, and a place called Punkaharju Ridge, a many-miles-long esker, or natural land bridge. Though I could not understand Finnish, I could sense it was important for my mother that we find a way to get to Punkaharju. After a lot of back and forth in Finnish, it was agreed that Cousin Erikki would drive us. Visiting an actual castle intrigued me. My childhood reading included all sorts of historical fiction set in castles. But it was the land bridge that drew my mother. Even in the self-absorption of my late teens, I could see my mother's pleasure at having arranged for a way to take us to that special place.

It was to be a long one-day trip driving east with the four of us and Erikki in his small taxi. We packed a picnic of dark rye bread and cheese. After driving several hours, we reached the beginning of the esker where Cousin Erikki drove more slowly. The road wound up and down and around. There were miles of water wherever I looked, more water than land. Pines stood sentinel on both sides. The water was close, sometimes only a few yards from the road. We drove up a gentle slope, around a curve, to a yet-larger expanse of blue, blue water. Another turn and the pine trees closed off the view of water for just a moment. Then another curve and more water. The trees reached up, straight, their branches filtering the sunlight. The breeze brought the scent of pine. I wondered how and when this came to be, this thin ribbon of land, making its way through so much blue water. I forgot that I was hungry. My mother opened the window and turned her face to the water and the pines. Every few minutes she said simply, "It's so beautiful."

Erikki slowed the car. Someone pointed to a good place to eat lunch. After lunch I found a place among the trees close to the water. I knelt on the ground, thick and springy with decades of pine needles, soft and warm and fragrant. I sat and watched the moving patterns of sunlight, which dappled the ground and my outstretched legs. I sifted handfuls of needles, watching them drop softly. I heard only the soft lap of water and birdsong. I lay down on my back. The sky was very blue. The tops of the pines swayed slightly. After a time, I turned so that my cheek rested against the earth, and I closed my eyes. My body settled into the warm needles. I hoped that I would not be found for a long, long time. Thought evaporated.

I do not remember much about the castle, but I cannot forget Punkaharju esker, that long winding ridge of land, rising from so much water, formed ten thousand years ago by the withdrawal of the ice. Something that day invited me; something in me changed. Eventually we drove west, back to Voikka, arriving very late. Aunt Saima had waited up for us. It was still light.

The Uses of Sorrow

(in my sleep I dreamed this poem)
Someone I loved once gave me
a box full of darkness.
It took me years to understand
that this, too, was a gift.[4]

Mary Oliver

At the beginning of my sophomore year, I met a seminary student from a Chicago suburb. He was intelligent, widely read, intense, and witty. He was also four years older than me. I had never known anyone like him. The boy I dated for almost two years in high school was kind and respectful, but we had little to talk about. Now here was an intellectual man, a true academic, who knew all sorts of things I did not know—and he was pleased to spend time with me. Because the college and the seminary were on one campus, we easily spent long hours talking over coffee and walking the golf course at Como Park at night. We talked about philosophy, theology, politics, and literature. I read the writers he suggested, writers I had never heard of. I wondered about Rudolph Otto's *mysterium tremendum* and the numinous, about Albert Camus, Soren Kierkegaard, and existentialism. In Blaise Pascal's *Pensées* I underlined, "The present is never our end. The past and the present are our means; the future alone is our end. So we never live, but we hope to live; and as we are always preparing to be happy, it is inevitable that we should never be so." The ideas were new and evocative to me. At twenty, I scarcely felt like the same person I had been at nineteen.

I walked with him to the homes of professors, where I sat in on conversations about theology and politics. At the home of the political science professor, I first heard the music of The Weavers and Pete Seeger. I fell in love with the seminarian and all the possibilities he presented.

4 Mary Oliver, "The Uses of Sorrow," in *Thirst* (Boston: Beacon Press, 2006), 52.

Throughout those many months of my sophomore year, I daydreamed that he would become a professor and marry me.

Then, a week or two before the end of my sophomore year, my hope for our future evaporated over conversation and coffee, a parallel setting to my falling in love with him. He was not unkind. Although I do not remember his explicit reasons for ending our relationship, it was probably about our growing physical intimacy—clearly not a direction we were supposed to go unless we were married. I was hurt, sad, and angry.

I didn't sulk, however. I took my pain and energy across the river to the University of Minnesota-Twin Cities campus, where earlier that spring I had enrolled in summer school classes: Shakespeare, Chaucer, and introduction to philosophy. The Shakespeare professor, wearing wing-tip shoes without socks, came to class smoking cigarettes and did not stop smoking for two hours. My paper on Falstaff pleased him. Shakespeare pleased me. I memorized the prologue to Chaucer's *Canterbury Tales* in middle English. I stayed on campus after classes, drank coffee, studied at the union, sat on the mall, and listened to students playing guitars and giving speeches about politics. I had begun the summer in anger and despair. Taking the intercampus bus to the university may have started as an "I will show you" gesture, but I ended the summer excited and energized for having stepped into a yet-wider world.

At the beginning of my junior year, I talked with a Bethel English professor about changing majors. I realized more fully that I had not enjoyed chemistry, and I had struggled to get an A. The homework took so much time, and I didn't enjoy it as I enjoyed my literature classes. Maybe God's will did not mean I needed to do something difficult, something I did not enjoy. I felt such relief. With the mentoring of that professor, I changed my major. I let go of my nursing plan and pursued an English and education major. I told my parents that I would be a teacher, a high school English teacher. I had begun to trust my own aptitudes and desires more than the messages of my Baptist upbringing. Even the expectation I should marry a pastor (or a seminary professor) had diminished.

Junior year, I moved off campus. I studied hard, sang in the choir, wrote for the school journal, and joined student government. I took a job at the nearby Jewish Home for the Aged, where I worked as a nurse's aide one night a week. My coworkers were mostly middle-aged women who were kind and supportive, teaching me what I did not know. They agreed with me that it was ridiculous I was not allowed to study between 9:30 and 11:00 p.m. when the ward was generally very quiet. One of them said crisply, "If I can read my magazines, I don't know why you can't study."

Though I loved my classes, one class (tellingly) troubled me: theology. When the seminarian had been in my life, it had been easy for me to let him carry my projections. I gave over my wonderings and my power, unconsciously expecting him to carry them. Being with him, I had pushed aside the too-small God of my upbringing. Now, not distracted by that intense relationship, my God questions resurfaced. Most of my college peers seemed content to claim their evangelical Baptist heritage with little critique, while I lived in continual questioning. I could no longer assent to the words, to what I understood the doctrine to mean. I could not claim the experience the words expected of me. My world had widened, yes, but it did not feel safe to let anyone know my doubts and wonderings. I was impelled to figure out God and theology on my own, just as I had tried to figure out getting saved. It was the pattern of my childhood, a pattern that included hiding my fear and shame.

At the close of junior year, I said goodbye to my graduating friends and walked alone to the house where I lived with four other women. It was late May. Lilac and apple blossoms filled the air with their spring scent, reminding me of evening walks with the seminarian the year before. The campus was empty. So was I. I needed to pack up and move to another house for the summer. I had a nurse's aide job I tolerated and an incomplete independent study on the miracles of Jesus due in two months. I did not know how I could write about miracles and still retain any integrity.

I had come to a wall. I had no way to articulate my struggle about my paper except by saying to myself, "I cannot believe these miracles happened." In the closed theological system that I inhabited, I did not see room to interpret the miracles metaphorically. No one had said to me that liberating statement I later grabbed: there are some things that are more true than fact. Confusion, fear, and shame silenced me.

Help Me

It's 11:05 p.m. and I am done,
  done with one more 3-to-11 shift
  at the Jewish Home for the Aged
Where I run the elevator, turn the lights on and off on Sabbath,
Where I am learning to keep meat and milk dishes separate,
Where at twenty, I hear prayers I do not know,
  and swearing that dementia can bring.

It's assurance for my mother,
  walking down the middle of the dark street back to campus.

More than textbooks and lectures, this job is opening me,
  still a somewhat practicing Baptist, but not for long.
Other nights I walk, most times south to Holy Angels,
  where the church doors are always unlocked.
I let the door close gently behind me.
Ahead the altar is lighted.
Pews are empty.
I sit for a very long time.
I know only that I need not think.

Here, too, I do not know the prayers.
What am I supposed to say when I light a candle?
Whom am I addressing?
Most evenings I just mouth "Help me."
And "Thank you," to those who keep the doors open.

1985

Inevitability

My senior year at Bethel College, I worked as a teaching assistant in the English department and completed my student teaching at North High School in North St. Paul. My master teacher went to the school basement most days to smoke with the janitor, perhaps giving me the advantage of learning how to be in charge. I graduated as salutatorian with an English and education major. It was 1962. I was poised to search for a high school English teaching position when the Tozer Foundation surprised me with a grant that would pay for two years of graduate school at the University of Minnesota on one condition: I needed to enroll that fall. Remembering how much I had loved my summer school classes two years earlier, I enrolled in several prerequisites and applied. Within a few months I was accepted to the graduate school of English at the University of Minnesota.

I lived with several women from Bethel in a duplex in St. Paul only a couple miles from the Bethel campus. Three blocks east was Hamline University where I often went to study. Some evenings, after classes and long hours of studying, I baked caramel rolls for my housemates and three young men from Bethel who lived two houses away. We phoned them just as I took the pans out of the oven, and then we sat around the kitchen table and ate the whole batch. If I had extra money, I would include pecans.

Only a few miles to the north was an Uncle John's Pancake House where I got a waitressing job to supplement the foundation money. On warm days I rode my bike, went straight to the restroom to wipe the sweat from my underarms, and put on my white blouse and yellow pinafore. The tips were good, especially from families whose small children inevitably made messes I cheerfully cleaned up. I hated the slow midafternoons. I could wipe off ketchup bottles only so many times. Sometimes I worked a double shift. In the winter when I did not ride my bike, I drove a small gray Fiat that belonged to Gladys and Ray. It had a sunroof through which I once tried to insert my bicycle. It did not fit.

I sometimes went back to the Bethel College campus for concerts and other events. But connections with professors and student friends were largely social; my spiritual longings were not conscious. I was focused on my graduate work, often anxious about how I was doing, feeling a bit like an imposter. I dated several young men. Two were planning to attend seminary. One of them I liked a lot, and I daydreamed that he and I might be together, but he went off to the Peace Corps. In my second year of graduate school, I was invited to teach freshman composition part time at Bethel. In the spring of 1965, while serving on a student and faculty planning committee, I met a smart, good-looking Bethel senior.

Though somewhat younger than me, B.'s intelligence, competence, and physicality was very attractive. He was taller than me, with brown hair and blue eyes, not classically handsome but quite good looking and certainly confident. Although he was from Menlo Park, California, many of his parents' Swedish relatives lived just north of St. Paul in rural Minnesota. He seemed at ease both in academia and the natural world. I was impressed that he had spent several weeks canoeing in the Boundary Waters of northern Minnesota, and that he could drive my seventeen-year-old brother David's classic MG TD with ease. This sports car, which I borrowed now and then, was not easy. Gas, brake, and clutch pedals were impossibly close together, making shifting gears a challenge, no matter the size of one's feet. B. was the only man I had dated who could drive this car as well as I could. I assumed a man ought to have the kind of competence in the physical world that I saw in my father and brother. But B. also had plans to attend seminary, Berkeley Baptist Divinity School in California, after he graduated. That clinched it.

We spent time together that spring, and in the late summer he went off to seminary in California. We began writing letters. A surprise to me, I passed my graduate exams with high scores. I thought about pursuing a PhD—but didn't. Although I did not experience much support from my professors, all male, I suspect that letting go of the possibility of a PhD had more to do with the California divinity student. Further graduate school might interfere with my hopes for a relationship with B. For the same reason, I did not follow up on an interview for a teaching position in a community college in Cleveland, Ohio. In late August I took a job teaching high school English in Roseville, a suburb north of St. Paul. I received my MA in English literature that December. With every exchange of letters with B., I imagined that my next teaching job might be in the Bay Area.

In 1965 all kinds of important things were happening in the larger world, building toward the Civil Rights Act and the events in Selma, Alabama. Listening to Bob Dylan; Joan Baez; and Peter, Paul, and Mary, I felt the stirrings of social and political activism. But my focus was B. and our developing relationship. We wrote letters, reams of beautiful, erudite letters, philosophical and literary, carefully shaped letters full of quotations that intensified the fantasy we were building together. As a child and teen, I had fantasized myself into the novels I read. Now at age twenty-five, I was creating a love story. I was falling in love with love.

I do not recall how or when we decided to get married. Perhaps a courtship of words on paper can have this effect. Was it via letter? More likely it was during one of my brief visits to California. The year before our wedding, we spent only a few weeks in each other's presence. I traveled to see him over a holiday and stayed with him and his parents. The rather formal way his mother treated me felt far from the emotional warmth I experienced with my mother and sisters. I was uncomfortable that his parents gave me the master bedroom and moved into the guest room. I was not especially happy or relaxed with B. during our visits. I think that without realizing it, I was not myself. I had begun to be tentative and careful, pushing my feelings aside. I was shaping my behavior to please him. Both of us were stepping into roles that our families, culture, and religion dictated.

B. returned to Minnesota in the summer of 1966. A month before our August wedding, we began to be sexually active, but there was little increase in our emotional intimacy. We spoke of our plans in practical terms, deciding that I would take the teaching job with the shortest commute from San Francisco. He would continue at seminary. I noted that much of our time together felt flat. We had none of the easy, witty conversation I had with my friends. And the deeper kind of conversation that our letters had promised, peppered with philosophical and literary quotations, did not happen in person. I had more glimmers of awareness that I was not being my real self with him. At some level, I was recognizing that our relationship was not solid. At a gathering of our friends shortly before our wedding, I noted that he was more alive in conversation with our friends than with me. I remember a sinking feeling. Yet, I said nothing to him. I do not know if I even considered trying to talk about what I observed. I pushed aside my perceptions and my anxiety. I was scrambling internally to salvage the relationship. B.'s maternal uncle, a Baptist minister who officiated our wedding, did not initiate significant conversation with us nor offer any premarital counseling to help us assess our relationship. I had few trusted older adults in my life, and if any friends or family noted anything amiss, no one spoke about it. We both looked so competent—surely, we knew what we were doing.

Our wedding took place at Calvary Baptist Church in St. Paul, not because B. or I had a connection to that church, but because weddings take place in churches. Photos show us flanked by three bridesmaids and three groomsmen, all in traditional wedding clothes, long white dress for me, tuxedo for him. We looked like two smart, successful, attractive people moving into marriage, everything seeming easy and positive. I cannot dredge up any details about the ceremony. I do recall looking at the display of gifts with my mother-in-law, making conversation about dishes. I was going through the motions. Having stepped onto this moving escalator a year earlier, I felt fated to stay on it.

However, the numbness that allowed me to move through the prewedding activities and the wedding itself evaporated on our wedding night at a local motel. Knowing that the next day we would begin our drive to San Francisco, we traveled a short distance to a motel on University Avenue. I must have believed that our wedding night would be different from the last weeks we had spent together—that the distance and disconnection would be dispelled. But connection, intimacy did not happen. We had no conversation about the wedding, our friends, or our families. No comments about how smoothly it went. No touching, no holding, no laughter. There were words. His words. And they clearly said he did not want to be with me. A future with me was not what he wanted. He turned away and got in the bed, leaving me standing there in my nightgown. I stood for a few moments, looking at his back. Then I went into the bathroom and wept.

The next morning, I sat across from B.'s mother at brunch, trying to make conversation about our impending car trip to California. I felt the full force of what had been set into motion. I looked at her, who assumed all was well with us, and I looked at B. This was the man with whom I was to drive to California the next day, the man with whom I was to make a life. I was devastated, but I gritted my teeth. I had to make it work.

We drove west. I remember coming upon the Grand Tetons, how they rise abruptly with no foothills, a row of amazing peaks. We hiked above the tree line to camp. I remember the fragile beauty of the meadow flowers, so small and vulnerable in the vast space. We set up camp by a small lake. I think it was Lake Solitude.

Over the next year, we tried to make a sort of life. We lived in an apartment in San Francisco several blocks south of Golden Gate Park on the eastern edge of the Sunset District. B. went to seminary, and I taught high school English in Daly City, the first suburb south of San Francisco along the coast. I made friends with other teachers. I enjoyed my students. I was pleased to teach teens who were African American, Latino, Samoan, and Vietnamese. Before the first day of class, I practiced pronouncing their names, so different from those of my students in Roseville, Minnesota. Every weekday morning, I got up to make our breakfasts, pack our lunches, and drive south to Westmoor High School. I was managing. We were managing. I was living the life expected of me.

Later that year, we drove back to Minnesota to spend Christmas with my family, driving straight through in twenty-eight hours. With us was a college friend, as well as my brother David, who had moved to San Francisco shortly after B. and I married. The four of us ate sandwiches and took turns reading aloud from Mark Twain's *Letters from the Earth* all the way from the Bay Bridge to St. Paul. I read Twain's piece questioning the purpose of God's creation of the housefly. That was as close as I got to whomever God was to me in those painful days. I did not let anyone in my family know how rocky our marriage really was. I carried my anxiety and shame in silence.

Then it was 1967. The Vietnam War filled the news, and the threat of being drafted into the military hounded every male over the age of eighteen. In the military system of conscription, college students had deferments that expired once they graduated. Being a seminary student had given B. a deferment, a 2-D classification. Although our first year of marriage had been difficult, I was not prepared for the depth of my anger and disappointment when B. dropped out of seminary. My anger was not about supporting us financially. I would have been teaching full time whether he was in seminary or not. I *needed* him in seminary. But I did not understand why.

As he was no longer protected from the draft by being in seminary, we scrambled. We researched possibilities for deferment. We looked at the Peace Corps but settled on the Volunteers in Service to America program (VISTA), which would give him a year's reprieve and the two of us a new and challenging experience. It was a crazy, intense time. David, who had entered a Peace Corps training program and later left when he could not give full support to the United States government's involvement in Vietnam, was still trying to get classified as a conscientious objector by a draft board in rural Minnesota. Protest marches continued to spread through Golden Gate Park, and Haight-Ashbury was overflowing with young people. It was the beginning of the Summer of Love.

In June of that year, I finished my first year of teaching in Daly City, and we let go of our San Francisco apartment. We had been married eleven months. We stored our household belongings with B.'s parents, packed up the essentials, and began VISTA training at the University of Oregon. Our training continued at the University of Alaska in Fairbanks, where, since grizzlies and moose abound in rural Alaska, I had to learn to shoot a thirty-aught-six. Little did I know the kind of survival the next year would demand.

A House on Stilts

I thought that I could make our marriage work.
Note the use of the singular.
If we just went to therapy together . . .[5]

Marilyn J. Benson

That year in rural Alaska may have been a means of military deferment for B., but for me it was a chance to save our marriage. I could not let go of the story I had unconsciously created—that saving our marriage was, in one sense, also about saving my identity and my soul.

Our training completed, our assignment was to live for a year in the small village of Lower Kalskag, a central Alaskan Yup'ik village with a population of seventy. It was located on the flat expanse of the flood plain along the Kuskokwim River, about a hundred miles northeast of Bethel, Alaska, and four hundred miles west of Anchorage. It was settled by Alaskan Natives who had converted to the Russian Orthodox faith in the nineteenth century and who in the 1930s had moved three miles south to put some distance between themselves and a small Roman Catholic community in Upper Kalskag. Both villages were accessible only by river and small plane. Because our time in the village overlapped with the VISTA volunteers we were replacing, we lived our first month in a storage room of the Bureau of Indian Affairs (BIA) school building.

In the mornings of that first month, a hot, mosquito-filled July, I vomited into a bucket at the side of my cot. I thought I was responding to the stress of change and would feel better as I adapted. But I continued to vomit. I caught the mail plane to Bethel and spent two days in the small public health hospital. I was pregnant. I was also frightened, not because I feared pregnancy, but because I knew that our marriage was not solid and I feared that my pregnancy would make things worse. After we told VISTA administrators that I

5 Marilyn J., Benson, *What Is, Is What Is, Is What Is*, unpublished poem, 1976.

was pregnant, they insisted we leave the program. B. wanted me to return to California to live with his parents or to Minnesota to live with my family. But I wanted the VISTA experience as much as he did. We discussed the pros and cons and eventually were able to present a united front and got permission to stay until the seventh month of my pregnancy. The VISTA administrator was supportive and clever in arranging VISTA business in Bethel at times convenient for me to receive prenatal care.

After that first month, we moved out of the storeroom and into a 24-by-24-foot log house on stilts. It was outfitted with an indoor manual water pump, a cookstove, and a "honey bucket," a five-gallon bucket we used as a latrine in a corner behind a curtain. Our house was heated by a wood-burning stove made from an oil drum. The village was close to the river, the major means of transportation. The house was on stilts because one never knew how high the river would flood when the ice broke up in the spring and jammed its flow.

As we stepped into our VISTA responsibilities, I realized in the village it did not matter that I had gone to college, that I had a graduate degree in English literature, that I was a teacher. While these achievements, the work of creating my identity as a young adult, had value in the culture in which I was raised, here they only served to shore up my ego. So much of what I had yearned for as a teenager, especially going to college, having a life of the mind, slipped to the side. What mattered here was not academic or professional. Rather, could I connect with the people of the village? Could I learn from them? Could B. and I listen well enough to collaborate with the village to create a project or two that would be truly useful to them?

This small community of people, with the natural resources that had supported their parents, grandparents, and remote ancestors, could not resist the powerful influence of the lower forty-eight. The subsistence culture was disintegrating. I remember an older villager, Pete Abruska, telling us that many young men of the village did not have the skills to support themselves through hunting and trapping. Most men left the village for weeks at a time to fight forest fires in the warm months. Their absence meant they were not home to fish for the salmon that fed their families and dog teams through the winter. And the scourge of alcohol almost guaranteed that some would not bring back their full salaries. Never had I witnessed so clearly the destructive impact of social and economic change.

As the months passed, B. and I found our way, sometimes together and more of the time separately. The villagers wanted a community hall, a place where they could meet without having to get permission from the BIA teachers, who controlled the only communal building in the village. B. organized a logging and building project with the village men. He wrote a grant to get building supplies. Then he went with the men up the Kuskokwim River to bring logs down to the village. Cutting the logs, transporting them to the river, bringing them to the simple sawmill, and building the hall gave B. a set of skills and a confidence that he carries with him to this day. The 40-by-40-foot community hall built on stilts became a place for the village people to have gatherings of all kinds, like watching the movies that arrived weekly by mail plane.

My project was continuing the preschool that the previous VISTA volunteers had begun. Like their parents, the Native children spoke little English. The children, usually a half dozen of them, met in our house every weekday morning. When I saw the materials for first grade provided by the BIA, I realized the children would enter first grade and be taught to read about Dick and Jane and Spot and Puff, riding tricycles, and Daddy going to the office, activities that had nothing to do with their lives in the village. I created other materials. We named colors and counted. I made games that asked them to match shapes. I read stories and listened to their stories. We looked at pictures and identified objects. In my queasy first months of pregnancy, some days the smell of fish that permeated the children's clothes and hair made me retch.

I had lived the first nine years of my childhood using an outhouse and a chamber pot, pumping cold well water at the kitchen sink, heating it on the stove, and carrying out wastewater. The lack of amenities was not painful. Our marriage was. I wrote detailed letters to my family several times a week, describing our life in Lower Kalskag but never anything about my feelings or my relationship with B. In my journal, I expressed my inner life—in pages of anger, blame, guilt, regret, and vows to be more loving. Only my college friend Gina, with whom I exchanged letters, knew my sadness and anxiety. I was too proud to let anyone in my family know that all was not well.

My parents sent many care packages, mostly dried fruit and small kitchen items, a paring knife, a peeler, a dish towel. And there was always a letter with family news. I was happy when we got a package, hoping that it included a loaf of my mother's homemade wheat bread. Even though I made our bread, her bread—even stale—expressed love. So did the packages, carefully wrapped in the dense fabric of clean seed-corn sacks, stitched closed, neatly, by my father.

My sisters, both nurses, cautioned me from thousands of miles away about not gaining too much weight. I did not tell them that I gained twenty-five pounds. Rather, I continued to write newsy letters about our life in the village and tried to encourage my mother to accept David's attempts to obtain conscientious objector status. My mother-in-law hosted a baby shower in Menlo Park and then sent the gifts to Alaska. The disposable diapers, size newborn, traveled around the back country for weeks, arriving too late to be useful.

On a practical level, B. and I worked together well enough. Our shared laughter about how we handled cultural differences brought us together. One family lent us a dog we named Piddles, who grew fat through the winter on what the villagers called "Eskimo ice cream." Early on, we were offered a treat that looked tasty—a soft white substance studded with blueberries and cranberries. In the presence of villagers, I innocently took a large spoonful of what turned out to be dried white fish, berries, and Crisco, which traditionally would have been fat from reindeer, caribou, or moose. How I wanted to spit it out. With all eyes on me, I swallowed it. We received many more such treats and passed them on to Piddles. Unfortunately, during a year when I could have eaten salmon every day, the smell of fish often nauseated me.

In December, when I was seven months pregnant, we convinced the VISTA administrators to allow us to stay, provided we pay for my medical care at the time of delivery. All was going fairly well until I stood on a chair to reach a high shelf. Unbalanced by the weight of my big belly, I fell and hurt my arm. Was it broken? When the weather cleared two days later, I caught the mail plane down to Bethel. The temperature was below zero, with only four to five hours of daylight. It was completely dark at 6:00 p.m. when I got off the plane wearing my Eddie Bauer parka, my fat Korean mittens (so named because they were the kind used in the war), my insulated pants, and my mukluks.

I waddled the few blocks to the public health hospital, housed in three metal Quonset huts, where, after examining my arm, the nurse told me that no one was there at that late hour to take an X-ray. "It's probably not broken," she said, "but come back tomorrow." I had brought a list of groceries. Not much fresh food was available in Bethel at any time, and even less so in the winter when everything had to come in by plane. At the one store that sold everything, I filled two bags with wilted heads of lettuce and oranges, anything sort of fresh for my developing baby. The next task was to carry these bags to the house where VISTA volunteers stayed when we came into Bethel.

The VISTA house, really a shack, was about a half mile from the store. Since my arm was beginning to hurt more, I decided to take the shortcut across the frozen tundra. As I came upon a large patch of ice, I began to regret my decision. In the dark—no streetlights in this frontier town of one thousand people—I shuffled slowly, hoping that my mukluks, with smooth moose-hide soles, designed for snow, would not fail me on the ice. Little tufts of dry grass here and there peeked up through the slippery ice, scarcely enough to give me some traction. Then, in the middle of the ice patch, I suddenly went down, not with a thud, but with a gentle swoosh. I sprawled face up, arms and legs outstretched, the grocery bags flung to both sides.

I lay there for a while in silence. I was not cold. The stars were very bright. I felt peaceful. I was not especially worried about the baby because my fall was slow and padded by all that insulation. When I turned my head in each direction, I saw my groceries scattered yards away. I did the only thing I could think to do. No pedestrians taking evening walks on the tundra in subzero weather would be coming past to help me. I sat up and skooched along on my butt, pulling the grocery bags with me. I gathered every wayward orange and head of lettuce. I deposited the first bag, slightly ripped, at the grassy edge of the ice patch. Then the second bag. It took me a few minutes to get my body upright, my feet planted, a grocery bag in each hand once again. Heading slowly toward the VISTA house, I imagined the story in my parents' hometown newspaper: "Pregnant VISTA volunteer, daughter of Gus and Bertha Benson of rural Bigelow, found frozen to death on the Alaskan tundra, a head of iceberg lettuce clutched to her chest."

The next morning, I found out my arm was broken, though not seriously. After being fitted with a cast, I flew home to Lower Kalskag with my oranges and lettuce. Two days later the doctor radioed new directions. There was no telephone service in the village. Apparently, my cast was to last about as long as the lettuce. After consultation, it was determined that the break was not serious, and that I could use a sling. I was told to remove the cast. After much soaking of my arm in hot water in the new plastic baby bathtub, we managed to cut off the soggy thing with a tool that looked a bit like my dad's tin snips.

I could not count on the mail plane to transport me close to my due date. Weather often made it unsafe for planes to fly for days at a time. So, I took the mail plane to Bethel in late January, several weeks before the baby was due. B. stayed behind in the village. In Bethel, I moved into a home for pregnant

Native women. Like these women, I wanted to be sure that medical care was available when I went into labor.

A few of the women spoke some English, but even without a common language, we enjoyed making meals and comparing notes about our pregnancies. A few days before my due date in late February, I went on bed rest, spending hours lying on my lower bunk bed, my feet elevated. With plenty of time to think, I began to feel frightened, realizing more fully that my body was going to do what it was going to do. I had to go along for the ride, whatever it would be.

B. flew down to Bethel a few days before I went into labor on February 26. I was still in labor thirty-six hours later. My cervix was not dilating. Those thirty-six hours were a very long time of pain, of trying hard not to cry out because I heard no Native women crying out, and finally, of being angry that someone kept telling me I had to bend over farther. How could I bend with a big belly, anyway? By the time the medical staff decided I needed an emergency cesarean delivery, it was too late to send me to Anchorage by plane.

The doctor struggled to insert the epidural needle between my vertebrae. The next thing I knew, I was looking down from a corner of the room. My body, draped in white, was face up, surrounded by four masked people. One of them was saying over and over, "We're going to lose her, we're going to lose her. She's got no blood pressure."

I was not aware of anything else. No long tunnel. No white light. No figure dressed in white coming to meet me. No music. Just the doctors and nurses peering at my body. Just the fear in their voices. Just the experience of watching, far above the action, from the corner of the room. A sense of calm, of peace. I did not tell anyone about this part of birthing until many years later. I have wished that this out-of-body experience indicated somehow the presence of the holy. Perhaps it does. Perhaps all the evidence I need is that the baby and I survived.

We named her Maja Kristine, Maja after my Finnish aunt. Maja (My-yah) is a Swedish/Finnish form of Mary, and Kristine is a form of the Christ. Ironic, that these names were chosen by B. and me, two lapsed Baptists. The first time I saw her I noted her fine reddish blond hair and her big feet—feet too big for the little black-and-white cowhide mukluks with red flannel trim made for her by Mary Valka, the postmistress at Lower Kalskag.

I don't know where B. was during labor and surgery. I do not recall if he ever said anything to me about what he was thinking and feeling during that stressful time. I imagine that he was frightened. A day or two after Maja's birth, he took a charter plane to visit another VISTA couple. I do not remember when he returned to Bethel.

Maja and I stayed in the hospital for eleven days, long enough for me to make a good start at recovering from surgery. She slept in a small bassinet next to me, making it easy for me to lean over to touch her, to gather her up and hold her close. I liked undoing her blankets to touch her slender legs and arms and marvel at her long fingers. Here was this small, beautiful person. She was alive. So was I. I was grateful. I had known that the two young doctors in Bethel were young and new to the public health clinic. After Maja was born, I found out that they had done only one other C-section prior to mine, and like mine, that one was completed during a phone consultation with doctors in Anchorage.

B. and I wanted to bring Maja home from the airstrip by dog sled, but Sam Parent, who owned the small local store at the airstrip, insisted he drive us the two miles to Lower Kalskag in his new pickup truck that had arrived the previous summer by barge. His pickup had limited use because the only available road was three miles of rough ruts between Upper Kalskag and Lower Kalskag with the airstrip between. It was drivable only a few months of the year. Maja, dressed in a yellow sleeper and wrapped in a yellow blanket, arrived in Lower Kalskag not by dog sled but in a yellow Ford pickup.

In March, April, and May, I continued the preschool in our house, often carrying baby Maja against my shoulder with one arm. After lunch, I made our bread, heated water to do our laundry by hand, and cooked our supper. Most days, diapers in various stages of drying caressed our faces as we walked from one part of our one-room home to another. Maja swung in the cardboard box and rope bassinet fashioned by B., bobbing halfway between the ceiling and floor, where the room temperature was between a chilly fifty degrees on the floor and the stifling eighty-five degrees at the ceiling. Many late afternoons, I sat with the older village women who came to see Maja. Three of them were frequent visitors. I made coffee, and then we sat, one of us giving the cardboard bassinet a little push. We didn't need to talk much to share our pleasure at being together. Mostly we smiled, nodded, and said, "Baby, baby."

The community hall and the preschool filled important needs, but it may be that our best project was the one we did together: my pregnancy and our daughter's birth. No *gussak*, as the villagers called an outsider, had ever stayed in the village with an infant.

B. and I left Lower Kalskag in June 1968 when Maja was four months old, having lived there a full year. Those months in a remote Alaskan village, living among Indigenous people, changed me. I still carry many images of the ways dominant culture's power damages a people's way of life, one that had sustained them for eons: buying snowmobiles that break down instead of using dogs to pull sleds; wearing rubber boots in zero-degree weather when traditional mukluks keep your feet very warm; using formula for their babies rather than nursing. I wondered about the small coffins resting on stilts high above the surface of the ground next to the Orthodox log church with its onion steeple. Those infants that died during the winter—could their deaths have been from dehydration after intense diarrhea, perhaps from drinking unsterile water from unclean bottles?

I saw how institutionalized racism and the bureaucracy and insensitivity of government agencies hurt people. Although the Bureau of Indiana Affairs schools provided first- through eighth-grade education in the villages, high school was not possible unless a young teen left the village and traveled to Oregon or Oklahoma to live in a BIA boarding school for ten months, leaving behind their family, their community, and their culture. We knew of only one young man who had left the village for boarding school in the lower forty-eight. I could not comprehend why there was not a boarding high school closer to home in Fairbanks, Anchorage, or Bethel. No one I asked had answers, not the BIA teachers nor the VISTA administrators. And then, once a villager had further education, there were few paying jobs in the village other than postmistress and school janitor.

Leaving Lower Kalskag, I was grateful to be alive, to have a healthy daughter, and to return to the lower forty-eight to teach again. At the same time, I carried, uneasily, my awareness that I had privilege, that I could leave, that I could make a comfortable physical life, unlike many of the people I knew in the village. But my overarching concern was about B. and me. Would he be willing to work on our relationship? What could I do to make it better? I was frightened and determined.

Death of a Marriage

We had heard about the assassinations of Martin Luther King, Jr. in April and Robert Kennedy in early June while we were still in Lower Kalskag. I remember that I was standing on the shore of the Kuskokwim River watching the villagers prepare salmon for drying when we heard about Kennedy. Now as we reentered life in San Francisco, the August 1968 Democratic National Convention in Chicago was exploding into violence. But it was our failing marriage that filled my horizon.

We rented a first-floor flat in a Victorian on Noe Street. Our daughter's birth had exempted B. from the draft, and in September he started graduate school at San Francisco State. I was welcomed back at Westmoor High School in Daly City to teach English. Maja was six months old. I had treasured being in the same space with her all day, every day, and I did not want to leave her. But I put my head down, dropped her off at the babysitter's house on my way to school, and pushed on.

There were few pieces of furniture in our flat, a sign perhaps that the trajectory of our marriage was unclear. We had scrounged a large wooden spool that we covered with a cloth and used as a low table in the living room. We sat on big floor pillows. Maja especially liked the one that had castors. We put her on it on her tummy and pushed her around the living room.

Early one morning, I found Maja leaning out of her crib, balanced, ready to pitch forward, headfirst, to the hardwood floor. I grabbed her just in time. Her perch on the top of the crib railing mirrored my precarious marriage.

My life was shaped by teaching and taking care of Maja. My weekdays were a routine: get up; make breakfast; make lunches for B. and me; dress and feed Maja; drive to the sitter; leave Maja; drive to Westmoor; teach five sections of English to ninth and eleventh graders; spend an hour of preparation time and lunch with my colleagues, men and women who were creative, witty, and collaborative; pick up Maja; find out about her day; drive home to our flat; and make dinner. My time at Westmoor and my time with Maja were good times.

One afternoon driving home from school with Maja in the car, I pulled up in front of our house to park. I was used to parking on hills in San Francisco, but the Noe Street address was the worst. It was parallel parking, facing uphill, on the left side of the street, in a car with manual transmission. That afternoon the rear bumper of my Volvo tapped the big American-made station wagon behind me. As I looked in horror out the rearview mirror, I watched the station wagon jump the curb and roll down the hill, finally bouncing a bit and settling crosswise in the middle of the narrow street, having stopped when it hit the rubber-covered bumper of a big pickup several car lengths down the hill. Panicking, I pulled Maja, now screaming, out of the back seat and rang the doorbell of our landlady, the owner of the station wagon. She came outside, followed by her handyman, the owner of the pickup. They both were adamant that the police did not need to be called. The station wagon had not been in gear, and the pickup was illegally parked. I could hardly believe my good fortune. Once in our flat, the adrenaline continued to flood my body. I lay on the living room floor with Maja, aware of how stressed I had been, how stressed I still was. I realized that I did not like coming home. I did not want to be in this space where there was so little love.

B. continued classes at San Francisco State, having decided to obtain a teaching certificate. He created a darkroom for his photography projects. The social life we had together was our infrequent drive to Menlo Park to see his parents, where I sat in the kitchen and tried to make conversation with his mother. Her perfectly appointed house, so different from my parents' farmhouse, felt formal and cold. I sensed she was disappointed that B. had dropped out of seminary, and I wondered whether she guessed how precarious our marriage was.

When we had been in the Noe Street flat for six months, B. told me he was moving out. Maybe his telling me was as abrupt as it sounds. I had recognized during those six months that he continued to move away physically and emotionally from both Maja and me. He spent hours in his darkroom. Very involved in his classes at San Francisco State, he had found a circle of friends. I was not included. I spent time with several teaching colleagues who were becoming good friends, almost always bringing Maja with me. I was angry, and under the anger, I was sad and hurt. But I also felt some relief. Living together was stressful. Alone with Maja I could relax. I could stop being vigilant.

In January 1969 I moved with Maja to a smaller flat on Twentieth Street in the Mission District. Across from our flat was the green expanse of Dolores Park, and down the hill through the park was Mission Dolores. I remember small, silly things from our time there, like the day a couple from our VISTA experience came to visit. While we were standing across from my flat in the park looking north toward the Mission, a dog ran up and peed on our friend's pant leg. I remember the foyer of our building had a black-and-white tile floor and large mirrors. B. took some photos when he visited Maja. In one, she is about fifteen months old, looking intently at the water in the toilet bowl, her hand poised to splash. Behind our flat was a small, shaded garden where I sometimes sat with Maja. But I cannot remember what the kitchen, bedroom, or living room looked like. There is a lot I cannot remember. There is a lot to which I was numb.

Other days I felt the pain. One day, driving home after a day of teaching, with Maja in the canvas car seat in back, I imagined driving my car over the curb across the sidewalk into a palm tree and the corner apartment building. "It would be better if we were both dead," flashed through my mind. But I kept driving.

I could not bear to stay long in that inner space of rejection. I clung to my belief that I could make the marriage work, even that I *had* to make it work, because letting go of the marriage went against everything I had been taught. Although I had read Betty Friedan's *The Feminine Mystique,* I was not the center of my life. I was a helpmate. I lived this role fully, exemplified by my doing the homemaking tasks, preparing meals, packing both of our lunches, and caring for Maja, all while working full time while he explored a career change. I felt resentful, but I was not able to recognize that I wanted what he had: the power to shape my own life. I could only work harder at being the good wife; it was my identity. I still lived my life within the culture and religion of my childhood, compelled to meet my husband's needs before my own in the same way I believed that I needed to meet my father's expectation—and Father God's. My relationship with my husband was entwined with the relationship with my father and with Father God.

After six months of living separately, we reconciled in August 1969. We began couple's counseling. I felt confused, anxious, and hopeful. We bought a three-story 1896 Victorian that had survived the 1906 earthquake that summer. Maybe we thought a house project would give our marriage a positive focus. Located on Twentieth Street a half block off Castro Street, it comprised four units with a wide view of the city and the Bay Bridge, and a steep stair out the back to a small garden. We three moved into the unit on the top two floors. We rented out the flat below as well as the two small apartments on the ground floor. David's girlfriend, Sally Anne, had moved from Lexington, Massachusetts, and the two of them lived with us for a short time, then rented one of the small apartments. Their presence through the following eighteen months supported me and buffered B. and me.

In the summer of 1970, B. and I made a road trip back to Minnesota with Maja. David and Sally Anne were spending the summer on the farm, and my sisters were planning to visit. The plan was for B. to drop Maja and me at the farm and then drive on to visit his extended family in central Minnesota. B. did spend several days at the farm, taking photos of summer farm scenes and my extended family. Some of the best photos of Maja's early childhood are from that visit. In one, she is wearing a little scarf, wisps of blond hair sticking out, picking green beans in the garden with Grandma Bertha. In another, she is wearing a purple dress with cream-colored lace that Sally Anne had made. She sits in the middle of the gravel driveway, her expression pensive.

I still have the photos B. took of each of my siblings with their spouses and children, each unit sitting on a wooden bench in the yard. He, Maja, and I took our turn; whether we would continue to be a little family was not certain. Many photos document the summer farm work: scenes of the farm buildings, and David and our father working in the shop. The photos are black and white, but I remember them in color.

I also have the iconic photo of that summer, a spoof of a Gothic family portrait that arose spontaneously while Sally Anne, my mother, and I were cleaning out a storeroom. We dressed up in what we had found and then gathered the men for a photo. Dad is in his striped overalls and a leather cap, holding a full-sized scythe upright, the blade prominent; Mom, in a print housedress, stands next to him. I am in the middle wearing a Little Bo-Peep costume from high school days—white ruffled pantaloons, a gathered print skirt, and a white hat. Little Maja in her OshKosh B'gosh overalls stands in front of me. Sally Anne, next to me, is in pigtails, wearing a sundress, looking as if she is fourteen. David stands against an antique motorcycle, arms around his dog, a German shorthair. A faded poster-sized version of this photo now hangs in my basement, where it continues to invite questions and comments.

Several people have commented that it looks like a shotgun wedding. But where is the groom? B., the husband, the photographer, is not in the photo. Not long after, he was hardly in our lives.

After many months of couple's counseling, the therapist said to B., "I don't hear anything from you that indicates you want this marriage." I do not remember what B. said in response, but the decision was made. In the following sessions, I was struck with the full realization that only two chairs were occupied, the therapist's and mine.

While B. and I had been going to counseling, I had been holding on to a smidgen of hope that things would change. As I struggled to accept his rejection of me, I focused on trying to understand *why* he rejected me. It was an old pattern. It echoed my wanting an explanation for why my father paid so little attention to me. Later, I became aware that trying to understand why B. did not want to be with me was yet another attempt at some kind of control, a refusing to accept reality.

I had thought I could manage our living together for several months while he found a place to live. I could not. At my request he moved out in November 1970, a short time before Thanksgiving.

One evening shortly thereafter, I was alone in the house. Maja was with B. for the evening. I had not made any plans for myself. I wandered around the large living room, looking out the big windows to the north, watching the lights of the city and the Bay Bridge come on. I was drawn to the books of nature photographs in the bookcase, remembering that I had given one of them to B. shortly after we decided to marry. I had inscribed it. Which one was it? I pulled out two Sierra Club books and sat on the floor. I opened *This Is the American Earth* with Ansel Adams's dramatic photos of Yosemite. No inscription. I opened *Not Man Apart* with Robinson Jeffers's poetry. No inscription. Confused, I looked more carefully.

Then I saw that the two front pages of *This Is the American Earth* had been carefully taped together.

B. must have taken the book with him when we had separated the first time and then brought it back when we briefly reconciled. Carefully, I separated the taped pages, and there was my inscription: "To B. This is ours to love and live upon. Christmas 1965." I lay on the shag carpet and wept.

More than any words between B. and me, those taped pages spoke the truth. He wanted me and every reference to me out of his life.

Later that evening, I paged through *Not Man Apart* and stopped at the photo of a forest clearing and the poem "The Deer Lay Down Their Bones," where Robinson Jeffers writes of his grief and despair, and describes the secluded place in the forest where deer come to die. The poem ends with the line, "The deer in that beautiful place lay down their bones: I must wear mine."[6] My marriage was dead; I had to wear my bones.

---

6 David Brower, ed., *Not Man Apart: Lines from Robinson Jeffers*(San Francisco: Sierra Club, 1965), 152.

PART II:
REORIENTING

Shaping a Single Life

The two years after B. moved out were a time of transition. David and Sally Anne lived with Maja and me for a year and a half. We laugh about their first "apartment," a cramped space under the stairs on the main floor of my two-floor unit. Later, they lived in one of the two small basement apartments, its entrance along the side of the house. This one was, in fact, illegal, with only one entrance and a tiny window no one could have squeezed through. Once, two-year-old Maja locked herself in their bathroom and David calmly talked her through unlocking the door.

In April 1970, David and Sally Anne married in a casual ceremony on the slope of Mount Tamalpais, overlooking the Golden Gate Bridge. The officiant had received his credentials by mail. I was happy for them, so glad they had found one another. Yet it was sometimes painful to witness their happiness. I was grateful to have them in my life and in my house—but it was not to last. In the spring of 1971, David and Sally Anne moved back to Minnesota to live on our family farm. The only family members who knew much about my life had left.

The pain of my failed marriage was mitigated by my teaching job. I was now at Serramonte High School in Daly City. I liked my colleagues, especially the three men with whom I team-taught ninth-grade English. I looked forward to our team planning and conversations. We four created innovative curriculum that used drama, skits, quasi-gymnastics, and more, which the students received enthusiastically. We introduced expository writing with the assignment to write a short essay giving instructions to a simple task of their choice. I recall the hilarity when, in a large group class in the theater, students read aloud their essays, and we teachers followed their directions literally. I remember lying on my back on the stage, trying to put my hands flat on the floor next to my shoulders, waiting for the next step in an incomplete set of instructions on how to do a push-up. Students were shrieking and laughing—shouting to the student reader, "No, no, first you need to tell Ms. Beckstrom to lie on her stomach . . ." The principal told us more than once that we made too much noise. In fact, he was pleased with our approach but felt he needed to pass on the complaint of another teacher. For several years, one of my colleagues adapted musicals that we performed for the entire staff satirizing our year of teaching. His versions of *Man of La Mancha*, *Peter Pan*, and *Camelot* were such fun. I usually got a lead since I could sing well. Maja remembers me walking around our flat practicing "C'est Moi."

Although colleagues became friends as well, and I saw many of them in social settings, only a few knew details of my marriage. The French teacher, Pat, probably suspected. When we were still living together, B. and I had camped once in the Coast Range with her and her husband. I can visualize B. striding far ahead down the trail and the three of us in conversation coming along behind, our separation foreshadowed.

Outside of work, my life was largely parenting. Five mornings a week during the academic year, I drove Maja nine blocks over the hill to Noe Valley to Teresa's house on Clipper Street. Some might have said that Irish Catholic Teresa and her husband, Maurice, had been sent from God. Their house was a consistent, safe place for Maja and several other children. When she began kindergarten, Maja went to school from Teresa's house. Teresa cared for Maja for eight years, from when she was eighteen months until she was ten years old and became a latchkey child. That house became the place of many milestones, one of which was Teresa's report one afternoon that Maja had used the potty. Maja told Teresa she wanted to do what Tanya, one year older, did. Knowing Maja was safe and enjoying her playmates, I sometimes stopped to meet a friend or to write at a coffee shop in Noe Valley between 3:00 and 5:00 p.m. on weekdays. Maybe once a month I invited a friend over for an early supper, leaving Maja at Teresa's house with Teresa's daughter, Mary, who was pleased to make babysitting money.

Meanwhile, I waited for B. to initiate divorce, thinking that since he was the one who'd left, he could go through the hassle of filing. But when he made no move for over a year, I found a lawyer. She helped me figure out child support and recommended that I ask for one dollar in alimony. I had been the major breadwinner during our time together and saw no need for spousal support, but my lawyer insisted. This small sum would apparently keep open a door if I ever needed it. But it was not the one dollar that kept a door open. Rather, it was my struggle to accept that I had been rejected so thoroughly and that nothing I had done or could do had changed this reality. I kept asking myself why I had wanted to be with someone who did not want to be with me. My marriage had turned out to be nothing like the fantasy I had constructed as B. and I exchanged love letters between St. Paul and San Francisco prior to marrying. Shame enveloped me. Shame for believing in the fantasy, and shame for struggling to accept my failed marriage.

Our divorce was final in October 1972. I was thirty-two. Still in therapy, I began to pay more attention to my dreams; two have stayed with me. In one, the sky has fallen, literally, to about three and a half feet above the ground, but it does not seem odd or limiting. I, and everyone else, are going about, bent over, living life in this reduced space. A young child is with me. I am holding her hand as we walk. I am not confused or angry. I accept this reality, and we are managing. In the second dream, the world is blowing up. Pieces are flying everywhere. I am standing to one side, watching, just interested, curious, and calm. I am not frightened. I am safe.

Words Neither Create nor Dissolve

I never wrote poetry about you.
Perhaps I felt that there had already been too many words.
First there were the letters, ordered in chronology,
Neatly packaged with rubber bands,
    masterpieces of theoretical love.
September 1965 to June 1966 we put on paper.
Are still on paper.
September to June proved paper thin.

We said the words.
But clergy have no power to create love.
Was love ever made flesh, or flesh love?

Then there were more words.
Three years of *How could you… But you said… If only…*
That climaxed in yet more words:
    Pursuant to Civil Code Section 4506,
    a Final Judgement of Dissolution.
But words do not dissolve any more than they create.
It has taken more years to make those last words flesh.
Now I can tell myself what was not,
So I can live what is.

1975

Speaking Truth

After finishing at Bethel, my college friend Gina went to graduate school for social work at Wayne State in Detroit and then moved to San Francisco where she got a job at the University of San Francisco Medical Center. As we entered new phases of our lives, our friendship deepened. Gina and I had countless conversations, but there are three I have not forgotten. What links them is her speaking the truth.

When Gina first moved to San Francisco, she rented an apartment on Diamond Street, just two blocks west of my house. We noted, as do real estate agents, that the summer fog rolled in from the Pacific Ocean just as far as Diamond Street, enveloping her in the fog and leaving me in the summer sun two blocks east. Metaphorically, however, I was the one in the fog. She and I often walked back and forth to each other's homes to have coffee and talk. One day over coffee in her kitchen she told me very directly that she could no longer listen to me talk about my soon-to-be ex-husband. She said I was likely dissipating the energy that I needed to do my work in therapy. I was taken aback and embarrassed. But I was not angry. I understood. She was right. I realized she spoke the truth—and I took her good advice.

The second conversation took place when Gina, three-year-old Maja, and I were on our way out the door to eat supper, something we often did. We had paused on the stairs of our flat, those stairs covered in ugly blue-and-green shag carpet. Maja was carrying her canvas bag filled with art supplies. She had spent enough time in a wide variety of San Francisco restaurants to amass a colorful portfolio of drawings. Having not yet decided where we would eat, I said to Maja, "Do you want to go to Bill's and have hamburgers or eat Chinese?"

She looked up at me and said, "Bill's."

I blundered on, "How about Chinese? Don't you think Chinese is a good idea?"

In the silence that followed, Gina said quietly, "Marilyn, if you don't want to give her a choice, why did you ask her?"

I took a couple of deep breaths and said, "Let's go eat hamburgers at Bill's." It was a powerful lesson. Gina treated Maja with deep respect. Her relationship with Maja helped me observe myself, making me a better parent and a better human being.

The third conversation took place in Gina's flat on Sacramento Street near the Presidio. Maja was playing on the floor with the collection of small animals Gina used in play therapy. I sat on the sofa. Saying she had something important to tell me, Gina said simply that she was a lesbian. We had been friends for years, yet she had not felt safe to tell me earlier about her sexual orientation. I wept. What must it have been like for her at Bethel College, that Baptist institution, where she was not accepted for who she was? I felt shame for my inattentiveness and self-absorption.

I was called to action. Within the next years, I became active in supporting gay and lesbian rights. When a friend of Gina's who was a journalist in the San Francisco gay press asked me if I would speak against the Briggs Initiative, I said yes. It was 1978, and California State Senator John Briggs was proposing a new law, Proposition 6, that would make it mandatory to fire gay and lesbian teachers and any other public-school employee who supported gay rights. Briggs stated that children were not safe with homosexual teachers, or with any teacher who supported homosexuals. In my file drawers somewhere, there is a copy of that interview with a photo of me, looking very mainstream in my short gray skirt and striped sweater. When the reporter asked me if I knew I could lose my job if the Briggs Initiative passed, I'm quoted as saying, "I felt I had an ethical responsibility to talk to you. . . . And I feel a little sad that anyone would want to take away my right to do that." The Briggs Initiative did not pass.

It was the same year that Harvey Milk was assassinated. Milk owned the camera shop down the street from our house and was a member of the San Francisco Board of Supervisors. He was the first openly gay elected official in California. He and San Francisco Mayor George Moscone were shot and killed by Dan White, another supervisor, who had initially worked with Milk, but grew hostile to the city's gay community. Maja, who was ten at the time, remembers that on the day of the shooting, I walked to the city bus stop to meet her when she came home from school, something I had rarely done. I was in tears. That night we joined thirty thousand people in the impromptu candlelit walk from our neighborhood in The Castro down Market Street to City Hall.

My relationship with Gina widened my world view and enlarged and deepened my sense of justice and compassion. What our friendship offered during those years in San Francisco was a parallel to my year in Lower Kalskag. I experienced another awakening to what I did not know—to what had always been there, and what I needed to learn.

Searching

Growing up, I carried two images of finding God's will for my life. One image was a railroad track. Finding God's will required a difficult crawl up the very steep embankment to the track, its direction already determined by God. And once on the track, I needed to be very careful not to slip off because getting back on was very difficult. Falling off, or "backsliding," was a common confession in those testimony times at the evangelistic meetings, a bit like letting go of the rope in the blizzard. In the second image, God's will was located somewhere out there in a forest, well hidden, like a bag hanging on a tree. My job was to search. There were lots of bags out there, waiting, but only one was meant for me.

It never occurred to me that God could be searching for me. Nor did I recognize that those two images contained no affirmation or even recognition of what my abilities and desires might be. Rather, in the fundamentalist worldview, God's will had nothing to do with who I was and everything to do with what God planned.

What invited me to claim my spiritual journey and seek spiritual guidance after years of not reaching out? Was it the pain, shame, and loneliness of divorce? Was it my awareness that I had not been able to love? Or be loved? Was it therapy? I spent a lot of time and money on therapy in my thirties. Was it that my reading and journaling were not enough? Was it a need for community? Was it a desire to understand how my life had come to this? I had lived for over thirty years, and what did my life mean, anyway?

I scrawled my questions, wonderings, and fears on scraps of paper, often the backs of extra classroom worksheets and handouts. I was searching, wanting a connection to whatever God might be. But most of my energy was focused on my messy marriage, separation, and divorce. During these years, my prayers were largely intermittent cries of help.

When I look back, I can see that I was slowly beginning to shape my own life. I began taking classes—the first class in 1971 on child development—that required me to record my observations and analyze Maja as a three-year-old.

Then, I turned to classes having to do with my work—curriculum and values clarification. Intermittently, I thought I might go on to graduate school in curriculum development or educational psychology. I met graduate students and faculty from UC-Berkeley and participated in a workshop for teachers about institutional racism, and another called Tools for Change that invited me to think about process as well as content in my teaching.

I loved the backpacking class for teachers. A colleague had invited me and two other teachers to plan an outdoor education program at my school that took students on camping trips. We camped in California's Coast Ranges, the Sierras, Big Basin, Point Reyes, and Death Valley. I especially loved our times in the mountains. During one trip in the high country of Yosemite National Park, I hiked the last mile to Cloud's Rest, separate from the group. Alone, and high above Yosemite Valley, looking down into the depths and across to the peaks of the Sierras, I crouched, awed, struck with the immense space around me and my finitude. Nearly overwhelmed, I crawled across the granite to safety.

Maja stayed with B. when I backpacked, but she joined our group twice when we did easy hikes to campgrounds and stayed in cabins. Her first weekend, I put her to bed in a down sleeping bag. When I came to check on her a half hour later, she was wheezing and struggling for breath. I was shocked and frightened. I pulled her out of the bag and wrapped her in blankets. How could I not have known? I made an appointment that week that confirmed her diagnosis of allergies and asthma. Twice a week for several years we drove to a Kaiser Permanente clinic for allergy shots. I was struck, then, as I had been other times, with the responsibilities of parenting—about what I did not know and what I needed to learn.

Maja's allergies brought a mix of experiences for us, including the visit of an allergy specialist who came to assess our home. I was able to act on some of his advice, like getting cupboards with glass doors for her books and her stuffed animals. Unfortunately, we had many square yards of shag carpeting that had to stay. And with some guilt, I never got around to regularly vacuuming the six-foot paper fish from Chinatown that was hanging from the ceiling in our living room. There were many visits to the emergency room. Many of them were in the middle of the night, after I woke to hear her wheezing. I remember that feeling of dread, getting up, quickly dressing, and carrying her in the dark to the car. Nights seemed to be when asthma episodes happened most often.

I think I have repressed the fear. I do remember driving home, parking, and trying to wake her, then carrying her half asleep from our usual parking place on Collingwood Street, a block away, and staggering in the door and up two flights to her bedroom, grateful that she was safe, and we were home.

In the next year, I experienced several small nudges that suggested that I might find my way to a spiritual life in the company of others, even a connection to organized religion. Although I had rejected the fundamentalist Christianity of my upbringing, I was acknowledging my longing to experience and understand the mystery that religion pointed to. My teaching colleague Peter took me with his family to Greek Orthodox services in Oakland. During the worship service, I thought about how Peter and other people I cared about and respected had made their peace within different faith traditions. Another colleague, Tom, had graduated from a Jesuit university. He did not seem intent on rejecting it all; rather, he had clearly enjoyed challenging his professors. My colleague Pat's husband, Leroy, was about to leave bricklaying to start classes at Starr King, the Unitarian seminary in Berkeley. And Sally Anne and her brothers did not seem damaged by her family's strong Unitarian roots. They seemed relatively healthy.

Whenever I could, I read. I spent hours in the bookstore on Castro Street two blocks from my house. I would settle Maja in the children's section as I went to browse. I read *Man's Search for Meaning,* Mary Daly's *Beyond God the Father,* then Maslow's *The Farther Reaches of Human Nature,* which led me to a workshop at the Esalen Institute, a retreat center for contemplation and personal development at Big Sur, California. I read Joseph Campbell's *The Hero with a Thousand Faces* and rekindled my love of the Greek myths from childhood days. These readings about human nature, psychology, and archetypal patterns of knowing were building toward something, though what that might be was not yet clear.

My daughter, like the texts I was reading, raised new questions in me and pointed me in new directions. One Saturday, I witnessed three-and-a-half-year-old Maja at play in the living room while I was upstairs cleaning. I often put classical music on the stereo when I cleaned. This time it was Brahms's *A*

German Requiem, quite loud. Realizing I had not seen Maja for some time, I went to find out what she was doing. Descending the stairs, I saw a long runway of our bath towels laid out end to end on shag carpet across the large living room. Arranged on both sides were her stuffed animals—bears, bunnies, lambs, dogs, and a lion. Maja, with her back to me, was sitting motionless to the side of one towel, next to her animals. In wonder, I crept quietly down the remaining stairs. When she sensed me, she put her finger to her lips and whispered, "Shhh, God is walking down the aisle." I was stunned—and felt a big nudge.

Within the year, Maja and I began attending the First Unitarian Universalist Society of San Francisco. The Unitarians felt safe, in large part, because they were familiar to me through my relationships with Sally Anne and Pat.

One Sunday, while I waited for Maja to come from Sunday school, I read an advertisement on the church bulletin board for a class called The Far Reaches of Human Experience. Offered by the University of California Extension, it was to be taught by Harry Scholefield, the minister of the Unitarian church, as well as Katharine Whiteside Taylor, a noted therapist and educator who would come to play an important role in my life. The ad mentioned she was a Quaker and had studied with psychoanalyst Carl Jung in Zurich. Later, I discovered she had taught at the University of California at Berkeley and had a significant role in beginning the cooperative nursery care movement. I looked at the reading list: Carl Jung, Martin Buber, and more. I signed up.

Cloud's Rest, Yosemite Valley

I climb the trail to the summit,
Letting the others go ahead.
They meet me on their return.
Now I approach.
Cloud's Rest, it's called,
A jutting granite ridge tapering into nothing
    1700 feet above the valley.
The trail stops abruptly, now only granite masses helter-skelter.
I lower my pack to the ground, prop it between rocks.
I take a drink and wedge my canteen.
I retie my boot laces,
    winding the too-long laces round and round.
I wait.
Their voices wane behind me.

The ridge ahead, the width of my Victorian house,
Tapers to nothingness.
Rocks wait, balanced on the edge.
I stay in the center, testing each step with a foot,
    then moving farther.
The Sierra stretches north and south.
Foothills slide west to meet the central valley.
Clouds mist between me and eastern peaks.

I crawl on hands and knees to the edge,
Keeping three contacts on the granite.
I wedge my back against the rocks
    and look.
At first, I cannot find them, the sheer face of El Capitan,
And the rising gray round of Half Dome.
Then I see a small, narrow scraping in the earth,
    the valley.

Granite and trees merge in gray and black-green,
No detail, only mass, color, shading.
No sound but wind.

My body, warmed by the rock, stands,
Sways out from the rock.
    wanting the air to take me in.
Sudden nausea sweeps up from my legs.
I crouch low, crawl back,
Lie flat, my face against the ancient granite.
I want to say a prayer, to name my fear,
My humble place in the world, my gratitude.
But no words are enough.

Sometime later, fingering the granite,
I find one small gray feather,
Soft and curved, a breast feather.
Its touch is gentle on my cheek.
I put it in my pocket, rise for one more look.
The valley is darker.
The shadow of the ridge shows on the eastern side.
I will have enough daylight to descend.

1977, edited 2019

Finding a Mentor and a Path

When I look at my life, I can name many pivot points. None seem to be as life changing as meeting Katharine Whiteside Taylor. In her class, we began by reading Carl Jung. I was drawn to his focus on the unconscious. In my own therapy, I had begun to see how much I had lived unconsciously, especially in my marriage. Though I was a novice, many of Jung's concepts made sense to me, such as how persona is the face we show to the world. I remembered the essay I had written in college, titled "Every Man's Mask," about what we humans don't reveal, and yet, how we want to be known. Jung's concept of the shadow also made sense—that hidden side of me, especially the parts I was afraid and ashamed of. The concept of individuation—the process of becoming whole—resonated deeply. My ego as the center of consciousness, the Self that was the totality of my being and included both what was conscious and unconscious in me, but also the collective unconscious—here was a psychology that went deep. My brain was swarming as I tried to understand. I was curious and excited. Perhaps I was finding a map for my life.

As the class progressed, one of our assignments was to write an essay reflecting on the theme of responsibility in relation to persona, shadow, ego, and Self. I jumped in. I wrote about my relationship to B. and how I had given over responsibility of myself to him—how I unconsciously expected him to meet my needs and desires, assuming he would point me to my life's meaning, in essence to God. I explained how I took responsibility for all kinds of less ultimate things in our relationship: teaching, supporting us for the three and a half years we were married, taking care of Maja, making his lunches, entertaining his friends. And all the while not understanding that my resentment was a clear sign something was seriously askew. I wrote that I had given him so much power, his acceptance of me and his rejection of me both "made" me and broke me. I wrote that I had often hated myself but knew no other way to respond except trying to be "good," doing all the things a good wife should do. I wrote that I had unconsciously believed because he was a man he had more awareness, greater perceptivity, and would know what was best. And I confessed that in giving over my choice, my power, I had blamed him for our failed marriage. All of this and more, I had expressed to my therapist, but I had never written it out. When I turned in my essay, I felt anxious and very vulnerable. Yet, I had told my truth.

Katharine responded to my writing with great generosity and full acceptance. Early on, she had encouraged students to make an appointment if we wanted to talk with her about the class. A few days after she had returned my paper, I asked if I could see her. Soon I was going to her house on Schrader Street for herbal tea a couple times a month. Getting to know Katharine as a teacher and counselor continued a time of transformation for me. My trust in her deepened over many conversations. I began asking her about being Quaker. She spoke of the Quaker practice of sitting in silence, waiting, and trusting the spirit. One day over tea, she simply said, "I wonder whether you might like the Quakers. Would you like to come to Friends Meeting and see?"

When I attended the San Francisco Friends Meeting on a Sunday morning in 1974, I felt that I had come home. I felt safe in this group of people. No one was telling me what I had to believe and what critical conversion experience I needed to have. Speech rose out of the silence as people waited for the Spirit and discerned whether to speak, when to speak, and what to say. Maja and I began to attend regularly. The Quaker community is not bureaucratic or hierarchical. Quakers with a tradition of unprogrammed worship do not ordain clergy, although there are "weighty Friends" respected for their wisdom. Each Sunday, Maja gathered with the other children at First Day School, and I joined the adults to sit in silence. After worship, when Maja and I left the big red brick meetinghouse on Lake Street, I often broke off a sprig of rosemary from the bushes by the stairs to put in my pocket. During the week I would find it, a pungent reminder of this place and these people. I had found community for both of us.

For eight years we worshiped with the Friends. I continued to have tea with Katharine twice a month. I told her about my fundamentalist Baptist childhood, my marriage, and the pain of having been rejected, the struggles of single parenting, and my dissatisfaction with teaching high school English and my new role chairing the department in a school of two thousand students with many diverse needs. I told her about the frustration of working in an educational system so resistant to change. I told her about my fears and my longings. And she listened. Although I did not know the phrase, I had found my first spiritual director. Philosopher-theologian Paul Tillich writes about the grace of suffering in his sermon, You Are Accepted:

> Grace strikes us when we are in great pain and restlessness. It strikes us when we walk through the dark valley of a meaningless and empty life . . . Sometimes, at that moment a wave of light breaks into our darkness, and it is as though a voice were saying: "You are accepted. *You are accepted,* accepted by that which is greater than you, and the name of which you do not know. Do not ask for the name now; perhaps you will find it later . . . *Simply accept the fact that you are accepted!*" [7]

Katharine's accepting presence in my life allowed me to experience the grace of transformation. A strand in the rope that I held was loosening.

Later, I realized the paradox. For many years of my life, I was struggling to accept—to experience and to trust my experience of having accepted Jesus as my personal Savior. And all the while, Tillich is telling me that I am accepted, that God had accepted me and continues to accept me. Oh my . . .

I read more Jung, Frances Wickes's *The Inner World of Choice*, and Robert A. Johnson's *He* and *She.* I knew the Greek myths and vaguely knew both stories Johnson used: the search for the Holy Grail and Eros and Psyche. But now, I immersed myself in a world where the text—story, myth, symbol, and metaphor—questioned me, so different from my study of literature where I was questioning the text. It might seem odd that my graduate work in literature had not impacted me personally the way my informal study of depth psychology did. But I was thirty-four when I began to read Carl Jung, not twenty-two. And my marriage, divorce, and parenting had broken me open. I felt liberated and grateful.

---

7 Paul Tillich, *The Shaking of the Foundations* (New York: Charles Scribner's Sons, 1948), 161-162.

At Katharine's recommendation, I bought the book *The Choice Is Always Ours: An Anthology on the Religious Way.*[8] It has been my companion ever since. The editors, three women, gathered prose and poetry from religious, philosophical, and psychological sources representing many cultural traditions. It was food for my hunger. I read, underlined, and copied quotations into my journals. Although I first read in graduate school the lines from W. H. Auden's poem "For the Time Being: A Christmas Oratorio," I was not ready for their power until I encountered them again: "For the garden is the only place there is, but you will not find it, / Until you have looked for it everywhere, and found nowhere that is not a desert."[9] Indeed, for decades I had searched for the garden everywhere except within myself.

The anthology traveled with me when I traveled. At the farm one summer in the late 1970s, it fell into a pail of water. Why the pail was there next to the table, I do not know. I grabbed the book and convinced my sisters to help me rescue it. We inserted pieces of the local newspaper between the pages and left it to dry. I did buy another copy, but I needed the original; it contained my underlining, my responses—a record and a witness—of my spiritual searching. I went back to it repeatedly.

During those years, I was part of a group that met in Katharine's home on Monday evenings for Jungian "active imaging," meditation, and conversation. Leaving our shoes at the foot of the stairs to the second story, we ascended to an airy, open room, carpeted in white, lit by a few candles. Through wide windows, we could see the lights sprinkled across the city and the Golden Gate Bridge to the northwest. I would find a spot, lie down, and slip into the silence. Katharine would read a section from Jung or another spiritual writer, and then lead us in an imaging experience, an extended time when I could let thoughts, feelings, and images come and go. Later, downstairs, we ate, drank, and talked. One Monday, as we shared wine, bread, and cheese, I thought to myself, "This is what holy communion is intended to be."

Things continued to shift for me, and in me, over the next few years. When I pick up my leather-bound journal that begins with June 1976, the first page reads, "How do I begin such a fine book? I think I have waited six

---

8 Dorothy Berkley Phillips, editor, *The Choice Is Always Ours: An Anthology on the Religious Way* (Wheaton, IL: Re-Quest Books, 1975).

9 W. H. Auden, "For the Time Being: A Christmas Oratorio," in *Collected Poems*, ed. Edward Mendelson (New York: Vintage Books, 1991), 353.

months to feel worthy of such a book. Thank you, Gina. This is a good birthday gift." At last, I was valuing my inner journey. I continued, "I need to work on three things, and they are all connected—my relationships with men, my own death, and my relationship with God." I had recently read Ernest Becker's *The Denial of Death*, and I must have been well into reading Becker's *The Birth and Death of Meaning* because the next page in my journal contains the following excerpt where Becker refers to William James:

> . . . [James] himself believed in the desirability of extending one's allegiance up to the highest level: Anything less than God is not rational (given the miracle of creation); anything more than the abstraction "God" (i.e., possession of certain knowledge about the actual Creator and his plan) is not possible. We can't know. . . .the nature of ultimate reality since we ourselves are transcended by it.[10]

In response I wrote, "I can affirm this. I think I have affirmed this all along. . . . sometimes covered over with various veneers." Amidst my struggles I was affirming the core, the central strong strand of that rope, while so many of the strands around it had been unraveling.

My journals from 1976 through 1978 are filled with records of my dreams and conversations with my therapist. In January 1977, I wrote: "What do you want for yourself this year? (1) to love and be loved; (2) to grow, (3) to find meaning." And then I added, "That I exist at all strikes wonder."

I continued to read. Carl Jung, James Hillman, Marie-Louie von Franz, more Jung. I was taken by his *Memories, Dreams, and Reflections*, grabbed by his famous dream, where a huge bird flies over a church and drops a large turd on the steeple. Here was a person, son, and grandson of Lutheran clergy, steeped in Christianity, who offered me a psychology, a spirituality, a cosmology, a way to think and feel about being a human being—a way to respond to the conservative Christianity of my childhood. Remembering the power of the two dreams I had shortly after B. and I separated, I began to keep a dream journal. I took my dreams to therapy. I went to seminars and retreats presented by Jungians, of which there was no shortage in San Francisco. I

10 Ernest Becker, *The Birth and Death of Meaning* (New York: Free Press, 1971), 189-190.

fantasized about studying in Zurich. At Katharine's home, I met philosopher Sam Keen and psychotherapist Robert Johnson. I wrote poetry.

I flew to Washington, DC, to attend a workshop about career change called What Color Is Your Parachute? Back in San Francisco, I was not yet ready to use fully the insights of the workshop in my own life. But I made a first step by working with my English department colleague Peter to create a series of weekend workshops through the University of California at Santa Cruz that focused on life and career planning for adults. And, important to both of us, these included a spiritual component. As we asked participants to think about what work needed doing in the world and what work they imagined they might do, I knew that it was my own life that I wanted to change.

Early in 1977 came the teatime with Katharine that I will not forget. As I described the educational psychology graduate program I was considering, Katharine paused. "Hmmm," she said. "I think you might like seminary." I was surprised and deeply touched. Though I was not conscious of it before she spoke those words, she had recognized and named my spiritual longing. And I soon came to realize how fully I had suppressed my desire to study theology. I did not record this conversation with her in my journal—rather, it is imprinted on my psyche. I know she must have said this to me in early 1977, because my journal that year includes many passages of wondering how I could possibly make seminary happen. My wonderings included lists of probable expenses, and the critical question: How will I support myself and Maja?

Within the year, I had crossed the Bay Bridge—to explore Pacific School of Religion, one of the eight seminaries in the Graduate Theological Union consortium, all but one located in a few square blocks nicknamed Holy Hill, on the edge of the University of California-Berkeley campus. I was thirty-eight when I applied and was accepted. I took a deep breath and applied for a one-year paid sabbatical from my teaching position. I knew I would need to return to teach two more years after the sabbatical. If I did not return, I would owe the school district two years of pay. I did not allow myself to fully absorb the risk I was taking.

I began seminary in September 1979. A week into the first semester, walking across the campus, I stopped in my tracks. I looked across the bay toward San Francisco and around at the seminary buildings. I knew, suddenly, why I was so angry at B. when he dropped out of seminary during the first year of our marriage. My conservative religious upbringing had left no room for women to consider theological education. It had never occurred to me that I could study theology. It had taken twelve years for my projections to fall away. Katharine's simple statement that I might like seminary had awakened me to my own deep longing.

Stepping Into the Story

When I began seminary in 1979, I was a practicing Quaker, still influenced more than I knew by my fundamentalist Baptist roots. I was excited about the smorgasbord of classes offered by the seminaries on Holy Hill, but I knew only that I wanted to go to seminary, not where it would lead me. I took ethics from the Jesuits, phenomenology from the Dominicans, and church history from the Episcopalians. I remember my professor at the Presbyterian seminary, Roy Fairchild, saying, "Prayer is paying full and fervent attention to all you know of God with all you know of yourself." As I reflected on my life, I could see how knowing myself was intimately connected to knowing God. I feared the God of my childhood—transcendent and judgmental. And I had hidden from God and myself—in large part by following what was expected of me. Now in seminary, I felt the freedom to question, wonder, doubt, and explore.

Reading the Bible Through was one of my first classes. It met five days a week, all day, during the last two weeks of August. Although we did not literally read every word, we were fully immersed in the text in various ways, including chanting the psalms. Near the end of the second week, we focused on the Gospels, the four accounts of Jesus's life and teachings.

One of the last days of class, we entered the classroom, bringing our Bibles, to find that all the tables and desks had been moved aside. Several benches had been placed in the middle of the large room. The professor announced that we would be enacting the Gospel of Mark. Pointing to a young man, he said, "This is Jesus." Indicating a woman instructor and himself, he said, "We are the narrators." He invited the rest of us to play all the other roles, encouraging us to take any part that grabbed us, both acting and speaking.

The Gospel of Mark moves fast. Most of my classmates stepped quickly into roles. I stood mesmerized as John the Baptist came on the scene. At Jesus's baptism I was still waiting at the edge of the crowd. Then came the call to Simon and Andrew in their boat (one of the benches). Another bench farther away became the synagogue, and yet another, the home of Simon and

Andrew. Jesus healed the leper, and then he healed the paralyzed man, carried by classmates on a "stretcher," another bench. For the following three chapters, I was swept along with the crowd.

Then came Jairus, begging for the healing of his daughter. Within that story is the story of the woman with the hemorrhage. Jesus, surrounded by a large crowd, walks toward Jairus's house. I began to press forward toward Jesus through the crowd. Then my body decided: I grabbed at his cloak. Jesus turned and said, "Who touched my clothes?" In the crush and confusion of people, his disciples chided him, "How can you say, 'Who touched me?'" I fell on my knees at his feet as the narrator spoke: "But the woman, knowing what had happened to her, came in fear and trembling, fell down before him, and told him the whole truth." Jesus replied, "Daughter, your faith has made you whole."

I came to tears. Jesus had already turned, and with the crowd, moved on to Jairus's house. I do not know how long I remained motionless, kneeling. Finally, I stood and moved through the rest of the Gospel of Mark—miracles, teachings, betrayal, crucifixion, and discovery of the empty tomb. The enactment ended with our standing in a circle facing outward and being sent forth.

I cannot explain what happened that morning. I had not looked ahead to chapter five and said to myself, "Ah, this is where I want to jump in." I was grasped in the moment by the story of the woman who had suffered a hemorrhage for twelve years and longed to be healed. I responded, not from my head, but with my body from my heart. Later, as I reread the text, I noted that the woman spoke, telling the whole truth. Her healing came through being touched and having her story heard and honored.

I have come to understand that falling to my knees that August morning was a way of telling my truth with the whole of me. My life had been broken open. My life was neither what I had imagined nor what I had hoped for. Without words, I was saying, "Right here is where I need to be. This is right. This is good. Wherever seminary takes me, I am fully in." The movements of Spirit are a mystery and a gift. When I was open, story had the power to transform me.

In seminary, I found new words, new concepts, that helped me see more clearly my religious upbringing. H. Richard Niebuhr's *Christ and Culture,* an exploration of the ways Christians have related to culture throughout history, helped me understand that I had grown up in a "Christ against culture" environment. He helped me see that there are several ways of experiencing and thinking about Christ and culture—and many ways to claim Christianity. In my first two years of seminary, it was as if I had begun to realize that the house I lived in had many more rooms than I'd thought—spacious rooms in the basement, rooms in the attic, rooms with windows and doors that opened onto porches and decks. All kinds of possibilities were opening within me.

At Pacific School of Religion, one of the professors facilitated a class in sacred movement; he invited us to put sticky notes on the parts of ourselves that we felt positive about and the parts that troubled us, that needed blessing. Then we moved about the large room, acknowledging our classmates and being acknowledged—in gracious silence. I put a sticky on my forehead, feeling positive about my mind. And a sticky on my thigh—I had always felt those thighs were a bit too thick. We walked around the room and met the eyes of our classmates, becoming part of a communal confession and absolution, an acceptance of ourselves, and of one another. It was so different from my early experiences of organized religion.

As I continued to meet regularly with Katharine, I spoke with her about my growing appreciation of being part of two communities—San Francisco Friends Meeting and the seminaries—where I experienced acceptance and at the same time invitation to wonder and question. One afternoon, she told me about Pendle Hill, a Quaker center for study and contemplation in Wallingford, Pennsylvania. She described it as an intentional community founded by Quakers in 1930 that offered hospitality to a range of people, many of whom were searching and discerning what might be next for them. One could spend a year or a term as a student, stay for a shorter time as a sojourner, or attend a seminar or retreat. One lived in community and participated in the practical work of the community; one could take classes and worship with the community. It sounded like a place where Professor Fairchild's words about prayer could be lived. Katharine said she thought I would like it. It sounded too good to be true. I wanted to go there, live there. But going there seemed out of reach. Yet, I trusted Katharine. Her previous suggestions had led me to the San Francisco Friends Meeting and then to seminary. I was ready to trust her again—but how might it work? How would Pendle Hill fit into seminary? Where would eleven-year-old Maja go to school? Who would manage our Victorian house and the tenants in three apartments? How would we get from San Francisco to Wallingford, Pennsylvania?

With the help of a seminary professor who knew Katharine, I arranged for an independent study at Pendle Hill that would fulfill seminary requirements. Maja would be able to continue fifth grade at a small Quaker school in nearby Rose Valley. My nephew would come to San Francisco to live in our flat and manage the property.

And so, amazingly, in the early spring of 1980, Maja and I flew to Minnesota, borrowed my parents' Volvo station wagon, and drove to Pennsylvania. I loved Pendle Hill immediately, as did Maja. On campus, she and I lived in a small suite with a bedroom and bathroom. Maja went to school in Rose Valley. I studied. And we both helped set tables, cook, and clean as part of the community. We loved the pottery studio, spending many hours together and separately, hand building pots and learning to use the wheel. I am reminded of one of the glazes called *runny nose* every time I see the pot that holds my pens and pencils. Each morning, I sat in silence in meeting for worship, grateful to be in a place where attention to spirituality was a consistent and acknowledged part of life.

Not long after arriving, I met Parker Palmer, the renowned educator whose work, based in the values and practices of Quakers, continues to influence me profoundly. Palmer, in turn, introduced me to the writings of the Trappist monk Thomas Merton. Though Merton had died in 1968, his work moved me so deeply, it was as if he were alive.

Indeed, through Merton, I found the words that redefined salvation. The words I most needed to hear are from his book, *New Seeds of Contemplation.* Fifty years later, its paperback spine has collapsed, and a rubber band holds it together. The book falls open to chapter five, "Things in Their Identity." The following passage, most of which I know by heart, comes to me again and again, sometimes when I hear or read the word *salvation*, and more often when I sit in my study, look out the west window, and see our big burr oak tree reaching up to the sky:

> A tree gives glory to God by being a tree. . . . It "consents," so to speak to His [God's] creative love . . . Trees and animals have no problem. God makes them what they are without consulting them, and they are perfectly satisfied. . . . God leaves us free to be whatever we like. We can be ourselves or not, as we please. We are at liberty to be real, or to be unreal. We may be true or false, the choice is ours . . . . we are even called to share with God the work of creating the truth of our identity. . . . To work out our own identity in God, which the Bible calls "working out our salvation," is a labor that requires sacrifice and anguish, risk and many tears.[11]

Merton's words liberated me. Rather like the Israelites in the wilderness, I had spent many years wandering. Merton's words redefining *salvation* unraveled more strands in that rope I had been given. Merton affirmed the anguish and risk I was experiencing in taking hold of my life. I could claim that the process of creating my own identity in God was good and right.

---

11 Thomas Merton, *New Seeds of Contemplation* (New York: New Directions Publishing, 1961), 29–32.

A Way Will Open

Early in my time at San Francisco Friends Meeting, I heard the iconic Quaker phrase, "A way will open." Taking a sabbatical from my teaching job and entering seminary was, I hoped, the opening of a way. After returning to San Francisco from my semester at Pendle Hill in the summer of 1980, I was desperate for another way to open, a way that would not lead me back to teaching and chairing the English department in September. What to do? Was there a way I could continue seminary part time? What could seminary lead to? How was I to make a living in the meantime? If I did not return to teaching, I would owe the school district the equivalent of two years of my salary in cash to pay back my year of sabbatical.

Then I spotted an opportunity. The Jefferson Union High School District was opening a federally funded teacher center as a resource for the five high schools in the district, including Westmoor and Serramonte. The position of director was advertised. Maybe this could allow me to continue seminary half time and begin to fulfill my financial obligation to the district. Knowing my colleague Peter also wanted to leave teaching, I called him. Maybe we could job-share. We had team-taught at Westmoor and then at Serramonte, creating a consensus decision-making process to run the English department, and more recently had created a university extension class on life and career planning. We were good partners.

Happily, Peter was ready to job-share, and we got the job. I could continue seminary, Maja and I could eat, and we would still be covered on the school district's health plan. But I was also anxious. Someone else would take the teaching job I would leave. If I went back to teaching, I would no longer have seniority. Phrases like "crossing the Rubicon" came to mind.

The Teacher Center was housed in a newly emptied San Andreas elementary school, located directly on the San Andreas Fault. The shifting tectonic plates beneath were an apt metaphor for the tenuousness of my life. Weekday mornings that academic year of 1980–81, twelve-year-old Maja caught a Muni streetcar at the corner of Market Street and Eighteenth Street to travel through the Twin Peaks tunnel to Hoover Middle School, while I took a BART train under the San Francisco Bay to Berkeley for class or drove south to work at the teacher center in Daly City. I was happy, although I suspect my anxiety expressed itself in fantasies that the big earthquake would occur while Maja was stuck in the L car under Twin Peaks. She was a latchkey child, heading to school with a key strung on a brown shoelace around her neck and tucked under her shirt. Often, she let herself into our Victorian before I arrived home.

One afternoon coming from Daly City, I turned onto our street to see a huge fire engine parked on the hill in front of our house. I left the car in the neighbor's driveway and ran through the gate and up the flight of stairs. In the kitchen stood Maja and two burly firefighters in full gear. It turned out to be a water emergency, not a fire. A valve under the kitchen sink had burst. Hot water had spewed, drenching the kitchen and leaking through the floor into the flat below. Maja, not panicking, had run a half block down to the corner store to ask the owner to help her call the fire department. "You have a smart daughter here," said one of the firemen. Hugging Maja, I collapsed in relief. I do not recall what fear-filled fantasies ran through my head when I saw the fire engine. But I know they were about Maja's safety—that I was fully responsible for her, for my decision to leave teaching, for arranging for her to be a latchkey child, for threatening her well-being. Holding our lives together was a balancing act that could easily crash. I knew I was choosing a course of action that to others looked impractical, even selfish.

I had calculated that it would take four years to pay back the school district working half time at the teacher center and taking seminary classes the other half, and I had only vague ideas of what seminary could lead to. I felt a bit like Jacob laboring for Rachel, who just might get Leah instead.

When Pendle Hill advertised a job for an administrator to manage its weekend programs, I wondered if another way might be opening. I asked Parker Palmer to write me a letter of recommendation. I did not get the job. Disappointed and sad, I was certain that the ideal job had just slipped away. As I read the gracious rejection letter, my fantasies of leaving teaching and living and working at Pendle Hill evaporated. A way had not opened. Parker had not yet written his book *Let Your Life Speak* where he suggests that a way closing can be as helpful as a way opening. I told myself to be grateful for the job I had and for the probability that Peter and I could work together for another year or more. Yet, I knew that my seminary classes took my best energy.

In early 1981, I received a phone call from a woman named Ruth Halvorson in Minnesota. My sister Shirley had given her my phone number. Ruth asked if I knew of ARC, the ecumenical retreat center that she and her husband, Loren, had founded, along with others, in 1976. She explained that the letters referred to Action, Reflection, and Celebration. I did know of it! Months earlier Parker Palmer had told me about the huge log house built by volunteers in the woods near Stanchfield, Minnesota, an hour north of the Twin Cities. Ruth's call was an exploration, she said. They needed someone to take her place doing administrative work and leading retreats while she and Loren, a professor at Luther Seminary in St. Paul, went on sabbatical. She had met Shirley and Shirley's husband, Ken, when they visited ARC. They had talked about my time at Pendle Hill and my desire to leave teaching. Ruth asked me if I would be interested in exploring the possibility of working at ARC. Elated, I said yes.

I visited ARC in April with Maja, and by the end of our stay, a plan was made for us to move to Minnesota that summer of 1981 to live at ARC for one year. Shirley and Ken and their two younger daughters would also move to ARC. Maja and I returned to San Francisco to make our plans to move. Peter would stay at the teacher center full time. I put seminary on hold for a year, not knowing if I would return. I depleted most of my retirement fund to buy myself out of the salary I owed the school district.

In early summer, David, Ken, and a friend drove out to San Francisco to get us. We loaded our belongings into my Volvo and an old Ford pickup truck pulling a U-Haul trailer. David had told me not to look back, but when our caravan crossed the Bay Bridge, I did anyway. I cried.

We drove straight east on Interstate 80 through Oakland, across the California Central Valley, over the Donner Pass into Nevada, and across Utah and Wyoming until turning north at Kearney, Nebraska. It was a route I had driven many times with B., David, or Maja. Just north of the Iowa border, we pulled into the family farmyard, two days and two thousand miles later. We were met by David and Sally Anne's two young children, Heather and Anton, holding up a huge hand-painted sign that said, "Welcome Home." I cried again.

What I Left, What I Took with Me

When I left California and San Francisco, I left much. I left a city alive with diversity, a city where I could walk to bookstores, the small local markets where I bought cheese at one stop and bread at the next. I left the ice cream shop on the corner of Castro and Twenty-fourth. I left the flower shop, the iconic Castro Theater, and a half dozen ethnic restaurants within walking distance. I left running in Dolores Park, in Golden Gate Park, and along Ocean Beach. I left the redwoods in Muir Woods and Big Basin, the beaches at Point Reyes. I left those drives up the coast to Mendocino and down the coast to the Big Sur. I left backpacking in Yosemite. I left my Victorian house on Twentieth Street with its wide view of the city and the Bay Bridge. I left the brilliant bougainvillea vine with its huge splash of red blooms that climbed the front of the house to Maja's bedroom windows on the third floor.

I left my work, my colleagues, my partnership with Peter. I left San Francisco Friends Meeting, that big brick house on Lake Street in the Richmond where I sat in peaceful silence with others Sunday after Sunday. I left tea with Katharine Whiteside Taylor. I left friends. I left my ex-husband, my child's father, wondering how we would parent Maja over such a distance.

Only later did I experience grief and loss. Displacement. I wrote to Katharine and stayed connected to several friends through letters and infrequent visits. But I feel regret that I didn't work harder to stay connected. So much of those years in San Francisco are experiences I share only with Maja, and bits with David, Sally Anne, and Gina. Sometimes, that part of my life seems like it belongs to someone else. I am struck with a feeling of loss when someone says, "I thought you had always lived in Minnesota." I am aware of how deeply I have been influenced by having lived in San Francisco for those formative years, 1966–81. Perhaps, I assume my experience of living there ought to show more clearly. San Francisco is where I found a spiritual mentor, the Quakers, and Carl Jung. It is where I began seminary. It is where my marriage disintegrated and where I learned to survive—and more than survive. It is where my rope began to rebraid with new strands. My values of inclusion and equity were shaped during those years. My political activism began in protests against the Vietnam War in Golden Gate Park and along Market Street after Harvey Milk's assassination. Living in the Castro, a half block from Milk's camera shop, amid gay coffeeshops, bookstores, and restaurants, was a gift that cannot be duplicated.

Those who know me well have asked me over the years about living in—and leaving—San Francisco. I did not leave San Francisco because I did not like it. I loved living there.

I left San Francisco because a way opened: to do work that focused on spiritual formation, to live in intentional community, and to be near my family—my siblings and their children, and my parents on the farm. After fourteen years in San Francisco and one year in Lower Kalskag, Alaska, I was returning to Minnesota, a divorced woman, and the mother of a daughter; not just a lapsed Baptist, but a Quaker. I was eager to continue to explore my own journey. Even though I knew the job was only for a year, a way had opened, and I was happy.

Action, Reflection, Celebration

Maja and I had left a busy city where buses growled up the Twentieth Street hill in front of our house late into the night, where Maja took the Muni to school, where my afternoon run out our door included hills, no matter which way I headed.

At ARC, we lived on acres of forest, ten miles from the nearest town. Maja and her cousins rode the school bus. I could run on miles of gravel road and meet only a couple of vehicles and fend off a couple dogs. We lived in a big log building that housed Maja and me; Shirley, Ken, and their daughters Sharon and Sarah; Judith Stoughton, an art history professor at St. Catherine University; and Richard Andersen, a recent graduate from Luther Seminary. Throughout the year, other staff and volunteers lived with us for shorter periods of time and many guests came on weekends and weekdays for retreats—all creating a lively intergenerational experience.

While Ruth and Loren were on sabbatical, our mission was to continue to carry forward the values and practices of the retreat center and community life: action, reflection, and celebration (ARC). As we welcomed groups for the weekend on Friday evenings, we told the story of ARC and invited people into community, a time of contemplation, communal prayer, carefully shaped programming, good food, and walks in the woods. Whatever programming people came for, hospitality was our central focus. We remembered to say what Ruth had told us, "Invite the guests to take a nap first, if that is what they need."

Although the learning curve was sometimes steep, I loved being part of an intentional ecumenical community, and I loved my work as program director and retreat leader. Every day brought new opportunities to meet new people and to wonder about spirituality. At meals, I listened to guests tell how they had discovered ARC and what it meant to them. The language of the inward journey—the life of prayer—and the outward journey—service in the world—felt true and solid—and Quakerly. As I met many of our guests, I appreciated that my year at ARC was giving me an unusual opportunity to get to know a wide range of people whose intent was to deepen their experience of the Holy and strengthen their acts of justice in the world. I wondered how I might shape my life in the years to come to include what I had found at ARC.

Every few days, a new group of people arrived, sometimes a church group on weekend retreat, sometimes staff from a church, seminary, or judicatory body. I was immersed in a community of people—clergy, lay, academics—where the focus was both spirituality and the institutional church. I began to learn the meanings of words *like judicatory, elder, deacon, conference minister, district superintendent, bishop*, and acronyms like *OSB*, *CSJ*, and *ELCA* (Order of Saint Benedict, Sisters of Saint Joseph of Carondelet, Evangelical Lutheran Church in America). I had come over two thousand miles to live in an ecumenical and interfaith subculture that I had first encountered at the seminaries in Berkeley.

In one of the first newsletters for which I was responsible, I wrote about my spiritual journey and shared an excerpt from T. S. Eliot's *Four Quartets*:

> We shall not cease from exploration
> And the end of all our exploring
> Will be to arrive where we started
> And know the place for the first time.[12]

I wrote, "I am certainly not at the end of my exploring, but I am recognizing that the place where I am, both inward and outward, is a place of great possibility."

At Pendle Hill I had looked forward to sitting with the Quaker community in unprogrammed silence every morning. At ARC, we entered a different kind of prayer time, sitting in a circle on cushions. Community members took turns shaping and leading morning and evening prayer. All were invited to participate, including the children. Maja and her cousins Sharon and Sarah stepped in to read, sing, and play their instruments. Some groups of guests joined us in what we had planned. Others wanted to lead their own prayer. On Sunday mornings during the Eucharist, we spoke the words and passed the bread and wine to one another. As the year went on, I became aware that I found the Eucharist more and more meaningful. As well, I was so happy to

---

12 T. S. Eliot, *Four Quartets* (New York: HarperCollins, 1971), 59.

sing. I loved the Quakers, but I had missed singing more than I knew. When I realized that Ruth and Loren intended to visit the Taizé Community in France on their sabbatical, I bought a couple of tapes of the community's brief, repetitive chants, some in Latin, others in English or French. I listened, and I sang along. I kept one tape in my car.

I thought about Christian community and being Christian in new ways. I remember a conversation with Sister Judith as I was getting ready to take Maja and Sharon to St. Paul for their orchestra rehearsals. I said something like, "We won't be here for prayer tonight." She responded with, "When the community prays, you pray with us, wherever you are." This felt revelatory. It was an invitation for me to let go a bit more of the religion of my childhood where the focus was on the individual person's relationship to God. Her words supported conversations I was having with Ken about community and the Hebrew scriptures' message about the people of God.

The retreat house, built amidst pine trees and not far from a creek, offered a peaceful setting for community members as well as guests. But it was a different experience to be staff. Many people commented, "It must be wonderful to live in such a calm and peaceful place." It was. I loved living there. Yet, we also found that living and working in a retreat center was hard physical work. We were rightly proud of our cook who came from Cambridge five days a week to make our bread, yogurt, granola, and main dishes. But it was our responsibility to prepare food, clean the kitchen, do laundry, clean the retreat house, and take turns feeding wood into the boiler in the middle of winter nights.

After we sent guests off on Sunday afternoons, encircling them and singing, "May the longtime sun shine upon you, all love surround you, and the pure Light within you, guide you on your way home," Ken and Sister Judith drove back to their teaching duties in St. Paul. Shirley and I collapsed into napping. Sunday night was the one night we had no guests. We often sprawled in the big living room with our children to watch *Masterpiece Theater*, eat pancakes or popcorn, and take turns pulling the sheets out of the washer and putting them into the dryer.

Although Maja once said something about how it seemed that only "really good" people came to ARC, she experienced significant loss in moving to Minnesota, and probably also depression. When she came home after the first day of eighth grade at the local school, she told me the math class would be a repeat of what she had learned the year before. After discussion with school personnel, we agreed that Maja would enter ninth grade.

Another concern for her was not remedied with as much seeming ease. She had also said during that first week of school, "Mama, they all look alike. And I look just like them." Her statement was not an expression of pleased surprise. Stepping into rural central Minnesota, she found that most of her classmates were as white and blond as she was. She had left behind her Asian, Hispanic, and Black friends and classmates. I often wondered what her new acquaintances would think if she told them about growing up in the Castro, about taking the Muni to school and, on the way home, wandering through shops on Eighteenth and Castro under the protective watch of gay men.

I had made a decision that I was sure was so right for me. I could only hope that eventually it would be a good decision for her as well. I promised myself that after we left ARC the following year, whatever my plans, we would not move during her high school years.

During the summer months leading to our departure from ARC, a guest arrived who was to challenge me to my core. A Southerner affiliated with the United Methodist Church, C. was a student at a seminary in Atlanta. As we connected over intense discussions of theology and church polity, I found myself drawn to him both intellectually and physically. We began a relationship, but our differences made me anxious. He took up a lot of space, physically and psychologically. He was younger than me, and our life experiences were vastly different. I sensed that neither Shirley nor Ken approved. I did not know whether I did either, but I had professional plans to make and pushed my concerns about our growing relationship to the edge of consciousness.

The end of our yearlong commitment at ARC meant moving back to St. Paul. Maja was registered for ninth grade at Derham Hall High School, a Roman Catholic girls' school. I registered for classes at United Theological Seminary. And we needed to find a place to live. Living in community at ARC with my sister and her family had been a positive experience, so Shirley, Ken, and I decided to look for a place that would house the six of us. I arranged to sell the house I still co-owned with Maja's father in San Francisco, and Shirley and Ken sold their house in a St. Paul suburb. It took several months to find the right place, a triplex in St. Paul. Located near a busy intersection with churches on two corners, I referred to it as north of the Greeks (Saint George's Orthodox Church) and west of the Romans (then Saint Luke's Roman Catholic Church). Maja and I moved into the second-floor flat; Shirley, Ken, and their daughters into the first-floor flat; and renters (usually related to us) were to live in the third-floor unit. Having secured housing, I turned my attention to finding a job. The little money I had left after having paid back my sabbatical was dwindling.

Pushed and Pulled: Taking Hold

If someone had asked me in the fall of 1982, "What is your intent in continuing seminary?" I do not know how I would have replied. I knew I wanted to follow where three formative events had led me: beginning seminary at Pacific School of Religion in Berkeley, living for a term at Pendle Hill in Pennsylvania, and spending a year at ARC Retreat Center. I was following my longing to study, to have conversations about spirituality—the kind that had drawn me to Katharine Whiteside Taylor—even if I did not know yet where it would lead me. While I was often anxious about how I would support Maja and myself, my deep desire was to find a spiritual home. I was realizing that the longing for whatever I called God had been part of my life as long as I could remember, perhaps present before recall. It was present in my doubts and wonderings in my childhood and had permeated my journals in my twenties and thirties, but until I said no to my marriage and took responsibility for my own life, I could not find a way forward that felt true and right. Now my longing was fully alive.

At United Theological Seminary, the class that challenged me the most was Christology. Our major assignment was to write about who and what Jesus was. Carrying so much baggage from my childhood, I did not know what to write or even think. I was drawn to Mark's Gospel, to the Jesus who seemed more human. Our Christology professor had said, "Start with your assumptions." It seemed to me that the Jesus of the first half of Mark did not walk around saying to himself or to others, "I am the Messiah." Rather, his ministry and identity were unfolding. My rough draft of that paper began with the statement, "Jesus didn't know either." Just as Jesus struggled to know who he was, what his ministry was, I struggled to know who Jesus was—and is. His identity would need to unfold for me. After identifying my assumptions, the assignment required me to assert my beliefs—a far more difficult charge.

I have a vivid memory of my New Testament professor, Henry Gustafson, his arm outstretched, hand pointing away from him, saying, "Jesus points us to God. Not to himself. Jesus shows us what God is like." Yes, this was more and more true for me. My view of God as judge was shifting. The God Jesus pointed to was inclusive, compassionate, fully present, just—and not judgmental. The Gospel stories about Jesus showed a life lived and a death accepted as a consequence of the life lived. The Gospel stories showed me a way to live.

I was realizing that deeply imbedded in the doctrine of my childhood religion was what New Testament scholar Marcus Borg calls the priestly story, "a story of sin, guilt, sacrifice, and forgiveness." In *Meeting Jesus Again for the First Time*, Borg writes that this is one of three macro-stories in the Hebrew and Christian Scriptures. He suggests two other powerful stories that resonated for me: the exodus and the exile.[13] I related fully to the exodus—that sense of liberation, of beginning a journey as I let go of fundamentalist theology. And having jettisoned Christianity in my twenties, in my late thirties I was coming back from exile, struggling to sort out what I might be able to claim. I felt like blinders had been removed.

I saw more clearly that I, and much of Christianity, had settled into the priestly story, where the death of Jesus solves the problem of sin. Who is going to pay for my sins? Because someone must pay. I can quote the words of the songs: "Jesus paid it all, all to him I owe." *Penal atonement theology* is a term for this—we are saved from damnation by Jesus paying the price—the sacrifice—that God demands. Even in childhood, I had wondered how this kind of a God was a loving God. But this was what I had heard from the pulpit again and again. Though my assertions and beliefs were changing, and I felt a sense of ease, the shadow of the old theology was not erased. It had been deposited in my bones, taken in with my food. I had more work to do.

In the early months of 1983, my second term at United Theological Seminary, a woman from one of my classes approached me and asked if we could talk. While I was at ARC I had shaped a career counseling practice. I thought that maybe this was what she was looking for. During a long conversation, it became clear that she was seeking a spiritual companion, not a career counselor. We had a second conversation, and within a few weeks,

13 Marcus Borg, *Meeting Jesus Again for the First Time* (New York: HarperSanFrancisco, 1994), 121-133.

we shaped a more formal relationship of meeting for an hour once a month. I asked her what she saw in me that encouraged her to approach me. She replied that I seemed "seasoned," and that although I had left organized religion, I was choosing seminary. Soon, another woman approached me seeking an ongoing dialogue about spirituality. These relationships marked the beginning of my work as a spiritual director. I was deeply touched to be sought out. These two women were seeking what I had found in Katharine, a listening presence, full acceptance—a companion. I was surprised, humbled, and grateful.

I knew then that I needed to be supported by others who offered spiritual direction. At that time, spiritual direction was not well known at United. I knew I needed to look more broadly—to find people familiar with the spiritual direction community in the Twin Cities. I began asking. Soon, at a workshop for clergy and therapists on the topic of shame, I met John Ackerman, a Presbyterian minister who was an associate pastor with a focus on adult spiritual development at Westminster Presbyterian Church in downtown Minneapolis. During a break, we talked. I told him I had been at ARC and was now in seminary. Taking a deep breath, I told him about the two women at seminary who were seeking spiritual direction. When our break was over, John said, "Let's talk more during lunch." Over the next hour, my thoughts wandered. Might meeting John be a door opening to what I needed?

It was. During lunch John told me he was looking for individuals offering spiritual direction who might want to be part of an ecumenical peer supervision group. He was hoping to form a group of both Protestants and Roman Catholics who would meet monthly to support one another—to offer consultation, to reflect on our own spiritual practice, and to learn from one another. He asked whether I wanted to be part of the group. Amazed and grateful, I said yes. At our first group meeting in the lower level of Westminster Church, our group was twelve in number. After a few meetings, six of us remained: John, Joel Wiberg (Lutheran clergy), Mark Scanell (Dominican), Joanne Dehmer (School Sisters of Notre Dame) and Virginia Matter (Benedictine). My new colleagues, immersed in the religious and spiritual communities of both Minneapolis and St. Paul, were to be my mentors and colleagues for years to come.

Though my peer supervision group accepted me fully, at times I felt like an imposter, and certainly a novice. What credentials did I have besides two women who had sought me out for conversations about spirituality? I was a lapsed Baptist and a recent Quaker. My advanced degree was in English literature. I did not have any specific certification from a training program. I was not a Roman Catholic or an Episcopalian, traditions that teach and honor the contemplative life. I was not an ordained Protestant. I had not even finished seminary. As well, it was only a few years earlier that I had named my conversations with Katharine *as* spiritual direction.

It was soon evident that the peer supervision group and seminary were opening all kinds of possibilities for me. Classes, book recommendations, seminars, and conversations all challenged me. I had begun to read Merton while at Pendle Hill. Now I added Hildegard of Bingham, Julian of Norwich, and Meister Eckart. I found Morton Kelsey's *The Other Side of Silence: A Guide to Christian Meditation.* I was drawn to Kelsey's writings as I had been drawn to Jung years earlier. Kelsey, an Episcopal priest, clearly steeped in Jung's writings, invited me to go deep, to wonder about my dreams, to meditate, to read scripture and other writings as a basis for active imaging—that Jungian practice I had learned first in Katharine's Monday evening gatherings. I was drawn to the Episcopal church.

Since leaving ARC, I had returned to worshipping with the Quakers. I identified strongly with Quaker founder George Fox's affirmation, "There is that of God in everyone." It counteracted early messages about my profound sinfulness that still arose, especially in the dark at 4:00 a.m. As a child and teen, I knew by heart the words to the song Shirley and I sang at church:

> Lord Jesus, I long to be perfectly whole.
> I want thee forever to live in my soul.
> Cast out every idol, break down every foe.
> Now wash me and I shall be whiter than snow.
> Whiter than snow, yes, whiter than snow.
> Now wash me and I shall be whiter than snow.

But when worshipping with the Quakers in St. Paul, I realized I had changed since I last attended Friends Meeting in San Francisco. What was so right in worshipping with the Quakers was listening in silence to the Spirit and the giving of oneself in service—an intimate connection between worship and my life of action in the world. The focus was on spiritual experience and service, not on doctrine and creed. This still rang true. But it was just as true that I missed ARC worship, especially the music and the celebration of the Eucharist. Maybe I wanted and needed aspects of a programmed liturgy.

As I moved through two years at United immersed in theology, church doctrine, history, and polity, all largely realms of the mind, I searched for a denomination with a contemplative tradition. At the same time, monthly gatherings with my peer group invited me to focus less on creed and doctrine and more on the experience of the sacred that clearly transcends human religious categories. I looked at the offerings of other Protestant seminaries. Few offered classes about spirituality. Thinking that United could offer a small remedy, another student and I put together a student-taught course in spirituality. Teaching the class gave me the opportunity to clarify my understanding of doctrine. I could finally assert my belief that doctrine is secondhand, partial, and inadequate. Creed attempts to summarize experience but does not create it; indeed, it often fails to make room for experience. Story, image, and metaphor are better choices for pointing us to the sacred. They are still removed from experience, but for me, not as far removed as doctrine.

It was a watershed moment. I mused about how we humans get to doctrine and creed, how we begin with experience, personal and communal. We tell one another about our experiences of the Mystery that is God. Over centuries our stories are collected and told, communicated through the scriptures and the traditions of communities of faith. As well, new stories are continually being told. Several of the strands of the rope that I had taken hold of in childhood were fraying and sloughing off. I was identifying the core strands that I could claim. I was beginning to braid a new rope.

If not the Quakers, with which denomination would I affiliate? For what ministry was seminary preparing me? Would I consider being a parish pastor? A chaplain? Did I need to be ordained? I knew it would be impossible to make a living offering spiritual direction. My head was filled with inner conversations.

As I continued to wonder and to explore church communities, I began to hope I could find a home within the Episcopal church. I attended Episcopal worship services and continued reading Kelsey. So much resonated with me. But when, in the late spring of 1983, I looked more fully at what an affiliation to Episcopalism would mean, I came up against a wall. I would need to do a year of seminary at an Episcopal seminary. There were none nearby, and I could not make a geographical move. Maja was a high school freshman in St. Paul, and I would not uproot her life again. I was disappointed and frustrated. Reluctantly, I let go of exploring the possibility of becoming an Episcopalian. I took a long look at the United Church of Christ, the founding denomination of both Pacific School of Religion and United Theological Seminary. I learned that the UCC emerged from a convergence of two groups in 1957: the Congregationalist Christian churches with Puritan roots and the Evangelical and Reformed tradition with roots in German and Swiss reformation theology. I became aware that UCC church structure is less hierarchical than that of the Methodists, Lutherans, and Episcopalians. Governance resided within local churches that associated with a conference. The UCC did not require its congregations or members to follow a creed. I breathed a sigh of relief. The denomination had a strong focus on social justice. I was pleased. A Congregational church in South Butler, New York, had ordained a woman, Antoinette Brown, in 1853, the first ordained woman minister in the country! So much looked right.

Though I did not see the tradition of contemplation that I saw in the Episcopalians, I could affirm much of the UCC. There was freedom within its structure. I began the process of affiliation. Though not as I had imagined it, I was finding a spiritual home. Not a perfect home but a "good enough" one. My decision was a practical one as well. I needed to find work that would support Maja and me. I understood that if I were to find work and function within the church as an institution, I needed a denominational identity and probably ordination as well.

As I began my final year of seminary, I met with the Minnesota Conference of the United Church of Christ's committee on ministry. Following an interview, I was accepted into the process that could lead toward ordination. I was considered "in care" and given a seasoned clergywoman as a mentor and advisor. The next step was to find a local UCC church in which to do my contextual education requirement, in other words, to serve as a student pastor.

Pushed and Pulled: Letting Go

It is striking that my relationship with C., begun during the last months of my stay at ARC, was unfolding against the backdrop of perhaps the most meaningful period of my life, personally, spiritually, and professionally. For almost four years, our relationship intermittently preoccupied me. It is painful to admit that my focus on him drained energy from other parts of my life, especially Maja during her high school years. Even now, I feel a stab of pain when I read advice to divorced parents who are beginning new relationships: "Your first loyalty is to your children." One December holiday, despite my guilt, I drove with him to Kentucky to meet his family, leaving Maja to celebrate Christmas with my sister's family. Guilt was a red flag, signaling that I was going against my values.

There was much about C. that I enjoyed and appreciated. He was intelligent and had an edge that could be fascinating. From the beginning, we had rambling conversations about theology, church history and polity, and especially about liturgy (order of worship), his forte. Only later, did I realize those times with C. were reminiscent of the conversations I'd had in college with the seminarian when I was a sophomore. And like those letters full of quotations that had traveled the US mail between B. and me in 1965, in all three relationships, I was giving over my power, my agency—that pattern so embedded in me, shaped by culture and religion. But with C., the red flags were becoming clear—the pattern was finally coming to full consciousness. Other factors arose. Not only was there a significant age difference, but we were at different places in our lives. I had married and divorced. I had a teenage daughter. He was in his early thirties and had committed himself to neither professional work nor a relationship. I had done both. I had stepped into adulthood in ways he had not. Though we were both seminary students, the trajectory of our lives had little in common. Any future I imagined with C. seemed fraught. I knew I had work to do, inner work, whether or not I stayed in a relationship with him.

My peer supervision group had helped me several years earlier to find my own spiritual director, Kay Vander Vort, a Roman Catholic laywoman. With the help of Kay and my therapist, I once again sought insight into my relationships with men. I looked deeper into my childhood, continuing to explore the power of fundamentalist Christianity. I saw more clearly how my father, B., and C. all embodied a patriarchal religious authority. And yet, at some level, even in childhood, there was a healthy part of me that pushed against it. I began to see that the disagreements in those relationships might have been about me asserting my agency. I stepped into a time of intense inner work, trying to understand and to forgive myself for choosing once again an unhealthy intimate relationship and letting my own agency slip away. I saw in my relationship with C. many of the same patterns that I had lived out in my relationship with B., the patterns that were rooted in my longing for a father who valued me and wanted to know me, and a God who accepted me.

As I look back, it seems obvious that I had yet to claim fully my own identity, my own spirituality, my own deep yearnings. I thought I had worked through that by getting myself to seminary. But no. My relationship with C. was a continuation of my overidentification with men, especially those who were seminarians or clergy, men who carried my projections, my spiritual yearnings. I was continuing to live out of the father/Father God struggles of my twenties. I thought I had jettisoned that old burden. I had not. It is telling that in the summer of 1983, my chaplaincy supervisor in the Clinical Pastoral Education program at Abbott Northwestern Hospital pushed me to think and write about my pastoral identity. Emphasis on "my." The supervisor had noted that, although I was very competent in many aspects of my chaplaincy work, I was not claiming the full pastoral authority that my role gave me. He had observed that I too readily deferred to men. Those many early years of experiencing men in leadership had shaped me more than I knew. Old patterns were embedded in my brain and my body.

During the academic year 1983–84, I prepared my resume and began to look for ministry positions. Because the UCC is a small denomination, I did not find much in the Twin Cities area. The few possibilities usually included working with children and youth. And although I had thirteen years of experience working five days a week with teens, I was a forty-four-year-old woman, and I did not look forward to teen lock-ins in church parlors. I had one interview. I did not get the job.

I had put a safety net in place: an application for a year's residency in chaplaincy at Abbott Northwestern Hospital, the same place I had done my required unit of Clinical Pastoral Education a year earlier. In the late summer of 1984, after graduating from United, I began my chaplaincy work in a chemical dependency unit at Abbott Northwestern. The position provided a small stipend that would support Maja and me for another twelve months and give me some time to sort out what might be next.

For six months, I cofacilitated groups and met with individual patients. My limited experience of chaplaincy a year earlier in a medical surgical unit had been rewarding, and I had imagined the possibility of continuing in chaplaincy. But hospital chaplaincy typically meant short-term relationships. I usually had one or two visits at most with a patient or family. I wanted more time with people. Working in chemical dependency, there was more time.

Twelve-step spirituality, the approach of the chemical dependency unit at Abbott Northwestern, was not entirely new to me. I had acquaintances who went to Alcoholics Anonymous and Al-Anon meetings. Yet I had not consciously applied the twelve steps to my own life. The six months I spent in the chemical dependency unit taught me that everyone is powerless in relation to something and/or someone. I was, as well. It wasn't alcohol or drugs. I recognized that my "drug" was C. I was still trying to make something happen that was not possible. I realized that I wanted C. to be someone other than who he was. I wanted a commitment of love from someone who couldn't give it to me. Just as in my relationship with B., I could not make C. commit to our relationship. I saw how our relationship was damaging to both of us.

Three memories about my relationship with C. are telling. I had a piercing moment of insight one sunny afternoon. We were sitting in my dining room. I was babysitting the child of a friend. The toddler was walking around my flat, exploring, with a pacifier in his mouth. C. began playing with the child. I watched as C. reached down to pull the pacifier from the child's mouth. Laughing, he held it a few inches away from the child. The child toddled toward the pacifier, mouth open, trying to retrieve it. C. let the child get close, and then quickly pulled the pacifier away, continuing to laugh. I watched. He continued. I was frozen, not wanting to believe what I was seeing. Finally, shaking with anger, I stood up and said, "What *are* you doing?" He did not seem to understand my anger at his manipulating a young child.

The second is not a specific memory but an ongoing awareness having to do with his not finishing seminary. From the beginning of our relationship, I realized there was some sort of difficulty about his finishing his seminary work. Whatever the barriers, whether academic or something else, they were vague. I could not easily understand them. I wondered why he could not do what he needed to do and move on into ministry. His not taking hold of this part of his life nagged at me.

A third memory is paired with my guilt at leaving Maja in St. Paul so I could spend a Christmas holiday with C. and his family in Kentucky. Staying in his family home with his parents and younger adult brothers for several days, I came to no clear insight, but rather a strong sense of anxiety. His mother seemed to be the dominant force in the family, and at the same time, C. and his brothers and father created an overwhelming presence of aggressive masculinity, teasing, poking, challenging, and shaming. It was an uncomfortable place to be. I remember going upstairs to a bedroom and sitting there, realizing I could not imagine stepping into this family. I could not imagine bringing Maja into this family. Within months, C. moved to central Minnesota to take a position at two small churches. His move gave us both physical and psychological space. Meanwhile, my professional work and my own therapy gave me the insight and courage to move toward ending our relationship.

In Alcoholics Anonymous, step five is often called confession. It involves admitting to God, to ourselves, and to another human being the exact nature of our wrong. Persons preparing to meet for a fifth step write an inventory of their wrongs. As I listened to fifth steps, I was amazed at people's trust, vulnerability, and humility. Here were women and men claiming the truth of their lives, seeking grace. I was honored to hear their stories and grateful for what I was learning. I will not forget the sixty-year-old man, divorced and estranged from his children, who knew exactly how many years, days, and hours he had been sober. The hardest thing, he said, was the feeling of pain and regret over how he had hurt his wife and children. Hearing him and others, I felt my shame and regret. It became clear to me that I needed to end my relationship with C. Still, it took me almost another year before I fully ended it. It took several years more to make full apologies to Maja for how my focus on C. had taken my energy and time from her during her high school years, and, as well, to Shirley and Ken, who were affected by my distraction and absence from our relationship.

Even before I asked if I could do my second six-month chaplaincy assignment in the mental health unit, I met John Martinson, the director of the Pastoral Counseling Center at Abbott Northwestern Hospital. He asked me if I was interested in pastoral counseling. Often called pastoral psychotherapy, pastoral counseling is a kind of psychotherapy that recognizes and honors the religious/spiritual tradition and formation of the person seeking it. Practitioners are trained both psychologically and theologically. Many pastoral counselors are also licensed as psychologists or marriage and family therapists. I recognized how much I loved my work as a spiritual director, meeting with an individual over a period of time. Could pastoral counseling be my full-time work? I explored with John how this could come to be. Did I need to get another degree, one in psychology? I knew that two of the staff at the center had degrees in psychology. But there was a path. I could complete the center's pastoral counseling training program when I finished my chaplaincy year. Then, I would meet a committee to be certified as a pastoral counselor by the American Association of Pastoral Counselors. Over time, with more training, I could be certified at a more advanced level. This sounded possible. John also asked whether I wanted to start seeing one or two people for counseling during the next few months and arrange for supervision. I said yes with little hesitation. I was recognizing that my temperament and skills were suited for pastoral counseling and spiritual direction.

During the next six months as I did chaplaincy work in the mental health unit, I began to see individual clients at the counseling center. My work fit me. I was letting go of my ideal ministry position, that of a parish pastor with responsibilities for adult spiritual formation. I stopped searching for a parish-based position. John Martinson's words of invitation were words I needed to hear.

Like finding the Quakers in San Francisco, finding the pastoral counseling staff at Abbott Northwestern felt like the right place and the right people. I finished my six months of chaplaincy in mental health and for the next year continued to build a load of pastoral counseling clients. Needing to make money while I completed training, I worked two days a week at Hazelden Pioneer House, the treatment center for adolescents and young adults, spending my days cofacilitating groups and hearing fifth steps.

The three other days I arrived at the pastoral counseling center at the medical office building on Twenty-sixth and Chicago by 8:00 a.m. I was often still at the office at 7:00 p.m. A colleague told me I needed to set my hours more realistically, that clients would fit the hours I posted. This was hard for me to do because I felt like such a novice again, but I limited my hours and built a full client load. Another colleague, a marriage and family therapist, suggested that I not only get certified as a pastoral counselor but also work toward getting licensed as a marriage and family therapist. By 1986, I was certified as a member of the American Association of Pastoral Counselors, on my way to being licensed as a marriage and family therapist, working in a profession I loved, and moving toward ordination. I had found my vocation.

After I completed the writing of my ordination paper in the spring of 1986, the next step was to meet with the Committee on Ministry, the administrative body of the United Church of Christ that decides if ordination is appropriate. I was anxious. Would I be approved? I have two strong memories of that interview. One is the challenge from a member of the committee who asked how it was that I was seeking ordination to a ministry of pastoral counseling when I was not in a church setting where I would offer Word and Sacrament (preaching and officiating at Eucharist). He quoted the specific language of the ritual of ordination. I knew that in many denominations a person only moves into specialized ministries like chaplaincy and pastoral counseling after a few years of experience in a parish. I also knew that the UCC ordained persons into chaplaincy. I said simply that I believed what I offered to the persons who sought pastoral counseling *was* Word and Sacrament. I wondered whether we might expand and enrich the meaning of Word and Sacrament. And that perhaps for some people, what a pastoral counselor offered could be more meaningful than what they experienced sitting in the pew on Sunday morning. In the faces of several committee members, I saw agreement.

The second memory was a comment about my written materials, made somewhat in passing by the same man who had challenged me earlier. He said something like, "The ideas in your paper are not very clearly presented. You use metaphor and story too much." I let that lie, making no response. A few days later, my mentor said to me as we processed my meeting with the committee, "You could have told him that Jesus had the same problem." I wish I had. Yet, what mattered was that I knew I had claimed my authority. I had spoken my truth.

The day of my ordination, August 20, 1986, I was happy. It was so right that I had chosen seminary. It was so right that I had chosen Pendle Hill and ARC. It felt so right that I had shifted my hopes and plans from parish ministry to pastoral counseling. I was content with the liturgy that C. had helped me create. I had chosen Thomas Merton's words from *New Seeds of Contemplation* as the basis for my reflection. "We are at liberty to be real, or to be unreal. We may be true or false, the choice is ours. . . . we are even called to share with God the work of creating the truth of our identity. . . . To work out our own identity in God, which the Bible calls 'working out our salvation,' is a labor that requires sacrifice and anguish, risk and many tears."

I had traveled a long way from my teen years, when I pushed against my father's attitude that college was a waste for a girl who was just going to get married. On ordination day I was a middle-aged woman, grounded in my vocation, surrounded by family and friends in a small United Church of Christ in south Minneapolis on a Sunday afternoon. David and Sally Anne had driven two hundred miles from the farm, bringing my mother and father.

Ordination gifts are often a special stole, a prayer book, a ceramic chalice and paten (the vessels used in the Eucharistic liturgy), or a beautiful cross on a silver chain. But the best gift at my ordination came during the worship service, during communion. After people had come forward to commune by intinction (dipping the piece of bread in the cup), my mentor and I brought the bread and the cup to my father sitting in the pew. Then eighty-four, he was using a walker after a back injury, though he still managed to position himself in the soybean fields to pull weeds and hoe thistles. He struggled to get to his feet. Beginning to weep, I offered him the cup. I could scarcely speak "the cup of blessing." And then I saw that he, too, was teary. I could not stay fully in that moment, for I needed to return to the table, lead the prayer of thanksgiving, offer the benediction, and greet people at the reception. Yet, in those few moments with my father, healing was fully recognized. I offered, and he received. And what he offered was equally profound. We did not need words. I did not need to say "Forgive me. I love you." I did not need him to speak. We stood together in sacred space, acknowledging the power of Spirit to heal.

A manila folder in my filing cabinet includes a copy of my ordination service. Over the years, I have often used the prayer of blessing when I have officiated in worship services, reminding me of my ordination and of the healing between my father and me that needed no words:

> May the love of God, the peace of the Christ, and the power of the Holy Spirit be among you, everywhere and always, so that you may be a blessing to all creation and to all the children of God, making peace and remembering the poor, choosing life and coming to life eternal, in God's own good time. Amen.

In the days following my ordination, I waited for C. to decide if he would drive east with me to take Maja to Brown University in Rhode Island. I do not recall whether he said he would not drive with me or if he just did not respond at all. I understood then that I needed to make my own plans. By that time, I had only a week to decide what to do. Maja needed to get to college. I made a reservation for her to fly. In late August, I left her at the Minneapolis/St. Paul airport. David and Sally Anne, visiting family in Massachusetts, picked her up from the Boston airport and drove her to Brown. I went home from the airport to flop on my bed and weep, and then to lunch with a friend whose son had left for college the year before. I wept for the loss of my daughter's daily presence. I wept for the hurt I caused her and myself by having stayed in the relationship with C. I wept for my struggling to let go.

In the next month, accepting my powerlessness, I was done waiting for C. to "come through." As I had when my marriage ended, I had waited for him to decide—for far too long. I decided. Letting go was the only power I had.

I asked him to come to my flat and retrieve a few belongings that were still at my house. It was late afternoon when he arrived. I had gathered his things together. He especially liked my blue coffeepot. I traded it for his antique brass spittoon. We walked out the back door at the same time. I went out for supper with several family members, a small part of me still questioning whether the kind thing to do would have been to invite him to join us.

Where I Needed to Be

In those years after 1986, there were days when I could hardly believe my good fortune. Maja was doing well at Brown University. I was living in community with Shirley and Ken in the big triplex. I had a job I loved with Abbott Northwestern Pastoral Counseling Center, with a salary, health insurance, and, once again, payments into a retirement account. In leaving teaching, I had also left the ten teachers with whom I had shaped our English department. Now, once again, I had colleagues, several of whom I would work with over the next decade and beyond.

I was where I needed to be. In *Wishful Thinking: A Theological ABC*, the Presbyterian minister Frederick Buechner writes, "The place God calls you to is the place where your deep gladness and the world's deep hunger meet."[14] I was deeply glad. I know that the individuals who came to see me for pastoral counseling might not have used the word *hunger* to describe what led them to me, but they did want something to be different in their lives. I knew from my own experience that finding a safe person who will listen and not judge is the beginning of transformation. In preparing the written materials for my first certification in pastoral counseling in 1986, I wrote:

> As a pastoral counselor, I listen to the person who sits in the other chair. I invite her to tell me her story. I hold it and honor it. I mirror it back to her. I wonder with her. I bring to her story the big story, the story of forgiveness, of grace, of acceptance. Only rarely does this mean that I use explicit religious language.

I also included a reference to what I had said in my ordination interview: that what I offered—human relationship—could very well be Word and Sacrament to the person sitting across from me, and that what we call God is experienced in many ways we do not traditionally acknowledge.

---

14 Frederick Buechner, *Wishful Thinking: A Theological ABC* (New York: Harper & Row, 1973), 95.

All human relationships can be experienced as spiritual practice, whether with intimate partners, friends, children, and perhaps most powerfully, with those with whom we disagree. Similarly, our relationships with all the created world can be spiritual practice. If I am open, each day offers me many invitations into the Mystery we call God. I do not remember when I found the Meister Eckhart quote, probably when I was at Pendle Hill:

> Apprehend God in all things, for God is in all things.
> Every single creature is full of God, and is a book about God. . . .
> If I spent enough time with the tiniest creature—even a caterpillar—
> I would never have to prepare a sermon. So full of God is every creature.[15]

I felt a sense of loss when I thought about my childhood. No one helped me to claim and name my experiences of the Divine in the natural, created world of the farm and my experience among the pines at Punkaharju. What the church claimed to offer in Word and Sacrament had been fully present for me in the created world all along.

My work as a pastoral counselor deepened with the arrival of a new colleague. A clergyman and therapist named Steve Tate moved to Minnesota to lead the new Samaritan Center for Pastoral Counseling, a branch of the Abbott Northwestern Pastoral Counseling Center that was opening at Wayzata Community Church in the western suburbs of Minneapolis. Steve, too, had grown up on a farm. One visit to the farm became a story often told by both of us. David pulled all of us, adults and children, into rounding up a couple dozen cattle that had gotten loose, resulting in us running about, shouting and laughing. Steve and I also shared a similar religious background. In him, I gained both a colleague and a friend. We worked together for the next nine years at Samaritan Center with a team of therapists, offering individual and couples therapy, retreats, workshops, and group Bible study. I loved the variety of the work and once again being part of a team, something I had left behind when I left teaching.

15 Matthew Fox, *Meditations With Meister Eckhart* (Santa Fe: Bear & Company, Inc., 1983), 14.

Steve and I created a series of Becoming Married workshops for couples, offered at the counseling center and in area churches. When we invited couples to think about the difference between falling in love and loving, I had plenty of personal experience from which to draw. I shared few personal details, but I could describe the excitement and wonder of falling in love, the probability of psychological projection, and the painful loss we feel when the projections erode. Steve always elicited nervous laughter from workshop participants when he suggested that some morning, one or the other would wake up to see their partner, still sleeping, snoring, mouth open, drooling. "If you think," said Steve, "'Not what I imagined, but he's/she's good enough,' it's love."

For me, *good enough* has become a phrase that works for much of life. It is an antidote to perfectionism, a liberating and compassionate reminder to accept things as *they* are, not to reject them because they aren't what *we* wished they were.

Steve and I also led retreats and offered adult education. What I enjoyed the most were the Transforming Bible Study sessions. These were modeled after a method created by the theologian Walter Wink. I had learned the method from Wink himself in 1989 when I had returned to Pendle Hill to attend a weekend seminar.

Wink's approach to Bible study had three components: critical issues, amplification, and application. The first, critical issues, is a careful look at the text. The second, amplification, was when Steve and I let our creativity flourish in inviting participants to enact the text. Jesus's healing of the bent woman resulted in our inviting people to walk about the room, bent over. We asked them to imagine what it might be to look at the ground all the time and not to be able to fully face another person. Application included asking in what ways participants feel "bent over." Where do we observe people in our community and in the wider world who are bent over; what systems are we part of that contribute to people being bent over? And what are the actions we can take to help heal? Week after week on Sunday evenings, I spent two hours with a dozen or more adults enacting scripture texts and finding more depth in their meaning than I could ever have imagined in those lapsed Baptist years of my twenties.

For several years I also facilitated a divorce support group. I heard women and men speak of anger, sorrow, judgment, stigma, and the struggles with finances, in-laws, and parenting. And although I was twenty years past my own divorce, those feelings were familiar to me. In conversation with my mother ten years after my divorce, I found out that her sister, who lived several hours away, thought I was still married. When I asked my mother why Aunt Aili did not know of my divorce, my mother replied, "She doesn't need to know." I did not tell my mother that I wished she could see and affirm *all* of me, even the part of me that disappointed her and gave her pain.

I wanted to say, "Can't you see that divorcing was what I needed to do?" I took a deep breath and held my sadness. She did not need me to judge or fix her.

My individual clients were mostly women, and their struggles and wounds often overlapped with my own. One day, early in my counseling practice, I sat with a woman who told me about feeling overwhelmed with children, aging parents, work, and tasks at home, a theme I often heard from the women who sat in the chair across from mine. Like so many women, she was taking care of everyone, often neglecting herself. I wondered how I might invite her to think about self-care. I looked at the basket of small, smooth Lake Superior stones on the table between us. I picked out more than a dozen and placed them in a circle, naming each person in her extended family as well as several colleagues and friends. Then I chose another stone and gave it her name. I invited her to place herself in the circle of care, to have compassion for herself, and to take responsibility for her own well-being. I wondered then—and still wonder—whether one can have compassion for another person if one does not also have compassion for oneself. When she left my office, she took that small stone home with her. She later told me that she carried it in her pocket for many months—a reminder of our work together. I reached for the Lake Superior stones in many future counseling sessions. Many have left my basket to live in pockets. My copy of Carol Gilligan's *In a Different Voice* left and returned to my office many times as well, a resource for my clients as it was for me in empowering women to claim our own voices, our agency, our power.

I lived immersed in rewarding work, almost always looking forward to each client. I did find, in the words of our consulting psychiatrist, that no one of us is omnicompetent. When I felt stuck with a client, consultation with my colleagues almost always freed me, which usually meant my client was also freed. I remember two clients I needed to refer, hoping they would receive what they needed from someone else. Sometimes it took the confirmation of my colleagues for me to realize that healing had taken place. And much of the time I knew that only my client and I would know the significance of the hard work we had done.

Many of my clients struggled with a history of abuse. A woman I will call Emily was a person with whom I lived the range of emotions and many consultations. More than once I felt inadequate and wondered whether referring her to someone else would be better for her. But I sensed that then I would become one more person who had rejected and abandoned her. Extremely depressed, she had not been working for several years. For many months I saw her twice a week. Early on she pushed the boundaries, coming late or going overtime by bringing up a new detail near the end of our hour. As she told me about her life, many painful details came to light. With consultation, I was able to receive and hold her stories, her pain.

One morning I was in a session with a client who had talked about suicide in an earlier session. As we talked again about her safety plans, I realized that we would probably go over the hour. I ended up running more than ten minutes late. Emily entered my office, clearly angry. She told me that I was just like everyone else in her life, taking advantage of her. I took some deep breaths, realizing that I needed to respond with great care. Not revealing any details, I apologized, saying simply that I had needed a bit more time with my previous client. She paced. I apologized again. After several minutes she sat down and began talking about her week. It did not seem that much happened during the session. The next week as she walked into my office, I could feel my anxiety rise, especially since she was on time. The first words out of her mouth were an apology for her anger the week before. I calmly accepted her apology. Then she changed the subject.

In the months that followed, Emily never spoke further about what had happened in that session that began late, or what might have happened for her in the following week. But she eventually went off her depression medication. She found a part-time job and started going out with friends. During the next months as I continued to bring my work with her to my colleagues for consultation, we spoke of how my receiving and holding her feelings without judgment, without attempts at explanations or excuses, was part of the response that had helped free her. After several months, she said she was ready to come every two weeks. Then once a month. Then we said goodbye. A couple years later, I received a card that I put in the file folder with other cards, a thank-you for our time together.

Somewhere in those years I read psychologist Alice Miller's *The Drama of the Gifted Child*, where she asserts that our wounds can be a gift to others—that in facing our own wounds with empathy and compassion, we are able to offer others what they most need. I know from my own life that what heals us is being seen and received fully by another human being, without judgment.

I Never Think of You That Way

Often when I go into my basement, I see the blue filing cabinet and remind myself that I have much sorting to do. The third drawer contains the essays I wrote for my seminary courses: Old Testament, New Testament, Christology, church history, ethics, phenomenology of religion, pastoral care, and more. Recently, I flipped through them, musing that I might just recycle them without reading them. From deep in the back of the drawer, I pulled out an essay from an Old Testament class with a feminist focus. (The course was part of a doctoral program I had started but eventually jettisoned.) The professor had asked us to write about a personal experience that would elucidate, in a current context, the struggles of women in the Old Testament texts. As I read, I was thrown back to the experience I had used as a basis for the essay, a conversation with my mother in 1988, two years after I had been ordained.

On a warm July Sunday morning in southwestern Minnesota, while my teenage nieces did errands in Worthington, Mom and I were worshipping with the Baptists. Mom would have loved to have her granddaughters come to church with us, but they were past the age of acquiescence. I had not been to Indian Lake Baptist Church for several years, even though I drove the two hundred miles from St. Paul to the family farm many times a year. The church had been my parents' faith community for almost fifty years and mine for eighteen. After the service, the congregants moved to the basement of the church for coffee hour, where my mother and I chatted with her friends. Some were women I remembered well; others were new to me.

After the coffee hour, my nieces Heather and Sarah were waiting for us in the old Volvo. Mom and I got into the back seat, and Heather pulled out of the driveway onto the county road. I was still thinking about coffee hour.

"Mom," I said, "I noticed that you introduced me to your friends at church as Maja's mother." I took a breath and continued. "I would like you to also say something like, 'Marilyn was an English teacher, but then she went to seminary, and now she is a chaplain and pastoral counselor.'"

The nieces stopped talking. I looked up and saw Heather's wide blue eyes in the rearview mirror. She looked at me so long I thought she might drive into the ditch.

Finally, my mother offered, "I guess I never think of you that way." She paused and then said, "I guess I think of myself as Gus's wife and David's mother."

My mother was not defensive. That was how she saw herself, and that was how she saw me. All I could do was take her hand in mine.

We drove the last mile to the farm in silence.

While my mother went to change out of her Sunday clothes, my nieces, voices animated, found Sally Anne in the kitchen, and told her what had happened on the ride home. I fled into the dining room, not wanting to hear the details of Aunt Marilyn confronting Grandma Bertha. I felt a familiar anger at the power of the early messages I had received while sitting in those Baptist pews the first eighteen years of my life.

Patriarchy had spoken loudly during that ten-mile ride from Baptist church to family farm.

The day Professor Carolyn Pressler handed back our essays, I asked to speak with her. We talked first about the legacy and the continuing power of the social, cultural, and religious systems that oppress women. Then, almost in tears, I told her my shame at having wanted the affirmation my mother could not give. That July morning sitting in the back seat of the car, I'd had no words to respond to my mother. As I spoke, I realized that my anger and my desire for affirmation had prevented me from owning the power of patriarchy in my mother's life and the losses she had suffered.

Carolyn affirmed how my mother and I both stood in the long line of women who have struggled and continue to struggle. All women. Everywhere. We spoke of women in the Bible. Women in the early church. Women in the contemporary church. Women who wrote the books we had read: Mary Daly, Elisabeth Schussler Fiorenza, Rosemary Radford Ruether, Elizabeth A. Johnson. And we spoke of my mother. As we spoke, my shame diminished and in its place compassion grew.

My mother and all women, as Mary Daly writes in *Beyond God the Father*, "have not been free to use our own power to name ourselves, world, or God."[16] In *She Who Is*, the Roman Catholic feminist theologian Elizabeth A. Johnson goes into greater detail:

> The internalization of secondary status then functions like a self-fulfilling prophecy. . . . This process is aided and abetted by male-centered language and symbol systems, key reflections of the dominant group's power to define reality in its own terms and a powerful tool of its rule. . . . Women have been robbed of the power of naming, of naming themselves, the world, and ultimate holy mystery, having instead to receive the names given by those who rule over them.[17]

Though not blind to the circumstances of her own life, my mother's seemingly simple statement, "I guess I think of myself as Gus's wife and David's mother," expresses in distilled form what Daly, Johnson, and myriad others have taken pages to say.

My mother, a Finnish girl who left school at fourteen, immigrated to the United States at seventeen, and became fully fluent in Swedish and English. This is the woman who raised me and my siblings to love learning and who once said, almost in passing, "I could have gone to college." I grieve for her losses. Although she was never able to acknowledge my ordination the way I wanted, I remember with gratitude that it was she who persuaded my father to allow me to go to college, the first person in my family to do so.

I can name, now, more clearly how writing the essay and the conversation with Professor Pressler not only relieved my shame and anger; it also created much more room for compassion—for my mother, for women everywhere, and for myself. Perhaps I will always struggle to carry the oppression of my early religious and cultural upbringing.

I put the essay back in the folder. This one I would keep.

---

16 Mary Daly, *Beyond God the Father: Toward a Philosophy of Women's Liberation* (Boston: Beacon Press, 1973), 6.

17 Elizabeth A. Johnson, *She Who Is: The Mystery of God in Feminist Theological Discourse* (New York: Crossroads, 1994), 26-27.

To My Daughter on Her Twenty-Sixth Birthday

The church ladies say to my mother,
        "Your girls sing so beautifully."
My mother answers, "I just give God the glory."

I wondered, years later, "Could God get the blame too?"

I dreamed once that I brought her
Ears of corn for breakfast,
Up the stairs to her bedroom
Where she told me to rearrange the furniture.
I refused.

My mother thanked God
For giving me to her.
I say to you, my daughter,
"God gave me to me and you to you."

I remember you at eighteen.
When I drove you to the airport.
You wore a black beret.
Your hair was short.
Your smile was wide.

We mothers, like Demeter, weep and roam.
My tears are mine and my mother's,
        and my mother's mother's,
Wept in Finland, years ago.

It can take many generations to set a daughter free.

In blessing you, I am blessed.
I will bless my mother also.
She has waited too long.

1994

Listening Into Discovery

> To listen another's soul into a condition of disclosure and discovery may be almost the greatest service that any human being ever performs for another.
>
> Douglas V. Steere[18]

When someone asks me what my work is or has been, it is relatively easy to answer if I say that I was a high school English teacher and then a marriage and family therapist. A bit more work is needed when I include pastoral psychotherapy, and more yet if I mention spiritual direction, this work I have done for forty years. I try to intuit whether I am sincerely invited to say more.

Spiritual direction can seem a bit strange to people. Almost always, the first question is, "So what is spiritual direction anyway?" The second is often, "Who comes to see you?" The second question is the easier of the two to answer.

I say, hoping to be inviting, "People like you and me." The answer to the first question usually includes something about people wanting to tell their story to someone who will truly listen. The word *direction* is not especially helpful. Often, I use the word *companioning*. Rather than directing someone, the process is that of listening, mirroring, wondering, and discerning. I often say that some people want a companion on the journey, someone who knows them fully and accepts them. One woman who came to see me for many years commented that each session was a time of "marking" for her, of noting and naming where she was in her inner and outer journey.

Conversation about spiritual direction often includes talk about what spirituality means. Almost always I am asked, "Do people talk about God?" It depends, I answer. I use whatever language—Higher Power, God, the Holy, the Sacred, the Divine, the Ineffable, Mystery, Love, the One, Grace, Ultimate

18 Douglas V. Steere, *Gleanings: A Random Harvest* (Nashville: The Upper Room, 1986), 83.

Meaning, Presence—suits the one sitting in the other chair. I believe that everyone has a spirituality, whether you claim a specific religion such as Christianity, Judaism, Islam, Buddhism, whether you consciously claim belief in a Higher Power.

A person in pastoral psychotherapy will likely talk about similar life concerns as the person seeking spiritual direction. One difference will be that in a spiritual direction hour, I will listen for the presence of the sacred in what the directee has been experiencing, or I might ask the directee to tell me about its presence—or its absence.

Often, I remind a directee that everything in one's life can be brought to our time together. Nothing about one's life is too mundane or too ordinary. In my early thirties, Katharine Whiteside Taylor paraphrased something Martin Buber had said to her: "Everything that happens in your life is an occasion to listen to God." When I began seeing my spiritual director, Kay Vander Vort, and meeting with my peer group in the early 1980s, I realized that Buber's words echoed what my new colleagues referred to as Ignatian spirituality—finding God in all things.

In a recent episode of decluttering, I found the journals I kept during the year I did the Ignatian Exercises, a process shaped five hundred years ago. I do not remember when I first heard of Ignatius of Loyola, perhaps in seminary in 1980 when I took an ethics class from the Jesuits in Berkeley. I do remember being amused when I heard of them, imagining they might be a series of physical movements like yoga. Doing the exercises that year included reading the assigned scriptures, sitting with the questions, journaling, waiting in silence, and meeting three times a month with Kay. Reading the journals anew reminded me again that my spirituality is grounded in ordinary day-to-day life, in how I live. Ignatius and his followers gave me another way to speak of our life journey—that of "contemplatives in action."

A spiritual direction relationship honors the unfolding of another human life, with deep respect for the integrity of the other and that person's unique process. I say to those who come, "This is your time." For many months after first meeting, one man would stop once or twice during our session and say he needed silence. Another brings the poetry he writes. Many bring their dreams, others the books they are reading. I remember one hour where we listened to the music of Leonard Cohen for much of the time.

One of the mysteries of offering spiritual direction is recognizing that often we do not know the full significance of what we have said to another person. Someone in the other chair says something like, "Last time when you said . . ." or, "I have been thinking about what you said . . ." Sometimes I can recall what I said, and other times I realize that what was recalled, I cannot claim to have offered. Presence has spoken through me. I hope that Katharine understood the significance of her saying to me, "I think you might like the Quakers." And later, her suggestions that I might like seminary and Pendle Hill. Those wonderings transformed my life. Katharine listened to me. Her listening guided me into disclosure and discovery—into a recognizing of my pain, my path, and my growing capacity for joy. One does not need to be a spiritual companion to listen. It is a gift we all need. And a gift we can all give.

Unlike much psychotherapy, a person might stay with their spiritual director for many years. I think of J., whom I first met with when she was single and in her late twenties. As a single woman, she had cherished time for spiritual practice: to go on retreat, to journal, to read, and sit in silence. When she married and gave birth to a daughter, she commented that she felt keenly the loss of time for her spiritual practices. I had noted over several months that she spoke often of her relationship with her young daughter. I could hear that this was where there was energy and joy in her life. I wondered with her whether she had noticed this herself. We named what was now a significant part of her spiritual practice—parenting. We spoke then of how this might be the time in her life when her daughter had become a sacred text. Now many years later, her two children are young adults who continue to be sacred texts for her.

At the close of a session with a directee, I often say silently to the Universe that brought me to this work of spiritual direction, "Thank you. Thank you, for the gift of listening to another human being who is exploring and wondering about the Mystery, the Sacred."

Tell the Truth but Tell It Slant

My spiritual directors' peer supervision group has been a consistent monthly commitment for over forty years. We first gathered at the invitation of John Ackerman whom I met while I was still in seminary in 1983. Over the years, we shaped a way of being together that became far more than bringing case studies for consultation.

Our schedule has remained almost the same for these many years. We meet once a month to pray together, to supervise each other's work, to read, to write, and to share. We go on a fall retreat, for years to ARC, and for the last ten years to the Benedictine Monastery, the home of group member Sister Virginia Matter. In May, we go to the Wisconsin farm owned by the extended family of group member Joel Wiberg to hike the pastures and trillium-filled woods. In recent years, our retreat days have included a nap.

Our peer supervision, our conversation about our directees is our major focus. Yet, it is more than talking about the person who comes for spiritual direction. Always, our conversation moves from the directee to the director, often with a question like, "What was going on inside you when . . ." Or "What was this like for you when . . . ?" Sometimes we ask all of us, "What have we learned today?" We ask for input about other aspects of our professional lives. Often, we ask the others for feedback about a retreat or other program we are planning. Sometimes, we work together. For five years, Joanne Dehmer and I team-taught the History of Christian Spirituality, part of the training program for spiritual directors at Sacred Ground Center for Spirituality in St. Paul.

And, we also share our stories. We have been with one another in life's pain and sorrow: deaths of parents, siblings, nephews; cancer diagnosis and treatment; Joel's wife Nancy's illness and death; and the breaking of our circle of five—John's death in 2013. We have celebrated: John's publishing, Joanne's jubilee (fifty years a vowed School Sister of Notre Dame), Joel's new relationship, Virginia's time in India, my second marriage. We know the joys and sorrows of one another's extended families and friends.

Every fall we assess our three-and-a-half-hour format for Wednesday mornings. We have made few changes. We begin with a brief check-in followed by prayer, then move to study or reflection using a video or book, or material from a seminar one of us has attended. In the final hour, one or two of us presents a case study of a directee for supervision and consultation by the group.

Sixteen years ago, we added a writing component, something akin to *lectio divina*, that monastic tradition of reading, reflecting, praying, and contemplating on a passage of Scripture. Our practice has deepened our experience of the Sacred and created greater trust and compassion among us. I believe it has invited us to bring more of ourselves out into the open. After prayer, we write. We have used song, poetry, prose, scripture, and art as the basis for our prayer and our writing. We write for about fifteen minutes and then share in turn. Here are a few of the texts and prompts we have used.

- Lines from Mary Oliver's poem, "Thirst": "Another morning and I wake with thirst / for the goodness I do not have, / . . . expecting to be told to pack nothing / except these prayers which, with this thirst, / I am slowly learning."[19] Write about your thirst. What are your prayers? What will you not pack?
- Questions for the first meeting in January: What name would you give to your journey of the past year? What metaphor or image?
- A paraphrase from Meister Eckhart: Let go of beliefs so that you can know and experience God. What are the beliefs you have let go of? What are the beliefs you continue to hold on to? And which do you desire to let go of?
- Scripture text: "I will not leave you orphaned. . . . the Holy Spirit, whom the Father will send in my name, will teach you everything. . . ." (John 14:18, 26) When have you been orphaned? Who found you? Whom did you find?
- Scripture text: "Thus says the Lord: Stand at the crossroads, and look, and ask for the ancient paths, where the good way lies; and walk in it and find rest for your souls." (Jeremiah 6:16) What is the good way now?
- Richard Rohr's *The Universal Christ*: "God is in deep-time cooperation with everybody who loves."[20] How and where do you experience this?

---

19 Mary Oliver, "Thirst," in *Thirst* (Boston: Beacon Press, 2006), 69.
20 Richard Rohr, *The Universal Christ: How a Forgotten Reality Can Change Everything We See, Hope For, and Believe* (New York: Penguin Random House, 2019), 100.

- In the "Time Before Death" (*Ten Poems to Change Your Life*), Kabir writes: "Jump into experience while you are alive! / Think. . . . and think. . . . while you are alive. / What you call 'salvation' belongs to the time before death. / If you don't break your ropes while you are alive, / do you think / ghosts will do it after?"[21] What experience might you jump into? What experience are you resisting? What are the ropes that hold you?
- In the Road to Emmaus passage, after Jesus's resurrection, he walks with two of his followers who do not recognize him until he leaves (Luke 24: 13-35). Who are those who have walked with you, those through whom the divine has spoken? Are there those who spoke to you whom you did not recognize at the time?

Rather than asking directly what is going on in one's spiritual life, the writing prompts broach the topic indirectly. In his book *A Hidden Wholeness* Parker Palmer writes,[22] "We achieve intentionality in a circle of trust by focusing on an important topic. We achieve indirection by exploring that topic metaphorically, via a poem, a story, a piece of music, or a work of art that embodies it. I call these embodiments 'third things.'" Palmer writes of how the soul is shy, and how our approach to soul needs to be indirect, reminding us of Emily Dickinson's poem, "Tell All the Truth, But Tell It Slant." The "third thing" may seem less personal than a direct question, but it can be far more personal. It can evoke great depth, as when parents describe how much more intimate their conversation with their teen is when they are both in the car and looking straight ahead. The invitation is indirect, offered at a slant. Similarly, my colleague Steve Tate in his retreat work with men, asks them to tell a story about their father—which almost always reveals deep feelings not accessible through a direct question.

During years of friendship and peer supervision, our group continues to grow deep in soul. For us, inviting the presence of the divine through the third thing has been a gift beyond any of our expectations and hopes.

---

21 Kabir, "Time Before Death," in *Ten Poems to Change Your Life*, ed. Roger Housden (New York: Harmony Books, 2001), 53.

22 Parker Palmer, *A Hidden Wholeness: The Journey Toward an Undivided Life* (San Francisco: Jossey-Bass, 2004), 92-93.

Beginnings and Endings

In 1992, at dinner in a Vietnamese restaurant in St. Paul, Maja and her partner Kermit told me of their plans. Maja was moving to Ventura, California, to live with Kermit. They had met one another in a journalism class during their last semester at Brown University. They continued their relationship after graduation. Maja had come back after college to an internship at Minnesota Public Radio in St. Paul. Later as a full-time employee, she hosted an arts program at the MPR station at Saint John's University in Collegeville. Every time it ran, I drove up Interstate 94 until I could hear the station clearly. Then I would pull off the freeway and park and listen. After Brown, Kermit had taken a job with a newspaper in Key West, Florida. Now he had a job with a newspaper in southern California. The plan was for Maja to join him and look for a print journalism job in California. They planned to marry within a year or so. I was very happy and not surprised. At the same time, I felt loss. Sitting across from Maja and Kermit, I could feel my body wanting to do the gesture I used with clients, of holding the infant close to my heart and then gradually opening my arms, allowing the child to grow and to leave, and to return, always encircled by arms of love.

When wedding plans began to be sorted in 1994, David and Sally Anne said, "Of course the wedding can be on the farm." During the spring and summer, I drove to the farm many weekends to help plant flowers and paint the outbuildings. I researched renting a big tent, tables, chairs, a dance floor, a porta-potty, and dishes from a company in Sioux Falls. Maja and Kermit were in California, but Maja's cousin Sharon, in St. Paul, was tireless in her attention to detail. We interviewed caterers, counted beds and chairs in the farmhouses, drew floor plans and yard plans. Knowing how readily I can come to tears, I asked my colleague Steve to join me in officiating. All I had to do was invite their vows and pronounce them married.

On the August weekend of the wedding, the farm was green and gold, the pond was full, and the Haralson apple tree, the backdrop of the wedding ceremony, was heavy with fruit. We mowed the east hay field to accommodate parking. We put up the big tent and dance floor, set the wood for the bonfire, and arranged the chairs for the ceremony so that guests faced south toward the pond and Iowa. Maja and Kermit's friends came and set up camping tents.

The farm was lush and beautiful. What was missing was my father. He had left the farm a year earlier to live in the local nursing home when my mother and David and Sally Anne could no longer manage his care. Over that year he had not returned. Maja and Kermit went into Worthington that morning to visit with him. He was fully lucid, shaking their hands and wishing them well. I was sad. I wondered, did he not want to come? Why? Here was an amazing celebration on the land he had chosen, the land he had worked for fifty-five years. I wanted him to be with us. I wanted him to share in our joy.

David and Sally Anne and the cousins played "Joyful, Joyful" on the handbells. Kermit and Maja read from their letters to one another. Steve spoke about marriage. Looking across the fields, we all joined in singing "Amazing Grace" after Maja and Kermit sang the first verse with Kermit on guitar. Inviting the wedding vows, I began to weep. After the ceremony, we planted a tree, toasted, ate salmon and wedding cake, danced to live Cajun music under the stars, and sat around a huge bonfire late into the night. I could scarcely hold my joy and gratitude.

Maja's father B. and his wife and other California relatives came. B. and I had not seen one another since Maja's graduation from Brown. I was anxious about spending two and a half days with him. I wished I had a partner to stand by me in the photos of Maja, Kermit, and their parents. I touched the old feelings of rejection, even though I was surrounded by family and friends who loved me. There was a moment when B. turned to me and said something like, "You've done a good job parenting Maja." I received his comment with gratitude, but I didn't want what he said to matter so much. But nothing could diminish my joy about Maja and Kermit. I was glad that we could celebrate their marriage at the family farm, this place that I had so loved in childhood, that I had fled in adolescence, and had come back to again and again in adulthood with deep love for the land and gratitude for David and Sally Anne's continuing hospitality. Maja and Kermit were at a beginning. A season of parenting had ended. A new season was beginning. The next day I would hug them, and they would leave for California. The parallel struck me. B. and I had left for California the day after our wedding. Although I knew Maja and

Kermit would have their own struggles, I had seen that their relationship, shaped over time, was one of deep intimacy. I was grateful.

By Sunday afternoon most of the guests had left. Those of us who remained went to take naps before we cleaned up the brunch dishes. Resting in the loft on a bed high in the peak of the farmhouse overlooking the pond, I heard the phone ring. A friend was calling to tell me that my dear friend Patrick, whom I had dated several years earlier, had died of a heart attack in the night. His body had been discovered only that morning by parishioners when he did not come to church to lead worship. I sat in the loft, looking out at the pond, the apple tree, the flowers. The night before I had celebrated the beginning of my daughter's marriage. I had eaten salmon and wedding cake. I had danced to Cajun music while my friend was dying of a heart attack.

At Patrick's funeral, I read Auden's "Musee des Beaux Arts," one of his favorite poems. It speaks of how I experienced Patrick's death in the next days and weeks— juxtaposed with Maja and Kermit's wedding celebration.

> About suffering they were never wrong,
> The Old Masters: how well they understood
> Its human position; how it takes place
> While someone else is eating or opening a window or just
> walking dully along; . . .
>
> In Bruegel's *Icarus*, for instance: how everything turns away
> Quite leisurely from the disaster; the ploughman may
> Have heard the splash, the forsaken cry,
> But for him it was not an important failure; the sun shone
> As it had to on the white legs disappearing into the green
> Water; and the expensive delicate ship that must have seen
> Something amazing, a boy falling out of the sky,
> Had somewhere to get to and sailed calmly on.[23]

23 W. H. Auden, "Musee des Beaux Arts," in *Collected Poems*, ed. Edward Mendelson (New York: Vintage Books, 1991), 179.

Icarus falls to his death. Life goes on for the ploughman. The ship has somewhere to get to. Patrick was forty-seven. He left his young daughter and son. He would never dance at his child's wedding or sing "Amazing Grace" with them.

I, too, had somewhere to get to. Yet, into the next weeks and months, and into the next year, I carried the juxtaposition of death and life, of endings and beginnings.

I Want All of My Life

Occasionally, I imagine that I might not have invited Tim Wulling for coffee that Friday evening in late November 1994. I might have gone home from the dance alone and avoided the risk of rejection. Two days before, I had found a lump in my breast while taking a shower. That afternoon I had seen a surgeon, who, after seeing my mammogram and examining me, scheduled me for a biopsy the following Monday morning. I had seen the look on the surgeon's face. I was scared. At work, my colleague Steve said it was probably just a cyst. This did not reassure or console me. As I drove home, I asked myself, "How could I have missed this?" At home at the triplex after work, I went down the back stairs to talk to Shirley. I also called my sister Gladys. I remembered that my musician friend, Roberta, who was in treatment for breast cancer, was playing music with her husband for a folk dance and potluck at our church that evening. I went. Tim was at the dance.

I had met Tim five years earlier when I began attending St. Anthony Park United Church of Christ. I had enjoyed getting to know him in casual settings. I had wondered intermittently if he might someday ask me out, but the impending diagnosis gave me impetus to ask him. I may have actually muttered, "What the hell! What have I got to lose?" when I went to find him as the musicians packed up their instruments. I found him in the church basement checking the old boiler to make sure it was working properly as we headed into the Minnesota winter.

In the chill dark, we walked the five blocks from the church to Lori's Coffee House on the corner of Cleveland and Buford. We shared personal history, my growing up on the farm, my years living in San Francisco, teaching, going to seminary, his years at Ripon College and graduate school at the University of Wisconsin, being in the army in Berlin during the Vietnam War, working in computer engineering at Unisys. I intermittently thought about my visit to the surgeon earlier that afternoon: "This is pretty crazy; this kind man does not know I am scheduled for a breast biopsy on Monday morning and that the surgeon says, from the mammogram, it's likely to be cancer."

Crazy and blessed too, that Tim said yes to "going out for coffee," even though he doesn't drink coffee. He nursed a hot chocolate through that first conversation marking the beginning of our relationship.

Though I was frightened, I managed the rest of the weekend with the support of my sisters and friends. I went to Sunday worship and told several people about the biopsy during coffee hour, including Tim. On Sunday evening, I had supper with friends and came home to write.

The Lump

Tomorrow morning the surgeon cuts into my left breast.
I found the lump four days ago,
Thinking about work, soaping my breast
          in the shower.

My friends ate supper with me.
They brought me a lavender night shirt
Covered with white stars,
Eight half-moon buttons up the front.
And a little porcelain pot for burning sage.

In August my friend died in his sleep.
Some people said, "Oh, I'm so glad he died in his sleep."

That means he did not suffer, I suppose.

I want all of my life.
Whatever's left.

November 20, 1994

Things moved fast. I had the biopsy. It was cancer. The surgeon said the lump was so large that a lumpectomy would deform my breast. He recommended a modified radical mastectomy. We scheduled the surgery for 7:30 the next morning. He told me to find an oncologist within the month. "You will need chemotherapy," he said. The three days in the hospital were a blur. I know my friend Susan came to see me. I remember vomiting from the

Demerol. I remember a woman, a breast cancer survivor, standing at the end of my bed telling me about a support group. I remember feeling far too nauseated to be civil. Maja did not come from California for the surgery. I had told her not to come. I said I had plenty of support. I thought I was protecting her. I was really protecting myself from thinking about dying from breast cancer, leaving my twenty-six-year-old daughter.

I came home from the hospital the afternoon of Thanksgiving Day. That same day, I walked with Shirley and Ken a half mile to the corner of Victoria and Summit, where we sat on a bench for a bit. I told myself "I'm not dead yet," something I'd tell myself numerous times during the next six months. I wondered whether Tim would want to see me again.

I remember peering down at my bony chest in the days after surgery, lifting the dressing and checking the incision, thinking, "Hmmm, they just cut it off. What do they do with a breast?" and then cringing a bit when I emptied the little plastic container of my body's fluid. Seeing my own blood or having needles stuck in me had never bothered me much. Yet seeing the pale pink fluid in the thin plastic tube, one end inserted in my chest and the other in the container, made me want to do the task swiftly. A new way for mortality to be right in front of me.

Tim called a week after surgery and asked whether I wanted to see the Penumbra Theater's production of *Black Nativity*. I did. For the next months, I held in one hand the reality of a cancer diagnosis, chemotherapy treatment, and an uncertain future. In the other, the possibility of a relationship with Tim.

I interviewed two oncologists and chose a woman I sensed could be with me through whatever was coming. She answered all my questions, took my many phone calls, and consulted with her colleagues. A few months into treatment, she told me I never had to read another thing about breast cancer. I did not follow her advice, but I still think of her with gratitude when my eyes find a breast cancer headline in the newspaper.

The next stage of treatment was six months of intravenous chemotherapy, every three weeks, at Abbott Northwestern Hospital. Gladys, a hospice nurse, came from her home in northern Wisconsin to be with me at the hospital and to stay the night. The significance of her profession was not lost on me. I began chemotherapy on December 24.

Chemo Solstice

Life is the destiny you are bound to refuse
until you have consented to die.

W. H. Auden

I have journeyed through Advent to this day
Of the coming of the light.
This morning before the sun rose
I lit thirty-one candles.
They were all I could find.

I am calling forth the light.

Today, the nurse will put the needle in my hand.
I see them, little lightnings, seeking out darkness
That grows in darkness.

Every twenty-one days until June.
I will go with open heart and hand
To this strange healing.

December 24, 1994

On a January afternoon, I sat again with Gladys, the day of my second chemotherapy treatment. I looked around at the many others receiving intravenous chemo. I was reminded of women in a hair salon. I went home to write.

I Want All of My Life

Yesterday was the second treatment.
A dozen recliner chairs line the room.
In this salon chemicals go in.
Hair falls out . . .

First Ativan for nausea,
Then Cytoxan, methotrexate, 5-fluorouracil
Into the vein of my right hand.

The first time I lost Thursday and Friday.
My sister said I vomited from three to eleven.
My friends said I called them.

I want to remember.
I want all of my life.

January 10, 1995

Sometime during those months of chemotherapy, my spiritual director asked if I prayed for full healing. I told her I could not do that. Why would God, or whatever name I use, choose to answer my prayer and not someone else's? So many women had breast cancer. I realized that what I *could* pray for was the openness to say yes to every possible outcome. Two Jungian analysts, Elizabeth Howes and Sheila Moon, write that prayer ". . .assumes the mystery of a presence, and of the possibility of grace (the unbidden abundance of God). . . . it is a continual yes-saying to the fact that there is a direction more encompassing than mine, a Purpose larger than mine, for which I can work. . . . and this decision to say 'yes' to whatever alternative seems to belong to Purpose, must be taken in advance before any of the specifics of moments are or can be known."[24] I realized I could not pray for full healing,

24 Dorothea Berkley Phillips, editor, *The Choice Is Always Ours: An Anthology on the Religious Way* (Wheaton IL: Re-Quest Books, 1975), 208.

but I could pray for openness. I could pray for the willingness to accept mystery and purpose larger than mine. Perhaps, I thought, this is the Jungian version of "not my will but thine . . ."

A few days later, I created a small shrine in the corner of my bedroom and began a morning and evening ritual of burning sweet grass in the porcelain pot Sister Virginia had made for me. In the dark hours of the night, I repeated the Jesus prayer, "Lord Jesus Christ, have mercy," sometimes on the inhale and sometimes on the exhale. Sometimes I just repeated "mercy." In a similar way I began to pray the words "Underneath are the everlasting arms" from a translation of Deuteronomy 33:27.

I reminded myself repeatedly of my mentor Katharine's story about meeting with Martin Buber and her paraphrase of his words to her: "Everything that happens to you is an occasion to listen to God." I do not interpret this as a statement that God causes specific events to happen. Rather, I hear it as an invitation to be open to the Sacred, to the Mystery, in all situations, all seasons. Breast cancer gave me daily occasions to be open, to listen.

Every spiritual tradition tells us to wake up, to pay attention, to listen. I was definitely awake. Yet, it was hard to listen, especially amidst the waves of emotions that swept through me.

In "The Guest House," the poet Rumi writes:

> This being human is a guest house.
> Every morning a new arrival.
>
> A joy, a depression, a meanness,
> some momentary awareness comes
> as an unexpected visitor.
>
> Welcome and attend them all,
> even if they're a crowd of sorrows,
> who violently sweep your house
> empty of its furniture, still,
> treat each guest honorably.
> He may be cleaning you out
> for some new delight.[25]

---

25 Rumi, "The Guest House," in *The Essential Rumi*, ed. Colman Barks, (New York: HarperOne, 2004), 109.

Rumi's poem was a source of solace for me in the next months of cancer treatment and getting to know Tim. I slipped and slid back and forth between hope and fear, anger and momentary acceptance, laughter, and weeping, cherishing the present moment and fantasizing my death from cancer. My friend Joan told me I could call her in the middle of the night. I did not make that midnight call, but I trusted that I could.

Before I started chemotherapy in early December, my niece Sharon and I went shopping for hats. I wanted to be ready for my hair to fall out. I bought two: a brown beret and a black-and-green crocheted hat with touches of red. The latter I thought would look good with my red and black sweaters. Trying them on in the store, I was pleased.

At home a few weeks later, I modeled my hats for Maja, who had come from California for several days. I paraded out of the bedroom wearing the black, green, and red hat. Maja looked at me for a few moments and then said very slowly, "Mom, I don't think you ought to wear that hat when you are seeing your clients."

"Why not?" I replied, feeling a bit miffed. It was my favorite hat.

"Well," she said, guiding me over to a mirror and pointing, "see, there, see the skull on it?" There it was. A skull. Probably a Rasta hat. In the store I had only noted the colors and the somewhat abstract design. We laughed, imagining what message I would have communicated had I worn the hat sitting across from clients.

For my fifty-fifth birthday in January, Tim gave me piano music—Pachelbel's *Canon in D* for four hands. He began spending evenings at my house, and I at his. The big, brick triplex where I lived had been built in the 1920s. It had its charms and its idiosyncrasies. One evening, early in our relationship, he appeared in my kitchen with some tools, suggesting that he could probably fix the old-fashioned flour bin that was stuck open about three inches. It was not especially useful, so I had been storing brown paper bags in it. He cleared up whatever was jamming it, getting it to close fully. This was the first of many small repairs at my flat. I, on the other hand, started bringing my garlic press to his house in St. Anthony Park.

In March of 1995, I wrote in my journal: "We have begun to talk about relationships. I told him about my divorce. I asked if he had ever considered marriage. He said he had never come close. Saturday I will meet his parents."

Death for Life

My father has stopped eating.
He spits out the ice chips.
He is ninety-two.

This morning when I light a candle
I pray he will find the door.

When he was seventy, he hurt his back,
Would not do the exercises,
Could not believe his body would betray him.
We found his hearing aid in the grass
    by the corncrib.

I want to see him one more time,
touch him.
Maybe he will open his eyes
and say my name.
Every morning, I drink my juice and take my vitamins,
Do two kilometers on the NordicTrack.
In four days, another chemotherapy.
Maybe he will let go that day.
I hang on,
His death for my life.

January 1995

Bertha Niilo-Rama and Gustaf Benson immigrated from Finland and Sweden in 1926 and 1925.

Bertha and Gus Benson over sixty years later (photo credit: Jim Brandenburg)

Bertha, Gladys (twelve), Shirley (five), Marilyn (two), Gus, 1942

Benson Farm, Bigelow (circa 1950), where Marilyn grew up, is still in the family.

Corn harvest 1942: Gus, Shirley, Marilyn, horses Bud and King

Strawberry harvest: Bertha, Marilyn, Shirley, Gladys

David, Shirley, Marilyn, 1949

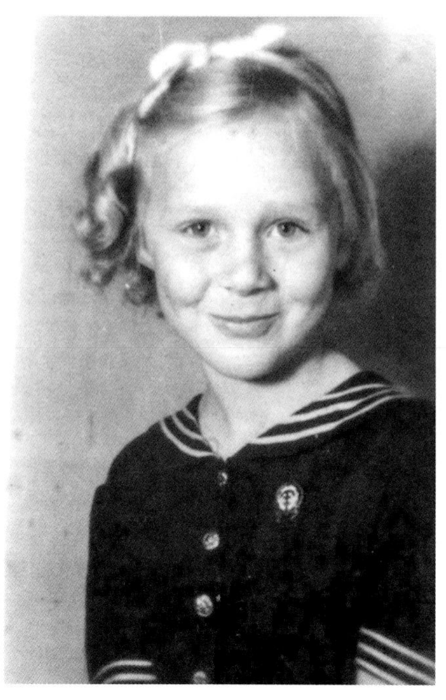

Marilyn, age eight

4-H Club, 1948-58

Rev. Walford Johnson baptizing Marilyn in Indian Lake, 1951

Marilyn and David coming home from school, 1957

Marilyn and the chickens, 1956

David and Marilyn, Bethel College graduation, 1962

VISTA house, Lower Kalskag, Alaska, 1967-68

Pregnant, 1967-68

Maja, age two

Marilyn, Maja, B., 1971

Teaching high school in California

Grandpa Gus and Maja
picnic on the farm

Home in
San Francisco

Living with sister Shirley's family at
ARC Retreat Community, Stanchfield, 1981-82

Seminary graduation: Bertha, Gus, Marilyn, St. Paul, 1984

Marilyn at Samaritan Center for Pastoral Counseling, 1987

Marilyn and Shirley at their families' shared triplex

“Hoeing the beans,” a task on the farm

Marilyn, with Maja home from college, Christmas 1988

Spiritual directors' peer supervision group (Marilyn, John, Virginia, Joel, Joanne) on retreat at ARC Retreat Community

Marilyn officiating at Maja and Kermit's wedding on the farm, 1994 (photo credit: Joe Rossi)

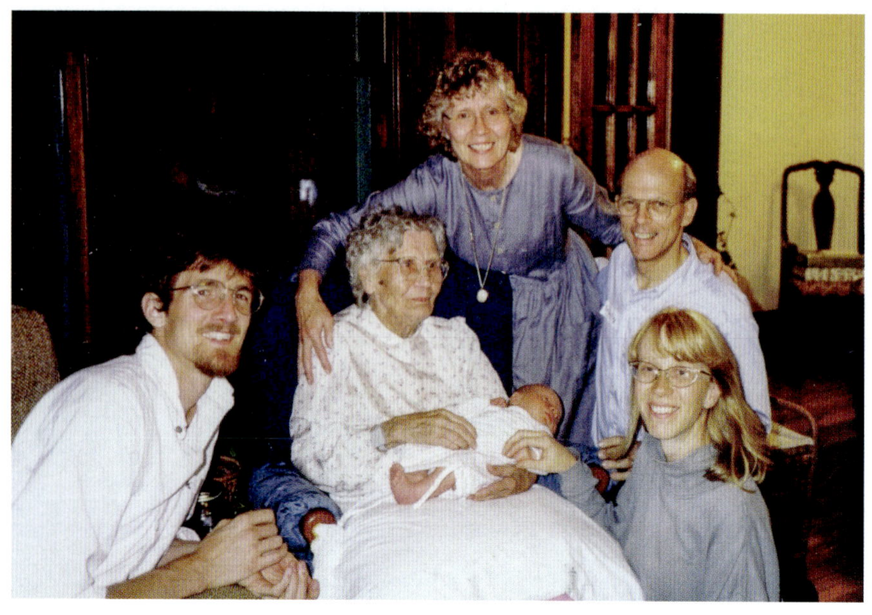

Four generations: Kermit, Bertha holding Eli, Marilyn, Tim, Maja, 1999

Marilyn with grandchildren, Alistair, Siri, Eli, 2007

Siblings Gladys, Marilyn, Shirley, David, 2008

Sally Anne and David's house on the farm, 2014

Tim, Sally Anne, Marilyn, David, Budapest, 2014

Maja and Marilyn, North Shore, Lake Superior, 2019

College friend Gina, Marilyn, Tim, Los Angeles, 2022

Fourth of July parade, 2023

Alistair, Eli, Siri, Maja, Kermit, Marilyn, Tim, North Shore, Lake Superior, August 2023

Tim and Marilyn with restored prairie on the farm, 2024

A Father's Death

Not six weeks after my cancer diagnosis and mastectomy, and as I was beginning chemotherapy, my father died at the age of ninety-two. It was January 1995, a bitterly cold month. I had gone to work the day of his death and worked eight hours. It seemed right to be working as he went to full rest—part of my father's legacy was hard work. We did good work, both he and I. David drove from the farm to St. Paul to meet with my sisters and me to write the obituary and plan the funeral. We sat around my dining room table and told stories, many stories—some joyful, others of regret.

I recalled how in my adult years when I called the farm, my mother, still the bridge between my father and me, was the one who answered the phone. If I asked to talk with Dad, I could hear her say, "Papa. It's Marilyn."

Between April and October, I'd ask, "Have you gotten enough rain?"

And he would say something like, "Oh, about three-tenths, but we need more."

Or in early July, "Did you get the cultivating done before the corn got too high?" During the ten years David bred Percheron workhorses, there was more to talk about. "Has Molly settled yet?" "Has Nellie foaled?"

I envied my brother's connection with our father. Though David left Minnesota when he was nineteen, he returned by the time he was twenty-four to work the farm. Alongside my father for many years, David heard stories of my father's younger years, stories of being in the horse infantry in the Swedish army, learning blacksmithing, swimming in the sea.

But I, too, was given an opportunity to meet my father anew. It was through watching him with Maja when she was a young child. When we lived in San Francisco, I drove with Maja to the farm every summer, often spending several weeks. Two photos from the early 1970s capture something of what I experienced then. My father leads Blooma, the family's well-loved milk cow, by a rope with Maja astride the cow's back. Both my father and Maja have wide smiles. That might have been the year that Maja made a wooden sign in elementary school of Blooma's name that Grandpa Gus posted above the cow's stanchion in the barn.

Another photo is of a picnic in the backyard. Maja, her cousins, and I had probably gathered firewood and hunted for green branches to cut for roasting sticks, just as I had as a child. The photo shows Maja, age three, sitting next to Grandpa Gus. Even in black and white you can sense his ruddy farmer tan, his thick shock of white hair, and their happiness. She is holding a very large hot dog with both hands, her mouth open. He is smiling at her. When I look at them, I smile, knowing that much of what my father could not give me, he gave my daughter. For her the farm was always joy. As a child, I could not understand that my father's care of the land and making a living for the family were his expressions of love. As an adult I wish I had said directly to my father, "I love the farm. And I am sad that I could not love the farm when I was twelve and sixteen and eighteen and wanted a different life."

At the time of my father's death, Tim and I were just beginning to become a couple. I was sad that Tim would know only stories of my father, and that my father would never know that, as my mother later said, "Marilyn found a good man."

Over the years I have come to understand that my father did not so much reject me as he was a man of his time and culture. In childhood, what stood out, what mattered to me, was that he was emotionally distant. But I came to see that he was known in our community as competent, hardworking, totally honest, and trustworthy. He fulfilled the expectations of providing for his family and participating in his community with integrity. My experience of his absence and rejection had taken root in my childhood fears of God and became entwined in my confused understanding of God, a God who was male, absent, and judgmental. The expression of healing came for me most fully in 1986 at my ordination service. Our tears and our wordless interchange when I offered him the cup were perhaps the best communication for the two of us, this silent Swedish farmer and his daughter who so deeply wanted his affection and affirmation.

My siblings and I planned his funeral with time to tell stories and evoke memories. We sang the Swedish hymn, "Children of the Heavenly Father," one verse in Swedish. Sitting in the pews were his neighbors as well as church members and our extended family of four generations. I kept thinking that although my father was a faithful member of that Baptist church, the 160 acres of southwest Minnesota farmland was the altar that claimed him every day of his life. Every morning, he got up, put on his overalls, and walked out the door to the farming tasks of the day. I can only trust that what those preachers never articulated, my father somehow deeply knew, that everywhere we stand, everywhere we look, we can see the footprints and fingerprints of God.

I shared many stories. Of being eleven, driving the tractor for haying, and making the big mistake: forgetting to release the big rope that connected the tractor to the sling of hay in the barn loft. I told how Dad did not berate me or scold me at the time, nor did he ever bring up my mistake in any other context. It was years later that I realized that he would show his irritation at small things, yelling at me when I made an imperfect turn in the hay field. But when the mistake was grave, he was able to find in himself the response that I needed.

I told also of finding the essay Paul Gruchow wrote in *Rosewood Township* where he describes how as a boy growing up on a farm, he stole matches. Up in the hayloft he lit one and dropped it accidentally. The hay exploded. The barn burned to the ground. His family were renters with few resources. He writes, "I was out of my mind with grief and fear." The landowner and the fire inspector arrived. His father told the truth about how the fire started. Yet the local paper reported that the fire inspector said the fire had started by spontaneous combustion. Gruchow names the compassion that came out of consideration for the child that he was. It was this story that invited me to feel the full impact of what my father had given me from the hayloft: wordless grace.

Six months after my father's death, we gathered with extended family and friends at the farm to bury his ashes. We four siblings divided the ashes and took some to the Baptist cemetery where we prayed and sang "For the Beauty of the Earth." Then, on Sunday afternoon at the farm, we walked along the south edge of the pond, across the dam, and into a wide-open field. At the center of the farm, we stood in a circle and took turns reaching into the bag. His ashes were gritty and not a single consistency. We sprinkled handfuls on the ground and tossed them toward the sky. Remnants stuck to my hand. On the black soil they created spots of light gray. I thought of the rain coming in the next days and my father's ashes sinking into the topsoil. This was the benediction I wanted for my father's life. He had finally returned to the land he and my mother cherished and tilled for fifty-six years.

On a recent May afternoon, I was planting basil and tomatoes in the small patch of sun on our boulevard. I thought of my father. Mixing in the compost from our backyard bin, my hands in the dirt, I could see his large hands in the black soil of southwest Minnesota. It was almost as if, for a moment, both our hands were in the soil, in a wordless connection—an affirmation of the sacredness of the land.

I remembered clearly again those warm summer afternoons in childhood when I walked through the fields to bring him his lunch and a quart of coffee wrapped in a dish towel. How I waited for him to signal where he would stop the John Deere tractor. How we sat side by side in the shade of the tractor tire and ate our lunch together. Only now in old age do I recognize that this, too, was communion.

Surviving

A month after my father's death, Tim and I and several others were invited to the cabin of friends near Ely, Minnesota, to cross-country ski over President's Day weekend. I looked forward to being with friends in the north woods. But before we left, my white blood cell count dropped significantly, a result of my third chemo treatment. I was hospitalized in isolation, a wide-spectrum antibiotic drip in my arm. The only people allowed to see me were medical staff who carefully washed, gowned, and masked before entering. I was to remain isolated until my temperature went down and my white cell count went up. Every morning there was a calculation: 1.0, then 1.8, then 10.4, my bone marrow jump-started by some new drug.

I called my sisters. I called my friends. I read mysteries. I read and reread the menus. I wrote in my journal. I slept. I prayed. I waited. The chaplain came. She asked whether I wanted communion. Yes, please. And then she asked whether I wanted a chocolate milkshake. I did!

I was in isolation five days.

Samuel Johnson wrote, "When a man knows he is to be hanged . . . it concentrates his mind wonderfully." A cancer diagnosis does the same. Shortly after the diagnosis, I made two lists in my journal: "Things I will take hold of" and "Things I will let go of." I would take hold of singing in my church choir, seeing my friends more, making more time for writing, and visiting Maja and Kermit in California. I would let go of finishing my Doctor of Ministry program. I asked myself whether I needed this additional degree to do what I loved. The answer was no. People to whom it would matter that I had a D. Min. did not matter to me. I could do my work of pastoral counseling and spiritual direction without it. I wrote a letter to the program chairperson and my adviser, informing them of my withdrawal, and then I called our church choir director and told him I wanted to join the choir. They say that she who sings prays twice.

Later that spring Maja and my niece Sharon gave me a gift. They made the opening of the package special, with a fire in the fireplace and tea and cookies. We sat in a circle that included my mother and Tim. The gift was a sculpture of a nude one-breasted woman, about sixteen inches high, done in a rough, dark brown clay. The artist had captured her power, planting her firmly on strong legs. I held the woman in both hands, feeling her weight, drawing my fingers slowly over her flat chest. I began to weep. Later my mother said to me, "She's ugly. I want her to be beautiful for you." I insisted the woman was indeed beautiful in her strength. In retrospect, I wish I had been able to receive my mother's comments and hold them in love.

By late winter and midtreatment, Tim had entered readily into the mix of my extended family and friends. Our relationship was not what some women with breast cancer experience. Some men leave their wives. Other men may stay but are repulsed by the flat chest and red scars. When a woman friend asked me whether I thought it bothered Tim that I had only one breast, I realized that I had not considered it would be a problem for him. All I could say was "I don't think so." With Tim, I did not experience myself as damaged or deficient. Rather, my diagnosis and his acceptance of me had opened me to love.

Not long after we met, I saw Tim's business card from Unisys, where he worked for many years. It read, "Thomas E. Wulling, Principal Logician." This physics major, this electrical engineer, was different from the men I had sought out earlier in my life. Tim met my breast cancer diagnosis like an engineer, which was what I needed. "Engineers," Tim once said, "do not see problems as failures, but as something to work on." I soon discovered that he had an aesthetic side as well. Following on the coattails of his father, an avocational letterpress printer, Tim set the type for several of my poems, printing them on cream-colored paper with a deckle edge and binding them with marbled endpapers and teal-green covers. They were—are—beautiful.

It had taken me a very long time to muddle through a parade of relationships with men—most of them seminary students, clergy, or at least English majors (I ask their forgiveness)—and lots of therapy and spiritual direction (I say thank you). I had chosen intimate partners with whom I tried to work out my own deeply buried needs, the unconscious projections shaped by my experience of my father and the patriarchal God whose acceptance and love I longed for. Again and again, I transferred my own desires and gifts to the men I fell in love with. Seeking out Katharine was the beginning of claiming my own spiritual path. It took me thirteen years to figure out that I wanted very much to go to seminary. And although my relationship with C. had been an enactment of the same unconscious pattern, I was learning. Stepping into the possibility of a relationship with Tim marked a clear shift. I could claim my own journey into ministry. I did not need a man to carry my projections.

Tim's presence in my life was a gift, in my personal life and in my professional life. Not only was 1995 the year of my father's death and my chemotherapy treatment for breast cancer, but it was also the year my place of work, the Samaritan Center for Pastoral Counseling, began to self-destruct, and more quickly than I would have thought possible. It was precipitated by the departure of the director. The new director could not recognize the gifts of the center's eight staff members or support how we had shaped a successful practice. Rather than inviting us into a common mission, he seemed to set about to divide us. I recall a lunch meeting with him early in his time with us when I realized I was being invited to side with him against my colleagues in the changes he wanted to make. Among his many edicts, he arbitrarily canceled an ongoing consultation with a family therapist with whom we had met for several years, not only for case consultation but also for processing our life together as colleagues. As a group, we had learned that shaping our working life together had a direct impact on the therapy we offered to the people who sought our counsel. The director's rejection of this was significant. Next, he canceled our consultations with a well-respected psychologist. I recall a tender, painful time when we staff members met at the hospital for one last bedside meeting with the psychologist, who was very ill. There were other edicts, including forbidding us to talk to board members. Nevertheless, several of our group of eight did appeal to board members. We received no help. We appealed to the administrator of the national Samaritan Center organization. Again, no help was forthcoming.

Within a year, all eight of us decided to create our own group practice and leave Samaritan to the new director. In this turmoil, Tim was there with the skills of an engineer, seeing a problem not as a barrier but as something to work on. My biggest problem in leaving Samaritan was the loss of my health insurance. I was still in treatment. I was living with a cancer diagnosis. No health insurance would cover my preexisting condition. Another staff member also needed health insurance. So, in creating our new organization,

Sanctuary: A Center for Psychotherapy, Spiritual Direction, and Education, it was clear that our new name was not only figurative. We realized we did not have the time to create a board of directors for a nonprofit, but Tim's careful attention to detail helped us to form a small for-profit business entity. We found office space in a variety of churches and told our clients we were starting a new practice. Most came with us.

Sanctuary was the creation of people who came together in distress and found a way into a new and good thing. It would be my home for the next ten years. My relationship with Tim was shaped in the crucible of my cancer diagnosis and treatment, my father's death, the disintegration of Samaritan Center, and the creation of Sanctuary. I acknowledge again the truth of Franciscan Richard Rohr's comment: what transforms us is great love or great suffering. I was experiencing both. Tim and I married in October 1997, surrounded by family, friends, and my Sanctuary colleagues.

PART III:

LIVING INTO ORIENTATION

More than Surviving

The last several months of chemotherapy I managed by writing and praying. Perhaps writing *was* praying.

Held

What's to blame?
Fifty-four years of chemicals with seven-syllable names?
Or hormone replacement therapy?
She told me to stop,
        the day we found the lump.

Where are you now?
You who slink through the spaces
Between my bones
Finding secret spots to leave your droppings?

Where might you go?
Liver, lung, brain?

My fingers run over my numb chest,
Along my ribs, down my arm.
Ah, at least my elbow is my own.

A bird sings outside my window.
I fall into the arms of God.

1995

My final chemotherapy appointment was on May 16, 1995, a few days short of five months since the first treatment on the December solstice, the coming of the light. I wanted to have an "end of chemo" party. It was a graduation of a sort and at the same time a commencement, a beginning of five years of taking tamoxifen, a drug that was to suppress estrogen and therefore, limit the chance of recurrence. I was ready to celebrate, even though a part of me thought, "Hmm, don't challenge the cancer gods. Be quietly grateful."

A few days before the party, my friend Roberta called. Her breast cancer had returned after the stem cell transplant. We cried together. I said, "I cannot have a party." She said, "You must."

The backyard and vegetable garden at the triplex were green. The lilacs on Summit Avenue would be past their glory in a few days. I bought a new dress, mauve with big pink roses. We borrowed lawn chairs and spread bright tablecloths. We baked all things chocolate. We bought wine and made gallons of horse's neck, my family's lemonade recipe, with lots of fresh mint and ginger ale. Friends came. Family came. My work colleagues came—three of them sweaty and tired after a camping trip, just in time to join us. It was a time of gratitude and impending sorrow.

Roberta died the following year.

I call it the Stalker, and it is always with me to a greater or lesser degree; I feel it when I go for my yearly mammogram. I know that familiar intake of anxious breath when I hear about women whose cancer reoccurs after fifteen years, twenty, twenty-five years. I know it when I see the email that invites me to the cancer support group that continues to meet.

Mammogram

My husband asks if I want him to come with me.
I say no.
By now it is almost routine.
Almost.

Two women in the outer waiting room,
            partners by their sides.
Are they survivors?

Will they get a call back, not the kind one wants?
Or will a letter come in the mail?

A letter that we open with trembling hands,
although we know bad news comes by phone call.

She says my name, smiling warmly.
Down the hall by the changing rooms,
she hands me a robe.
Take off everything to your waist, she says,
Put everything in the lockers across the hall.
Be sure to put the key in your pocket.
The waiting room is around the corner.
It should only be a few minutes.

I undress.
Waffle weave robe is much too large.
I take my belongings to the lockers in the hall.
Hang my sweater, blouse, and purse,
Stuff my gloves and scarf in one parka sleeve,
In the other sleeve, my bra,

Which, now, slips out onto the hall carpet,
prosthesis leading the way.
No witnesses to this mastectomy humor.
Once I asked if I would be billed for only one breast.
She'd heard that too many times.

Around the corner one woman waits.
We smile.
I reject the magazines and look out the window.
The technician calls my name.
Apologizes for her cold hands.
I hold my breath.
Cold metal pinches.

I hold my breath.
A second pinch.

In the dressing room I use the spray deodorant,
Dress, dump my robe in the laundry basket,
        gather my purse and gloves.

Now the two men are waiting alone.

I stand there remembering.
Not just the day of diagnosis.
But later, year after year,
Those tense times, after the mammogram,
        waiting for the courtesy reading,
When, with intake of breath,
I let go of my husband's hand,
        rising to meet the results.

I cannot find my car.
Then I remember, "Elevator to P2
        and turn left."
Exiting the ramp, I don't know where I am.
Behind me a car honks and honks.
I drive.
Ah, Smith Avenue and the long hill up to Summit.
Now I know my way home
        where I will wait.

2014

Recently at a family dinner, one of my grandchildren, now a teenager, asked whether any of us adults ever wondered what our lives would be like if we had made different choices for college, for marriage, for a job. We had, of course. They fantasized. What if Maja and Kermit had not gone to Brown

University and had not met in that journalism class the last semester of their senior year? What if Maja had not written about growing up in the Castro District in San Francisco for that assignment? What if the professor had not read it aloud to the class? What if Kermit was absent that day and did not hear it? They tried for a few moments to step into that impossible world of not being. And what if . . .?

For myself, I have stopped wondering about the coming together of my cancer diagnosis and inviting Tim out for coffee. Breast cancer broke me open, made me risk, opened me not only to loving Tim and being loved by him, but also to receiving the support and care of family and friends in ways I had not previously allowed. I accept this mystery with gratitude.

Learning to Love

On a recent morning, Tim asked whether I wanted to see the surveyor's diagram of the lot our church sits on. I had never seen a surveyor's diagram, a certificate of survey. Tim was part of a small group working to resolve the problem of water leaking into the church basement during heavy rains and fast snowmelts. I spent the next fifteen minutes looking at land elevations and drawings of probable rain gardens and underground sinks to control water absorption.

There are so many things I would not know about if I had not met Tim. I suspect there would be many things he would not know about had he not met me. He and I are not the only people who have noticed our differences. When Tim and I planned our wedding in 1997, we asked Maja and Kermit, both journalists, to each write a reflection to be shared during the marriage ceremony. To my great joy, they had moved to St. Paul in 1996 when Maja was offered a job as a religion reporter at the *St. Paul Pioneer Press*. Kermit's work as a freelance journalist made it possible for him to work wherever he lived. We gave them journalistic freedom, saying we would first hear what they wrote at the wedding—the same time as everyone else. They spoke of us as a bowling ball and a ping-pong ball.

Tim grew up in La Crosse, Wisconsin, the middle child of educated middle-class parents. His father, Emerson, was a Harvard-educated, college English professor and well-known avocational letterpress printer. His mother, Jean, a second-generation graduate of Wellesley, was an active volunteer in the local library, the Republican party, and the Community Concert Association that brought renowned classical musicians to La Crosse. Tim played tennis, got confirmed in the Congregational Church, passed the exam for an amateur radio license when he was sixteen, was a Boy Scout, did not date, graduated from Ripon College in physics, and went on to graduate school at the University of Wisconsin–Madison with an NCAA tennis scholarship. When the draft loomed during the Vietnam War, he enlisted and spent three years in Berlin repairing electronic equipment.

Tim came back to the United States to find an electronics engineering job that advertised "long hours and low pay, in exchange for good experience." From there, he moved after seven years to Unisys, where he stayed for twenty-five years. Note the trajectory of Tim's life: a steady, more traditional journey, not so much risk—until he married me.

Three hundred miles of old Highway 16 (now Interstate 90) separate La Crosse, Wisconsin, and Worthington, Minnesota. But more than that separated Tim and me. Both of my parents left school in their early teens. My father emigrated from Sweden in his early twenties after serving in the Swedish horse artillery; my mother emigrated from Finland at seventeen, fleeing hunger in the aftermath of the civil war. They each arrived in the United States with a single piece of luggage. My mother's, a wooden case, was built by her carpenter father. She sat in the back of a one-room schoolhouse to learn English. My early exposure to classical music was my mother's listening to the Ames, Iowa, radio station and the simplified classical piano pieces I learned. I went to college with minimal financial support. When I moved to San Francisco in 1966, I did not exactly drop out and tune out, but I lived the next fourteen years, except for a year in the Alaskan bush, embedded in much social and political change. I joined the teachers' union, went on strike twice, and took Maja many times to Golden Gate Park to protest the Vietnam War. I got divorced, left my secure job, and took seven somewhat rambling, risky years to attend seminary and find my second vocation.

I was drawn to Tim's "bowling ball" qualities—and his embodiment of the textbook definition of *inertia*, the tendency of an object that is not moving to remain at rest and of an object in motion to remain in steady, predictable motion. Far from seeing it as a bad thing, I consider his so-called inertia a centered, grounded quality—in short, a gift. Perhaps he was drawn to me in part for some of those "ping-pong ball" qualities: spontaneity, high energy, quick to move, ready to risk, eager to explore something new. A Jungian scholar I knew in San Francisco implied that in the spiritual discipline of marriage, one would be invited to grow more fully if one's partner happened to be significantly different.

Tim and I are both introverted, although the direction of his energy flow inward might go deeper than mine. When we first talked of marriage, he wondered whether he would still have time for his solitary projects. Years later, he says he does, and that what has been added is family connections, a social life, and deeper relationships with others. I am the one to initiate social events for us. I ask, "Shall we see if Maja and Kermit and the kids want to come for supper Sunday night?" At Christmas, I am the one who says, "Let's invite the extended family for Boxing Day again this year." In the summer, I say, "Shall we go to the North Shore for a week?" I would suggest inviting friends for dinner or to a Rose Ensemble concert.

Some years ago, David asked, "Do you two want to go to Labrador on a freighter and then drive across Newfoundland?" Another time David asked, "Do you two want to go to Greece with Sally Anne and me to pick olives?" Both times I said yes within twenty minutes. Tim took longer to decide, although about Newfoundland and Greece and much else, he has said yes. I have asked Tim more than once whether he would have asked me out for coffee. He says, "Probably not." I am glad I altered the trajectory of his bowling ball.

As introverts, we are good at going our different ways. Now that Tim is retired, he goes to the coffee shop to meet with others about investing money to reduce carbon emissions, to the church basement to meet about community solar power, and to his computer to Zoom meetings with St. Paul 350, a local chapter of 350.org, the nationwide organization working to mitigate the effects of climate change. I was employed a bit longer than Tim. I closed my counseling practice with Sanctuary in 2003 and ended my teaching at Sacred Ground Center for Spirituality in 2010. Now I go to the coffee shop to write and return home to meet with my writing group or join friends with whom I am reading Kathleen Dowling Singh's *Unbinding* and Richard Rohr's *Immortal Diamond.* Several hours a week, I offer spiritual direction, welcoming those individuals who come to sit in the chair across from me to wonder about the presence of the Mystery in their lives.

But just as we go our separate ways, we also come together: Sunday morning worship, the Transition Town planning meeting once a month, a book group where we have discussed *Strangers in Their Own Land, Ten Poems to Change Your Life, Don't Even Think About It,* and *Between the World and Me.* I forward him pieces from the *New York Times*. He sends me links to what he is reading online about climate change from Richard Heinberg and Rob Hopkins. Over breakfast, we discuss Franciscan Richard Rohr's daily meditation. In summer we sit on the glider with a glass of wine and try yet another time to recall all the names of the perennials we planted in our rain garden.

We are together in our love and commitment to Maja and Kermit and their three children—Eli, Alistair, and Siri. We became grandparents at the same time. We look forward to our weekly dinner with whomever is around.

The grandchildren have left the nest. We carry the memories of being an integral part of their lives, so grateful that most of their childhood was spent in a house seven blocks from us. We fed them around our table once a week after school and were able to participate in many of their activities. In sunshine and rain, Tim and I stood together to watch Eli and Alistair compete in cross-country. We sat together at Alistair's piano recitals and Siri's violin recitals. Now we text, sit on the love seat to chat with them on speakerphone, and look forward to seeing them when they come home for the holidays.

At our weekly dinners with Maja and Kermit, we have more time to hear what is going on in their lives. Conversations are especially interesting when you sit down with two journalists. We were fascinated to hear Kermit's stories about his trips to the rift valley in Ethiopia in preparation for his book *Fossil Men*. He can make complicated science accessible to lay readers. Later, his research about ancient brains intrigued me. On a phone call from Maja I heard ancient grains, not brains. As the interested and supportive mother-in-law, I did a bit of research and initiated a conversation with Kermit by talking about teff, einkorn, and amaranth. Kermit, who was washing dishes when I initiated our conversation, doubled over, and laughed for five minutes.

Maja had the religion beat at the *St. Paul Pioneer Press* for three years until she took a leave when Eli was born. After she returned to work, she began a beat that focused on children and parents, including outings in the greater Twin Cities area. Sometimes, I accompanied her and the children. My favorite was the dog sledding story. Memories of living in Alaska. I freaked when she let Eli and Alistair, probably ages eight and six, ride the SpongeBob SquarePants Rock Bottom Plunge at the Mall of America without an adult. They loved it. I probably held my breath the entire time they were zipping up and down and around the cavernous mall. Maja's many years of experience as a journalist and her curiosity make her job as a producer for Minnesota Public Radio a good fit. She says she appreciates my opinions about the show, about what works well and what does not. I am quietly happy when I hear the closing line of a show, "This show was produced by Maja Beckstrom."

Part of me knew some of what I needed and wanted back in 1974 when I wrote about a relationship that had begun and ended within a year.

A Perennial, Please

It's a fragile flower that we bloom,
I had forgotten there is no stasis for a flower.
Even mountains only seem not to change.
I want to plant a redwood tree,
Or an apple tree,
At the least, a perennial.

Back then, I did not yet know the significance of my unconscious longings. Like so many others, I lived as if love was largely about romance, about feeling attracted to the other. I was attracted. He was attracted. That was enough to begin. In that relationship and several others, I was not aware of how much was unconscious in me that I needed to claim: my own power, my own gifts and desires, my own spiritual path, and how much my relationship with my father and with a patriarchal God was shaping my intimate relationships with men.

In *We: Understanding the Psychology of Romantic Love,* the Jungian analyst Robert A. Johnson writes " . . . one of the great needs of modern people is to learn the difference between human love as a basis for relationship and romantic love as an inner ideal, a path to the inner world."[26] Inviting my projections to fall away has been, and continues to be, work that is both psychological and deeply spiritual. Johnson continues, " . . . we have taken the imago dei out of the temple, out of heaven, and suddenly relocated it here in our midst, contained in the relationship between two human beings."[27] I tried this, several times. It does not work. In my relationship with Tim, I do not claim that all projections are resolved; rather, I trust that I have done enough of my inner work so that I can come to our relationship capable of commitment, affection, and yes, joy.

---

26 Robert A. Johnson, *We: Understanding the Psychology of Romantic Love* (San Francisco: Harper & Row, 1983) 48-49.
27 Robert A. Johnson, *We: Understanding the Psychology of Romantic Love* (San Francisco: Harper & Row, 1983) 60-61.

Scott Peck writes: "I define love thus: The will to extend oneself for the purpose of nurturing one's own or another's spiritual growth."[28] His definition sounds like work. And it is work, good work. It is also grace. It is taking me a lifetime to live part way into the depth of its meaning.

---

28 M. Scott Peck, *The Road Less Traveled: A New Psychology of Love, Traditional Values, and Spiritual Growth* (New York: Simon & Schuster, 1978), 81.

Reclaiming

As a child, I loved the farm. Despite its daily demands, despite the always-present fear of closing the chicken house doors in the dark, it was a vast, ever-changing playground in all seasons. But as a teenager and as a young adult, the farm was a place I wanted to be *from*. I respected the lives my parents had created with the land, but I knew I did not want to be a farmer's wife. So, off I went to St. Paul and then to San Francisco, determined to find a new way, my own way. Only in my thirties did I see more clearly how the farm had nurtured my curiosity and creativity and provided space and time for a deep connection to the natural world, a grounding for my spirituality. I recognized that I had always experienced the natural world as sacred text, although I would not have used those words at that time.

After David moved back to the farm with Sally Anne in 1971, Maja and I visited every summer and often at Christmas. In touching back to my childhood through Maja, the sense that the farm had narrowed my life evaporated. For Maja and her cousins who played in the grove, climbed to the roof of the old chicken house, and hunted asparagus along roadsides, the farm was joy—as it had been for me when I was young. But their attitude about chores was different than mine had been. They could scarcely wait until they were old enough to help, to "walk the beans" with the grown-ups, that communal, summer task of hoeing thistles along the soybean rows. Now, as an adult, I could value what Maja anticipated: walking the beans as an important ritual, a labor made lighter by conversation about books, movies, and politics, with water and snacks at the end of a long row, and a leap into the pond when the work was done.

In my thirties I also began to read more about the land. David recommended the fiction, poetry, and essays of environmental activist and farmer Wendell Berry. In Berry's writings I found an expression of a sense of place, of home, and an honoring of the land. I saw this also in David and Sally Anne's farming practices, which built on my father's work. As a teenager, I was aware that my father's practices were different from those of many other farmers. I remember being in the car on our way to a 4-H Club meeting, and hearing my dad comment—kindly, but not favorably—on a neighbor's cornfield, where the topsoil had eroded down the rows into a gulley at the bottom of the hill. My father used crop rotation, understood water flow, built terraces of soil on hillsides, and did not plow or plant up and down inclines. In some ways my father, with his attention to the health of the land, was before his time, although some might have said he was old-fashioned.

In the 1980s, David, Sally Anne, and my father and mother began to work toward getting the farm certified as organic, a certification they held from 1988–2002. They grew organic soybeans and buckwheat, which were shipped to Japan where demand was high for tofu and buckwheat products like soba noodles.

David and Sally Anne's care of creation encompassed more even than the land. Their care for others was expressed in Sally Anne's work as a Montessori preschool teacher and head of school, and David's twenty years as a county commissioner. Their generosity and hospitality to me, to other family members, and friends has continued for more than fifty years. Many years ago, we three mused: If all else collapsed, I could always join them growing potatoes on the farm. Later, we half-jokingly imagined our old age retreat, The Terminal Moraine Nursing Home and Montessori School, its name a pun about the terminal condition of life and the geologic formations called *terminal moraines*[29] found in southern Minnesota—and a tribute to Sally Anne and David's care for others.

Returning to the farm as an adult and a parent helped me understand more deeply the sacredness of the earth. We humans have not treated the land with reverence. We have not worked with its natural processes, but against them, often with the attitude of subduing and conquering. We have not understood that we are part of the natural world. When I drive the two hundred miles from St. Paul to the farm, I see the damage done by the monoculture of industrial agriculture and the overuse of herbicides and fertilizers. Farm buildings and trees have been razed to the ground; weedless fields of corn and soybeans are planted fence row to fence row, although there are few fences now. In the last two miles, on County Road 4, almost to the farm, I point to old farmsteads where even the trees have disappeared. I say, "That's where

29 A terminal moraine is an accumulation of earth and stones carried by a glacier and deposited at the point of the glacier's furthest advance.

the Kleevers used to live; that's where the Mutzigers lived; and there, that was Jens and Anna's farm."

From a mile away I can see the trees of my family's farm. The big maples that, in my childhood, marked the east boundary of the orchard, still rise. To the south, the catalpa and the two big maples are there, and two of the big spruces to the north. Yet there are many changes. The chicken house and hog shed are gone. The trees planted in memory of my parents are large now—a birch for my mother and a burr oak for my father. What used to be the orchard is now a wide swath of grass stretching from David and Sally Anne's earth berm house past raspberry patches and rhubarb beds to the pond, the fire pit, and the picnic tables under the trees. The big pink rock in the pasture where I played as a child was drowned by the three-acre pond long ago. The paths I walked to take my dad his afternoon lunch have reverted to prairie, part of the University of Minnesota bee project. The cow yard, too, will soon be planted in prairie.

My conversations with David and Sally Anne, stretching over fifty years, have been shared during long walks around the ponds, through the alfalfa, and the restored prairie. We continue to pass books back and forth. I recently gave David psychologist Bill Plotkin's book *Nature and the Human Soul* for his birthday. He gave me Timothy Egan's *The Worst Hard Time* about the Dust Bowl years. I am struck by how David and Sally Anne have lived their values of sustainability and accountability—values my parents lived by and bequeathed to all their children. The sacred, natural world that I discovered on the farm in childhood is still here, all these many years later. The teen who wanted and needed to leave grew into an adult who is grateful to return and to claim those early experiences.

My love for the farm has also been deepened by others who have appreciated and documented the natural world of southwest Minnesota. During what came to be called the "farm crisis" in the 1980s, the *St. Paul Pioneer Press* did a series titled *A Year on the Farm*. Journalist John Camp and photographer Joe Rossi[30] spent many days documenting the life of my parents and David and Sally Anne and their children Anton and Heather. In 1986, the series won a Pulitzer Prize for feature writing. We were delighted. We celebrated with the staff of the paper, all of us wearing T-shirts that proclaimed the Pulitzer Prize. In 1990, the Blandin Foundation published the book *Minnesota: Images*

30 Not to be confused with Joe Rossi, the Minnesota football coach.

of Home with photographs by Jim Brandenburg and text by Paul Gruchow. The book features two photos of the family farm: one titled *A Farm Still Life: Grain Scoops, Grain Screens, A Crib of Corn*. The other is of David in overalls, seen through the haze of grain dust, shoveling corn into the sheller. It is titled simply *Shelling Corn*. These ordinary scenes of my father's grain scoops, their edges worn down, and the physical task of shelling corn are made memorable in black and white. When I walk down the hall to my study I look to my right and see Brandenburg's photo of my parents—my dad in his overalls, sitting outside at coffee time, a cookie in his hand; my mother, her hair in a kerchief, leaning to pour him a cup of coffee. I look left to see Joe Rossi's photos of Maja and Kermit's wedding at the farm. I see the pond, the fields, Iowa in the distance, family members playing the handbells against the backdrop of the Haralson apple tree.

Though I have lived in cities most of my adult life, I continue to find sanctuaries of wildness near me. The St. Paul campus of the University of Minnesota, just a block from my home, contains a farm, part of their agriculture program. I walk there many mornings and evenings, a spiritual practice that frees me from thought, judgment, ego, and plans. In the spring there are cows and calves, ewes, and lambs. This past spring, I counted thirty-nine lambs! A small patch of prairie near the water tower comes to life in late spring. In summer, I note the bee balm, joe-pye weed, and milkweed in full bloom, reminiscent of the acres of restored prairie on my family's farm. I stop to read about the trees—how the larch loses it needles in the fall, and the black walnut is toxic to other growing things. I note the one Ponderosa pine on the campus. These are small learnings that open me to ask the question that the natural world continues to pose: "How is it that there is anything at all?"

Sometimes, I walk past a parking lot on the south edge of the campus, just blocks from the house I share with Tim. I am reminded that from 1963 to 1965 I parked the little gray Fiat there and ran to catch the intercampus bus to my graduate school classes on the Minneapolis campus. I was a young woman then, trying to outrun the fundamentalism of my youth and everything associated with it. Silently, I say thank you for this spiral trajectory of my life.

Bread Is Sacred

In a memory from childhood, I am running from the school bus, down the lane past the spruce trees, across the east lawn to the back gate, then around the house and into the kitchen to meet the scent of freshly baked bread and my mother's smile. I run very fast so that I might get there before my sister and brother and be the one who gets the crusty heel of a fresh loaf. A thick piece, still warm, spread with butter and jam—maybe strawberry or raspberry—was such pleasure, a closure to a school day and a transition to feeding the chickens. Homemade bread was a constant in my childhood home.

My mother was known for her bread—for her golden loaves, for light dinner rolls with smooth rounded tops, and especially for the Swedish tea rings that she made for holidays and special occasions. First, she rolled out the sweet dough spiced with cardamom, and spread it with butter, cinnamon and sugar and sometimes raisins or dates. Then she rolled up the dough into a long tube, shaped it in a ring, placed it in a round pan, and made uniform cuts along the outside edge of the ring to allow the dough to expand and reveal the filling inside. For very special occasions she drizzled it with icing. I remember seeing a photo in the local newspaper, *Worthington Daily Globe*, of her and other church women. My mother is holding up a tea ring. Only later did I note that it was always identified as a Swedish tea ring, though my mother had certainly learned her baking skills from her Finnish mother and Finnish sisters. In her community of mostly Swedes, my mother understood intuitively how to subordinate her Finnish heritage to the dominant culture.

My mother brought loaves of bread to the pastor and his wife and to her Finnish friend who lived in Worthington. She taught us girls to make bread. As part of our 4-H Club, Shirley and I baked bread for many county fair competitions. Bread was part of every meal and every little lunch and coffee time between. But for my mother, bread was more than physical sustenance, more than an opportunity to showcase her skills. I never saw my mother discard a piece of bread. Potato peelings, carrot tops, and strawberry hulls went to the chickens and other scraps to the dog or into the slop pail for the hogs. But every crust of bread, no matter how dry, was dunked in coffee or saved for bread pudding. Bread was precious. Bread was sacred.

The sacredness of bread for my mother was born in her early experiences in childhood. One of nine living children, she had experienced hunger in Finland, eating bread made from cambium, the inner bark of birch trees, when there was little grain. When she was still a school-age child, shortly after the Finnish Civil War, she said goodbye to three sisters who went to Sweden, where they hoped life could be easier. Before she emigrated, my mother believed that America would be the promised land. The farm in the sand hills of Nebraska that she and my father rented did not fulfill that expectation. But the black soil of southwest Minnesota gave my parents hope that they would never be hungry. And we never were.

After 4-H Club, I did not make much bread, except for those caramel rolls I baked during graduate school. I still have the index card with that recipe. I did not make bread that first year of my marriage to B. when we were living in San Francisco. But during the year in the Alaskan bush, I started to again. I looked forward to baking. I could not tell my family my fears and sadness about my marriage, but I could tell them about the bread. With the scent of yeast and the feel of the warm dough, I felt connected to my mother, to my family far away. I looked forward to the packages my mother and father sent, stuffed with the practical, including packages of dry yeast and dried fruit, wooden clothespins, and dishrags, and often a loaf of bread. I knew that it took many days to get to Bethel, Alaska, and then it could be many days before the mail plane could land at the airstrip. The arrival of a package was the silent arrival of my parents' love.

When Maja and I lived in San Francisco and then St. Paul, I made bread for us. With chagrin I remember that it took me a while to realize that the whole wheat bread I sliced for Maja's school lunches was too thick and dense to appeal to a child.

For a time during the 1980s and '90s, my brother David planted wheat. When I visited the farm, I knew I would eat Sally Anne's bread or my mother's bread made with freshly ground wheat. I remember sitting at the big kitchen table next to my mother and sorting the wheat kernels for grinding, removing chaff and any stray sticks or small stones. Organic wheat ground a few hours before baking makes really good bread.

I have continued to make bread regularly. I eat the heel of one loaf when the loaf is still warm. The other loaf I give away, often delivering it, sometimes still warm, to Maja and Kermit's house seven blocks away. Less often I make the sweet bread, using my mother's recipe I know by heart—two cups milk, six and a half cups of flour, and always freshly ground cardamom. For years I shaped the sweet dough into two Swedish tea rings. Then, during the years my grandchildren came to visit after school, I often made the sweet dough into three loaves, two with cinnamon and brown sugar rolled into the dough, one with just the cardamom. And if I could arrange it, I baked on a Tuesday to have the bread come out of the oven a short time before the children arrived. I always sent a loaf home with them. I do not know how my daughter and son-in-law and grandchildren will remember bread. I hope with pleasure—and the assurance of being loved.

There is something deeply creative about making bread. It is a form of gestation—of bringing together seemingly inert ingredients to create something new. I think about my mother who likely made bread every week of her adult life. For her, it was both a responsibility and giving of herself. I can imagine that for her as for me, she sometimes began baking in frustration, anger, or sorrow. And in the process over hours, in handling and shaping the dough into baked loaves, feelings are released, perspective shifts. Something is created—loaves of bread—and a heart lightened.

My mother would not have baked the bread used in Holy Communion in the church of my childhood. I think she would have liked to. It would have been a way of connecting her sense of the sacredness of bread to her religious practice. Rather, the wife of a deacon would have baked the bread. My father was never a deacon, but a trustee, with the practical skills and knowledge to care for the church building and grounds. At my church in St. Paul there were several years when women, sometimes men, baked the bread that we used in Holy Communion.

Holy Communion, known in many traditions as *Eucharist*, is meant to be a meal, remembering a meal. Jesus's last supper was the Passover meal shared with his disciples. Of the major functions of a clergyperson in the United Church of Christ denomination, it is Holy Communion that I deeply love. Even though I believe that what I offered in pastoral counseling and spiritual direction was and is sacramental, officiating at the Communion table in a worship service is a public act of radical hospitality, an inclusive act. It is an offering of the bread of life to all. I think of the many times that sharing bread has been sacred for me—many times as the one who invites and countless times as the one who receives. Approaching the altar on Sunday mornings to receive the bread, saying "Amen," in response to the deacon's words, "The bread of Life." Sitting in a circle at ARC at Sunday worship, offering the bread and cup to the person sitting next to me. Looking into my father's eyes at my ordination as I offer him the cup. Giving leftover pieces of sourdough to the teenage boy and his mother, saying, "God is generous." Sharing bread and wine at Katharine's house in San Francisco after meditation. Eating rye bread, cheese, and cucumber, bought at outdoor markets in Finland, with my mother, sister Gladys, and Maja. Offering warm caramel rolls to my graduate school housemates. Sharing lunch with my father, sitting with him in the shade of the tractor wheel. Breaking bread together. I cannot name them all.

Homemade bread is not fast food. I once tried to time how long each step could take: mixing, kneading, first rising, punching down, second rising, shaping the loaves, third rising in the loaf pans, baking. About six hours. I have tried to slip bread-baking into a busy day, kneading while looking at the clock, setting the timer for Tim to punch down the dough while I walk to the shops. But much better is having a span of several hours that lets me enjoy the process, kneading as long as it takes and not rushing the rising, looking forward to the scent of the bread baking.

A few years ago, we bought a KitchenAid mixer. "Aha," I thought, "I suppose a machine can do the mixing and the kneading." It does do the work, but I missed the slow process of touch, that rhythmic, mindful motion of kneading, the sensing when the dough is ready to be put to rise or put in the pan. So, I have gone back to kneading, more fully aware that its sensory experience connects me to the living yeast, my mother, my childhood, and to that Mystery I call God. It has taken me years to claim fully that connection between bread and the sacred that my mother knew in her body without ever naming it.

The Power of Story

The power of storytelling grabbed me early and has not let go. In childhood, stories were my entertainment, my means of escape from painful feelings, and my window into a larger world. In adolescence, I read about girls who went to college and women who had careers that shaped and validated my own desire to go to college. Without such stories, would I have made it there? I think not. I then followed my love of reading, my love of story, to undergraduate and graduate degrees in English.

But stories were also a source of deep anxiety. I grew up in a family and a religion where everyone around me believed that the stories of the Bible were not only very important, but they also mattered in an existential way. How they were understood was a matter of life and death, heaven, or hell. For the most part, everyone around me took Bible texts literally. When was it that I began to question literal interpretation of Bible texts? Not as a young girl when I lay in the double bed with my sister in the west bedroom, frightened and reciting to myself Luke 17:34: "One will be taken and the other left behind," certain that I was the one who would be left behind. Not that dark November evening as I watched for the lights of my parents' car, fearing the Rapture had occurred, that Jesus had returned and taken my family but not me. Yet, even as the terror of the Rapture caused me so much anxiety, at the same age I also knew that Jesus was not literally a vine, and that people were not literally branches. I was eleven or twelve when I tried to explain the difference between the two seemingly contradictory Genesis creation stories to my mother, asserting they could not both be true. Though it frightened me to challenge the Bible, I wanted my mother to engage with me about the stories. I needed her to respond to me. I needed her to ease my confusion and fears.

It was in college that I turned away from church and the Bible. During my junior year, I procrastinated so long on writing a paper about the miracles of Jesus I had to carry an incomplete into the summer. I finally wrote the paper, but it was a turning point: I hadn't believed what I wrote—I *couldn't* believe what I wrote. My understanding of Baptist theology required me to take literally the Bible stories of Jesus's miracles, which I could not do. I was both miserable and relieved to hand the paper in. Perhaps if I had found the courage to talk with my professor about my doubts and struggles, he would have been supportive, not judgmental. Perhaps then I would have been able to write a paper that had integrity.

While I rejected the stories and doctrine of the church that had shaped me, I followed my love of reading and story to teaching high school English. During those years I met Katharine and began to read Carl Jung, Joseph Campbell, Mary Esther Harding, and Robert Johnson, among others. I resonated with the depth psychology of Jung. I found meaning for my life in the myths that I read. I paid attention to my dreams, those stories from my unconscious. I was not consciously aware of it, but at a deep level, there was a door opening, a door into another way to be with story—all stories. I was preparing for seminary without knowing it.

In my first seminary class, when I enacted the Gospel of Mark with classmates, the story of the bleeding woman who touched Jesus's cloak grabbed me at a level deeper than conscious thought. Without forethought, I *became* the woman who sought the healing of Jesus. Entering the story gave me insight I could not have found any other way. There began my conscious journey of exploring how I might approach the profound, messy collection of stories we find in the Bible.

As I moved from teacher of literature to pastoral counseling and spiritual direction, I moved from being present to one kind of story to another. In pastoral counseling and spiritual direction, my work is listening to the other person's story, entering it to understand and to accept. Here, also, there is setting, character, plot, and theme, although we do not use these words. Wondering together, we look for understanding, threads of meaning, openings for growth, choices to make. The reward in my work is being present to people reshaping their own stories, integrating parts of their story into a whole. And, though not always explicitly, this process invites them to bring their personal story to the Big Story—the story of grace, of liberation, of oneness, of healing and transformation, so much of which is at the core of every spiritual tradition.

In 1989, thirty-five years after the conversation with my mother, came an invitation to wonder again about the Genesis creation stories that my twelve-year-old mind could not reconcile. My spiritual director, Kay, asked me to write a reflection on the creation stories for the Theological Insights program, a series of seminars at the St. Catherine University in St. Paul. These seminars for women were modeled after the work of women at Harvard Seminary. I was pleased to be asked and a little intimidated. I wrote and re-wrote. My reflection became an essay, "A Story of Healing," included in the book *Walking in Two Worlds.*[31] Recently when I pulled the book off the shelf and reread my essay, I did not say to myself, "Oh my, did I really think that then?" In fact, most of it still resonated.

In the essay, I described what I learned as a child from the interpretation of the Adam and Eve story in Genesis 2: I was born into original sin; I was subordinate to men; and Eve (i.e., woman) was to blame for Adam's sin—therefore, for everyone's sin. I wrote that it had taken me a long time to believe that God celebrates the created world as good, although that is stated so clearly in the Genesis 1 creation story, where God declares creation good again and again. I wrote that the Adam and Eve story shows us that as humans, we make choices, and that our choices can separate us from God.

As I reread the Genesis 2 story recently, I thought about how the story of Eve and Adam reveals what it means to come to conscious awareness of ourselves, an inevitable process of being human. A child begins in symbiosis with the mother and slowly becomes aware of not being one with its mother. We have no choice but to separate, to come to consciousness, to make choices. We individuate. We will make choices that are nurturing of life, ours and others, and other choices that are damaging to ourselves and to all the created world. We cannot help eating from the fruit of the tree of the knowledge of good and evil. I sometimes think of that first bite of the fruit (often thought of as an apple), and then subsequent bites, as consciousness unfolding, an amazing drama in every person's life. This is what it means to be human.

But there is more to the story of the human journey. I have come to believe that in our essence, we are not, nor have we ever been, separate from the Mystery that we call God. Orthodox priest Anthony Bloom says, "It is not God who is absent." I can choose to be absent. I can choose to be present.

31 Kay Vander Vort, Joan H. Timmerman, Eleanor Lincoln, eds., *Walking in Two Worlds: Women's Spiritual Paths* (St. Cloud, MN: North Star Press, 1992).

And every spiritual tradition finds a way to say that we are One, that we are connected, that the *I* my ego insists on is not my essence. And that all creation is connected, is One. How do I write about the ineffable, the indescribable? Sister Virginia, my colleague and friend, who studied with Thomas Keating and Bede Griffiths, tells of Bede extending his hand palm up, saying that all spiritual paths meet, just as his fingers meet in his palm, in silence, in Oneness.

We need the metaphorical to even begin to point toward the Mystery. Many times, sitting in the pews, I have wanted clergypersons to acknowledge that they, too, are sorting out the literal and the metaphorical. I want the preacher to acknowledge the power of story and metaphor, that we can take scripture seriously without taking it literally. I want the preacher to know and say that some things are truer than facts. I want the preacher to know and say that the truth of Jesus's story of the Samaritan woman at the well is far more important than whether these events literally happened as described.

Brian McLaren's approach to the Gospel stories in his 2022 book *Do I Stay Christian?* is liberating. He writes: "I call the alternative to the conventional literalist approach a literary approach. If we take the stories seriously as literary artifacts, we do not need to take them literally as factual accounts."[32] He continues in detail, with a powerful interpretation of the exorcism and swine suicide story in Mark, Luke, and Matthew (Mark 5: 1–2; Luke 8:26–39; Matt. 8:2–34.) He writes, " . . . could it be that demons were the best available explanation ancient people had for what we call mental illness." And he continues, "In this telling, the miracle in the story, the magic in the story, wasn't an exorcism. It was love. Kindness drove out shame and self-hatred." One does not need to try to reconcile the details that differ in the three stories to recognize that love and kindness have power to heal.

And so also with Genesis. Both creation stories are true: Creation is good. At the same time, as we move to consciousness and choice, we will make choices, and what we choose will often separate us from God, other humans, all creation, and our true selves.

When Maja was a child, we read C. S. Lewis's The Chronicles of Narnia together. She loved those stories, as did I. In Narnia, Aslan the lion, although often terrifying, is the manifestation of the Christ, a wise, just, compassionate presence. I remember breathing my gratitude to Lewis for his presentation of Sacred Presence—a presence to whom both Maja and I were strongly

32 Brian D. McLaren, *Do I Stay Christian?* (New York: St. Martin's Essentials, 2022), 114.

drawn. Ironic, that the Bible stories that were part of my childhood did not, or could not, touch me in young adulthood until I first found meaning in Greek mythology through Jungian psychology, and the world of Narnia. It is a circuitous journey.

When I think about story, I see how it has been an integral part of my professional life and my personal, spiritual journey—the two woven together. By turns, struggling with story and welcoming its power has been at the center of "working out my salvation." That rope I took hold of in childhood and then let go of in young adulthood could only be reshaped and made new through my experience—through my own lived story.

Return to the Garden: Reclaiming the Hebrew and Christian Stories

Over time I have reclaimed the stories of the Bible—in seminary, in my own preaching, in listening to others, but the most powerful reclamation happened when I *told* the stories. In 2004, I began to teach the children at my church using the Godly Play curriculum. Shaped by Jerome Berryman after the principles of Maria Montessori, the curriculum had grabbed Maja's interest in 2001 when her son, Eli, was three. After having observed a Godly Play class at the local Episcopal church, she signed up for the training and began to shape the program for children ages three to eight at our church. I, too, was drawn to the curriculum's deep respect and trust for the child's own experience of God's presence. Within the next year, I was trained, and for the next ten years, I was a Godly Play storyteller in the class for the five-to-seven-year-olds.

Godly Play class time begins by welcoming each child at the door and asking whether they are ready to sit in the circle. Once the circle is formed, the storyteller begins. All eyes are on the center of the circle where the story takes place, with the storyteller placing and moving the props that are part of the story. There is silence except for the storyteller's voice. Once the story is told, the storyteller asks the "wondering" questions, leaving plenty of time for responses: What part did you like best? What part do you think is most important? Is there any part of the story we can leave out and still have all the story we need? Where might you be in the story? The children readily answer the first question. They are often very astute about the second. The third question often takes a while, as they try leaving out various elements, as does the fourth. The storyteller does not tell the children what to think or feel. Rather, the approach is an open invitation to wonder. When I began training to be a storyteller, I noted the language of *I wonder* and how I used that phrase as an invitation so many times in pastoral counseling and spiritual direction.

After hearing the story and participating in the wondering, the children choose which of the stories they will engage in for their "work time," hands-on work with the elements of the stories: small wood figures and structures, rocks, pieces of different colored felt, and more. Each story has its own props and sits on a tray on a series of shelves in the classroom—at child level. The children have time to dwell in the story, to retell it in whatever way works for them.

For many months, one child chose the Genesis 1 creation story every Sunday for children's work time, delighting in spreading out the pieces of felt, first black, then the blues for sky and water, then sun, moon, and stars, next brown and green, and eventually birds, fish, mammals, and humans. The Flood captivated children with its many animals, the tiny ramp up to the door of the Ark, the Ark itself, and Mr. and Mrs. Noah. The Great Family, the story of Abraham and Sarah, is the first of many stories presented in the desert box, a low box on rollers filled with several inches of very fine sand. So popular was the desert box that we storytellers devised a system to make sure that each child had work time with stories that take place in the desert.

There are prop sets for the stories of the Exodus, the Ten Commandments (named The Ten Best Ways), and the two stories of the Ark of the Covenant, the first with the movable Tent and the second one with the Temple. The many parts of these two stories—candle stand, basin, altar, and a curtain to separate the Holy of Holies from the remainder of the structure—create miniature worship spaces. It is fascinating to watch children build the structures and recreate the story for themselves. As the story is told, a small wood figure of the high priest is placed in the Holy of Holies, with the reminder that only the high priest is allowed in this special place. I remember a wondering time with second graders when one boy commented that we didn't need a priest to enter the Holy of Holies to pray, " . . . because we can pray to God wherever we are." "Wow," I thought, "listen to children." Jesus's words from the Gospel of Mark came to me: "Let the little children come to me; do not stop them; for it is to such as these that the kingdom of God belongs." (Mark 10:14)

Godly Play also includes the stories of individual characters: Abraham, Sarah, Jacob, Joseph, Moses, Ruth, Samuel, David (always a favorite with the children). I remember one Sunday morning when grandson Eli bumped us fully out of the story of God's call of Samuel. Several times in the night, Samuel hears his name and thinks that it is Eli the high priest calling him. But it isn't, and the high priest encourages Samuel to answer. When I came to the latter part of the story where the High Priest Eli and his sons, who had clearly not followed God's ways, were about to be punished, I spoke the words, "Then Eli and his sons were struck dead." At that moment grandson Eli improvised, collapsing silently in a heap. It took some time to get us all back into the story.

One of my favorite stories is the Great Family, the story of the call of Abram and Sarai, the one family in Ur who "believed that all of God was in every place. . . ." In telling that story, I took care to set the scene: "The desert is a dangerous place, the sand always moving, so it is hard to know where you are. There is little water." Then I would begin to move the figures of Abram and Sarai, and their many sheep and servants, slowly, leaving Ur, traveling along the dark blue yarn of the Tigris and Euphrates Rivers toward Haran and eventually into Canaan where God makes the seemingly impossible promise that they will have a child. They will be the parents of a great family. This last part is the best part of the story when I speak of Abraham and Sarah (now renamed) saying, "Then Isaac and Rebekah had children, and their children had children. . . . And this went on for thousands of years until your mothers and fathers had children . . . " And then I take a handful of sand and let it slowly trickle out as I conclude, "Now you are part of that great family which has become as many as the stars in the sky and grains of sand in the desert." Then I take my eyes away from the desert box and look directly at the children. They smile at being included in the Great Family.

Jacob is one of my favorite Hebrew Testament characters. I recognize my own capacity to manipulate when I read about him tricking his twin Esau to get Isaac's blessing. His struggle in the desert with the angel/messenger at Peniel, the face of God, has been my companion for a long time, reminding me of my struggling. If someone asks me for a favorite story from the Bible, I often choose Jacob's reconciliation with Esau. Jacob, now owning his betrayal of Esau many years earlier, is returning home. Although he is surrounded by his wives, children, animals—all signs of his wealth—he is a chastened and frightened man as he approaches his brother. Esau welcomes him with forgiveness. Then Jacob says, "Seeing your face is like seeing the face of God." Many faces have been the faces of God for me—some were face-to-face meetings, as with Katharine, and others were imagined meetings—with Thomas Merton. And many more, so often the face of a child.

The Godly Play Christian Testament stories begin with Advent and the Nativity and move quickly to Jesus's baptism, his ministry, miracles, and parables. The parables are stored in boxes, each one wrapped in gold foil. They are presented to the children as precious gifts to be unwrapped and wondered about. In the parable of the Great Pearl, the storyteller asks, "I wonder what could be so precious that a person would exchange everything for it?" The wondering time often begins with the children sharing what is precious to them. They might start with naming prized possessions, but almost always they move to naming a parent, a sibling, a friend. The Good Samaritan parable creates lively discussion when the children answer the question: "Now I wonder who is the neighbor to the person who was hurt and had everything taken from him, and was left by the side of the road half dead?" With the older children, after the first, more obvious answer, the storyteller can place different combinations of the characters (traveler, Samaritan, Levite, robber) side by side and ask the question, "Who is the neighbor?" again to deepen the conversation. Children have a more nuanced ability to see possibilities than adults realize.

Jesus is introduced in each story with a simple sentence: "There was once someone who said such wonderful things and did such amazing things, that people followed him." This opening statement said again and again, becomes both expository and liturgical. Both Christmas and Easter are presented as Mystery. The story of Lent is told using six wooden plaques, Faces of Easter. We tell the children that we need a long time to get ready for Easter because Easter is such a great Mystery. The last plaque of the Faces of Easter has two sides, one side showing crucifixion and the other the risen Christ. In the telling, the storyteller illustrates that one cannot pull them apart and then puts the plaque down with the face of the risen Christ visible, saying "This is the Mystery of Easter, and that makes all the difference." Telling the Christian Testament stories has helped me let go of my strong need to understand. I can let the Mystery be—most of the time.

When I began to tell the stories to the children in 2004, I felt a strange homecoming. I recalled what Katharine had said about going home to rural Kentucky for Christmas in adulthood and reclaiming the power of Nativity stories. She said she no longer argued about whether they were literal or metaphorical. Rather, she could allow the power of the stories to touch her fully. Coming back to the scripture stories through Godly Play has been a similar experience for me.

Except for the enactment of the Gospel of Mark that first term of seminary, no seminary class ever invited me to enter the stories as fully as does telling the stories in Godly Play. The question "Where am I in the story?" rarely, if ever, surfaced in those four years of seminary. I did find invitations in Anthony de Mello's book, *Sadhana: a Way to God: Christian Exercises in Eastern Form,*[33] where he invites the reader to imagine entering the story. In leading retreats, I found various ways to ask the question, *where are you in the story?* The Ignatian Exercises, the approach to Christian Scripture shaped by the Jesuits, invites one to enter the stories. As does the amplification process in Walter Wink's Transforming Bible Study method that I used many times in the 1990s. Yet, for me, the Godly Play stories are the most powerful, especially when I am the storyteller. Perhaps it is that to tell the story well, I need to enter the story fully. I need to know the story so well that I can tell it without notes and without hesitation. I have needed to live in the story a long time to tell it truly.

Even though I loved the Bible stories in childhood, especially before I began to struggle with the question of literalism, I do not recall being invited to enter the story—to wonder what it might have been like to be the prodigal son being welcomed by the father or the lost sheep being found by the shepherd. Perhaps the invitation was offered, and my young ears were closed. I think, rather, that I got stuck in that other story—the priestly story, the story of my terrible sinfulness and Jesus needing to suffer and die to save me from hell. No one in my childhood or teen years wondered about the other two macro-stories: Exodus and Exile—liberation and returning home. Those stores were about the Hebrew people, not about us Christians.

Entering the stories continues to confirm for me that the Bible is an amazing collection of many different peoples' attempts over many years, to say something, always partial, about their experience of the Mystery, the Holy. We will continue to tell the old stories and our new stories. So says the banner hanging above the outer doors of our church: "God is still speaking."

---

33 Anthony de Mello, *Sadhana: a Way to God: Christian Exercises in Eastern Form* (St. Louis: The Institute of Jesuit Sources, 1978)

Blessings of Ordination

Even though I have been ordained for almost forty years, it does not sit easily with me. It is not a dominant part of my identity. When people ask me about my work, only rarely do I say more than that I was a high school English teacher and then went to seminary in midlife. What are the messages embedded in me that make me hesitant to claim pastoral identity? Perhaps it is not one thing, but several woven together, including messages I cannot even name. I know I still carry the residue of my early religious upbringing, where women had no leadership role. I carry also having been a member for several years of San Francisco Friends Meeting, part of the strand of Quakerism that eschews clergy. I carry the awareness that although I am ordained, I have not been the more public, traditional clergyperson serving in a parish. And probably in the mix is my intermittent sense of not being good enough.

My career shift—or if I use the words many clergy use, my *sense of call*—was long and indirect in its coming, revealing itself slowly over seven years of transition. And although I found mentors and colleagues (and they found me), I was not part of a church where members and leadership offered financial and emotional support to enter and complete seminary. My journey was rather like jumping from island to island in an archipelago while it seemed that many of my contemporaries in seminary had chartered a boat and knew where they were headed.

In 2011, the pastor of my church asked whether I wanted to note the twenty-five years since my ordination. I said yes. As I began planning the liturgy and my reflection, I remembered how I had felt a bit like an impostor when I began writing my papers for ordination in 1986. I had asked myself, "How am I to write about my sense of call?" I could not easily claim that my call was from the Minnesota Conference of the United Church of Christ, which felt like an abstraction, or from the small congregation in which I served only the one year of my internship during seminary. I had not experienced any kind of epiphany, of being chosen, as some people might. Nor was there any clergyperson in my family whom I experienced as a mentor. As a child I had never imagined being a pastor, unlike two Roman Catholic friends who, clearly wanting to be priests, enacted the Eucharist for their siblings.

During my chaplaincy work in chemical dependency and mental health, I came to realize that my call was from the fifty-year-old man in treatment for the fourth time. In offering pastoral counseling, my call came from the woman who had finally grown strong enough to leave an abusive marriage and from the women and men who struggled with depression and anxiety, with shame and despair. I was called by the two women who sought me out for spiritual direction while I was in seminary. All these people and many more were the community that called me. Though their voices would not be heard at my ordination service, they were present to me. As I wrote my reflection, I remembered my mentors as well as the hundreds of women and men who had sat across from me in my office and told me their stories. I knew that my gifts had fit my work. I had found the place I needed to be.

When I finished speaking that Sunday morning in 2011, my heart was full of gratitude—but there was more to come. Pastor Victoria came forward. When she asked me to sit on the chancel steps and called the children forward, inviting them to surround me, I began to weep. I understood why she had called them. I knew these children and they knew me. As a Godly Play storyteller, I had blessed each of them at the end of class many times. Being blessed by them was so right.

"Gently," Pastor Victoria said, "gently put your hands on Marilyn." Jackson reached out his hand, smiling shyly. Ian touched me with the back of his hand. Five-year-old Fred, who often exuberantly threw himself at me for a blessing at the end of class, reached out his hand. In the group were my grandchildren, nine-year-old Alistair and five-year-old Siri, who snuggled against me.

The children's hands that Sunday morning of celebration were the right hands to mark twenty-five years of ordination. Church dignitaries were not needed in 1986 nor in 2011. The people who came for pastoral counseling and spiritual direction could not be physically present then or now. But the children with their open faces and sticky fingers were also my community of faith, and they represented many others. These children to whom I told the stories, to whom I told the big, best story of healing and liberation, could offer a full blessing.

Claiming the Cross

One recent morning when I walked into my study to meditate, I picked up a small olive wood cross from a shelf on my bookcase. The cross, several rocks, and a shell rest in front of an etching of Carl Jung's statement, "Bidden or unbidden, God is present," a reminder of why I sit in meditation. As I sat down, I wondered why I had picked up the cross. I typically pick up a shell or a rock.

Given my story, it is not surprising that the cross is a Christian symbol that hasn't resonated for me in a positive way. Even today, I do not wear one. It is so easy for me to start hearing those Baptist hymns, "In the cross of Christ I glory," and "Beneath the cross of Jesus. . . . Lift high the cross," and slip into the confusion of substitutionary theology, where God the angry Father demands that a sinless Jesus must be sacrificed for my sins, our sins. I grew up with the words of John 3:16 etched into my psyche: "For God so loved the world that He gave his only begotten son that whosoever believeth in him shall not perish but shall have everlasting life." Belief, accepting Jesus as Lord and Savior, seemed largely about getting saved from hell and getting to heaven. I came to a time when I could not believe in a God who needed to kill Jesus, who sent Jesus into the world to be killed. I could not believe this, even though at the same time, I feared God's judgment of my sins and my unbelief. I struggled. What to do about the crucifixion and resurrection—central to Christianity.

Marcus Borg helped me. In his books *The Meaning of Jesus: Two Visions* and *Speaking Christian* I found a theology of the cross that makes sense experientially and intellectually. I understand that Jesus's death on the cross was the result of what he preached and how he lived. He was executed because he challenged the injustice of both the political and religious powers of his time. The powers needed to get rid of him. The crucifixion of Jesus was a political act.

And it is more. Marcus Borg writes: "The story of the empty tomb means that death could not hold Jesus, could not stop what he had begun."[34] Death

34 Marcus Borg, *Speaking Christian* (New York: HarperOne, 2011), 112.

could not then, and does not now, stop the power of love, of the path Jesus showed us. Borg goes on to say that it is not important whether the tomb was empty. Rather, what matters is that Jesus's death and resurrection changed things. That " . . . the followers of Jesus, both then and now, continued to experience Jesus as a living reality after his death."[35] Out of Jesus's death and resurrection, life comes, transformed life. For me, following Jesus means living with compassion and justice in community with others. I no longer see the cross as what saves me from hell, but as what invites and challenges me to live, to serve, to love, to follow Jesus. His death and resurrection are archetypal, inviting me to understand this universal pattern of transformation in my life, in all life. And to live it. What belief means has changed for me. Believing has to do with what and whom I set my heart on—what and whom I give myself to.

Several years ago, a Jungian therapist spoke of the cross in yet another way. I do not remember exactly what he said, but I recall him standing in front of us with both arms outstretched—a stance of wide-open arms. He invited us to consider that the cross opens our hearts, in a sense breaks our hearts open. The cross, symbol of Jesus's life, death, and resurrection, breaks me open to compassion, inclusivity, and justice.

Perhaps I had picked up the cross because, without knowing it consciously, I was letting go of the theology of substitutionary atonement.

---

35 Marcus Borg and N. T. Wright, *The Meaning of Jesus: Two Visions* (New York: HarperCollins, 1999), 135.

God Loves You Even More

When my grandson Eli left for a college visit, I gave him two twenties and told him to put them in his shoe in case he lost his wallet. I also told him I would hold him in the Light, something I say often, in person, in greeting cards, and by text. Is it universal, the joy that we have for the lives of grandchildren? Eli was born on September 9, 1999, a date easy to remember. I must have been extolling his six-month-old beauty yet one more time when my friend John Ackerman said to me, "Marilyn, God loves you even more than you love Eli." And I exclaimed, "No! How can that be?" This reminder has accompanied me for all the years of Eli's life and the lives of his siblings, Alistair, born in 2002, and Siri, born in 2006. Often when I am with them and experience that swell of joy and gratitude at their being in this world, I remember John's words. And I say thank you for them and for John's affirmation. My grandchildren are my sacred texts.

I did not, could not, imagine what it might be like to *have* grandparents. My parents' immigration had cut off any possibility of me knowing my grandparents. I did spend two days with my father's mother on the family trip to Sweden when I was nineteen. She spoke Swedish, and I spoke English. In my childhood, there was no grandparents' house where Christmas and Thanksgiving were celebrated. Our closest relatives were an aunt and uncle who lived in Nebraska, whom I saw a couple times a year. I had a childhood friend whose grandmother lived on their farm in her separate house. She was a large, formidable Swedish woman who was the church pianist and often looked sternly at the two of us if we whispered during worship. Yet, she welcomed me into her home, and there were times when I stayed at her house so I could participate in a church event.

At every visit to the farm during Maja's childhood, I saw the joy my parents found in Maja and their other grandchildren. There never was a doubt that Maja could stay for weeks with Grandma Bertha and Grandpa Gus while I flew back to San Francisco to begin preparing for teaching in September.

To be a witness to the growth of a child is a gift. I keep journals about my grandchildren. At family birthday gatherings we often read favorite stories. The children especially like to hear about their early years. Eli created an imaginary friend—a teenager. His intent was to circumvent the rule: no playing on the back deck by the alley unless you have a grown-up with you. This was also the period when he took on the persona of Frances, the badger character, in the children's book *Bread and Jam for Frances,* telling us as he stretched out his hands, "See my little badger paws."

Alistair carried a large paper bag around collecting interesting bits and pieces. He also hid things. The stapler was gone for a long time. The banana was found when it began to smell. Tim retired just before Alistair started kindergarten. When Alistair was asked in kindergarten screening where he had gone to preschool, he pointed to the Jean Lyle Children's Center shirt he was wearing and said, "Here. But I'm retired."

Siri heard many stories about Grandma Bertha, my mother, who had died before Siri's birth. On the refrigerator is a photo of my mother in the last years of her life, a joyful expression on her face, holding baby Eli. I often told Siri that Grandma Bertha loved children and would have loved to have held her too. When Siri was about two and a half, she asked, "Grandma Bertha come back?" "No," I replied, "Grandma Bertha got very old. Then she died and went to be with God. That's where she is, with God." She turned to Tim and asked, "You old?" Tim said, "Yes, kind of old." Then Siri asked, "You go to be with God?" After a deep breath I said, "Boppa Tim will someday go to be with God but not for a long while, probably when you are a grown-up woman."

Over the years, the time we spent with our grandchildren shifted. When they were infants and toddlers, we did childcare, spending several days a week with each of them. When they attended nursery school, we picked them up and took them to our house for snacks and playtime. I loved settling Alistair in the stroller, taking Eli's hand and walking him to nursery school. I recall walking along streets and in parking lots with Eli, listening to him note the differences in hubcaps and wheel covers. I am fascinated by how children make sense of things. Siri, at age three, identified the garbage disposal as the garlic exploder. During their elementary and high school years the grandchildren came once a week for supper. Eli and Alistair especially liked the roast beef I made. There is so much that I did not get to do with Maja when she was a child that I got to do with our grandchildren. On weekday mornings in San Francisco, I was probably already thinking about my first class, when

I would drop Maja at Teresa's house from where she would go to preschool and elementary school.

Watching our grandchildren continues to invite me to wonder and marvel at human development—physical, mental, emotional, spiritual. And it affords me the opportunity to recall parts of my life and to be introduced to new experiences. Those summers when Eli and Siri acted in Shakespeare productions in a local park were a time for me to remember how much I enjoyed teaching Shakespeare's comedies to teens. I have a great photo of Eli in *A Midsummer Night's Dream*, struggling to stay in character while wearing a large carboard box painted in a brick pattern that portrays the wall through which the lovers communicate.

Teenage girls did not participate in sports when I was growing up, although I did play second base in our grade school's softball team. Maja was not especially interested in sports. Drama and music were her interests. Then Eli discovered sports, especially sports statistics. I have saved for him a few pages of the many sports events he fantasized in our basement during his school years—pages and pages of teams, players, and statistics in his small, neat printing. During the boys' high school years, we watched Eli and Alistair compete in cross-country running and Nordic skiing. Later, when Alistair was at Carleton College, we enjoyed following his track career, watching him run the 800 and with his teammates, the 4-by-400 relay. I now understand a bit about running, like what makes the 800 a difficult race. And I learned, how for Eli and Alistair, sports created a positive community with strong bonds and opportunities for excellence, leadership, and enduring friendship.

When I was a school-age child, I took piano lessons from Miss Headley who lived next to the post office in Worthington. I continue to enjoy playing simple classics, hymns, and Christmas carols, and I look forward to singing in our church choir. It is music that can bring me to tears, to a deep sense of awe. Alistair's piano recitals have given me joy and anxiety. He plays as though he is running the 800. And Siri can move from playing Irish fiddle one week to a classical recital piece the next.

My involvement with grandchildren brings me happy memories of childhood and early adulthood, but it also brings regret. I regret that I did not involve Maja in backpacking or camping after we moved to Minnesota. I let go of something that was life-giving, that experience of the Mystery in the wilderness, although I found it again and again at the family farm. Through friends, Alistair and then Siri found Camp Widjiwagan, the YMCA camp in Ely, Minnesota. Many summers they canoed the Boundary Waters Canoe Area of northern Minnesota or backpacked in the Bighorn Mountains of Wyoming and the Rockies of Montana and Alberta. Siri did one semester at High Mountain Institute in Colorado where she did several trips into the high desert. Those were the months that she and I exchanged frequent emails of news and poems having to do with nature—poems that speak to how wilderness invites awe and a sense of oneness with nature.

Over the years, two experiences—our church's family camp and the family farm—were extended times together. For twelve years, we took the grandchildren and Maja to a week of family camp at Pilgrim Point Camp on Lake Ida near Alexandria, Minnesota. Eli was just five our first year; I got up at 6:30 all week, mostly cheerful, to pitch softballs to him. When he was a young teen, he stayed up late to create the scripts of the annual camp skits that included a dozen boys ages five to fifteen. Siri joined us as a toddler. Camp was an intergenerational experience that created friendships that all of us, adults and grandchildren, have maintained.

Once they were teens, trips to the family farm became more difficult to schedule. During those visits, the grandchildren roasted hot dogs, swung in the barn, paddled in the pond, cleared brush, lolled in the hammock, lay in the grass to look at the night sky, and delighted us with their skills of barrel-rolling. Our videos document Alistair and Siri balancing on the fifty-gallon oil drums, moving their feet to roll the barrels across the wide lawn. Alistair learned to use a chainsaw. Both Eli and Alistair's first experiences of driving a car happened on the farm with Tim as instructor.

Eli has graduated from Dartmouth in New Hampshire. Alistair has graduated from Carleton College in Northfield, Minnesota, an hour south of St. Paul. Both are working in Boston. Siri is a freshman at Carleton. Tim's conversations with them about math and physics during their high school years and my taking them out for breakfast to talk about the novels and plays they were reading has shifted. Now we have coffee dates and breakfasts and lunch when they come home, and weeks at the North Shore on Lake Superior in the summer and again after Christmas. And we text.

In my work of spiritual direction, often those who sit across from me in the other chair tell me that their first experience of what God might be like was their relationship with a loving grandparent. May it be so for our grandchildren. Giving our time and our full presence to our grandchildren has given us a continuing window into a fuller experience of being human—infant, child, teen, and young adult. I suppose I am not alone in realizing that in my parenting I was often not present, my consciousness and my time focused elsewhere. I have wanted to give to my grandchildren what I could not give to my daughter. They have given me so much. They continue to be my sacred texts, revealing the Mystery.

Our grandchildren's presence in my life invites me again and again to reflect on my own childhood, and to own both its pain and healing. In one of my journals about Alistair, I wrote of overhearing an interchange between him and Eli. Six-year-old Eli asked four-year-old Alistair if he was afraid. Alistair said simply, "No, God keeps me safe."

One might think, "How naive. He'll learn to be afraid." But for me, this conversation revealed that Alistair was experiencing what every child needs—a trust in life, a trust in being loved and cared for. I believe that those adults in the Baptist church of my childhood had good intentions. Yet, fear dominated then, and fear can wave its hand from deep in my psyche, saying, "Still here."

It is then I try to recall my friend John's words, "God loves you even more than you love Eli."

Renewing Baptismal Vows: God's Beloved Child

Around the font the children cluster.
She asks him to pour the water.
My grandson, at thirteen, is inches taller than her.
He lifts the pitcher very high.
We are silent.
The long silver stream splashes into the silver bowl.

Before each blessing, she asks,
  "May I touch your face?"
When she reaches up to brush aside his long blond hair,
  that hair that may be his gentle rebellion,
I begin to weep.

Later, I wait my turn.
My face is already wet when she brushes aside my hair,
  touches my face, and says,
"You are God's beloved child."

In my Gideon New Testament, it says I accepted Jesus
  as my Savior on June 14, 1947.
I was seven and do not remember
  what happened in Bible School.
I probably knelt on the linoleum floor in the church basement.

Four years later, on the muddy shores of Indian Lake
I stand with my sister waiting our turn.
Our feet are bare, our dresses white.
She is fourteen. I am eleven.
On the shore the choir is singing.

Chest deep in the lake stands Rev. Johnson.
Does he have a black suit just for baptisms?
Shirley goes first, through the shallows,
A deacon holding her hand.

Now my turn.
I rest against his arm.
Close my eyes.
White handkerchief over my mouth and nose,
Back and down, down, and up
   in a rush of water, warm and murky.

Wading to shore, mud between my toes.
Hair dripping, white dress clinging.
Choir singing "Shall We Gather at the River."

When I was five, Shirley had her tonsils out.
   I did too.
When I was eleven, Shirley was baptized.
   I was too.

Did Rev. Johnson touch my face
   with gentleness and say,
"You are God's beloved child?"
I do not remember.

2015

A Mother's Death

I read somewhere that the first parent we talk about in therapy is the easier of the two with whom we can come to healing. While my relationship with my father was fraught with my experience of a judgmental God, I worked things through enough to know that our relationship was healed. My relationship with my mother is more complex. In childhood I took her love for granted, though I think that unconsciously I expected her to somehow take away my fear of a judgmental God. I needed her to be more powerful. It is telling that when I began menstruating, she did not explain anything to me. When I asked her about this years later, she said something like, "You were so smart. I guess I thought you knew, you know, from Shirley." I remember thinking, "But I needed you. I needed my mother."

Though my mother did not have the power to mitigate my fears, she was a person of great strength and courage. I wish I had told her more often how remarkable it was that she emigrated from Finland at seventeen and made a new life. She learned English, and enough Swedish to communicate with my father's Swedish family. Although she lived down the country road from her sister Maija for the first thirteen years of her life in Nebraska, she was ready to move with Gus two hundred miles north to buy a farm and make a life far from her only family in the United States. In southwest Minnesota, she learned to adapt her Finnish identity to thrive in a strong subculture of Swedes.

My mother had stopped attending school at fourteen when she and her family thought that she would soon emigrate. She understood how much I wanted to go to college. Interested in my classes, chapel services, and new friends, she came to campus several times to hear convocation speakers. She welcomed my friend Gina warmly when I brought her home at holidays. When I left home after a visit, she always gave me ten or twenty dollars, simply pressing the bill into my hand. Her twenty dollars was worth a lot more than the twenty dollars I gave to Eli when he left for a college visit.

My mother's relationship to God was at the core of who she was. It truly was the bread of life for her, sustaining her all her life. Yet, I saw that part of her theology caused her pain. For many years, perhaps all her life, she felt deep concern that David was not saved. Many times, I encouraged her to look at David's life, not at the words he said or did not say. When he sought conscientious objector status during the Vietnam War, he was explicit that he did not claim his pacifist standing based on belief in a Supreme Being, a radical stance at the time, and a first in Nobles County. I wrote passionate letters to her from Lower Kalskag, Alaska, defending David for living with integrity. I do not know whether she ever fully let go of her worry about him being saved. I hope she did. I hope that in experiencing David's care for her during the thirty years they lived a few yards apart on the farm, she knew who David was by how he lived and loved.

The second core part of my mother's life was our nuclear and extended family. I saw her delight in being with her sister Saima the summer we traveled to Finland. When she was thirty-eight and pregnant with David, her sister Maija's death was a huge loss. Over the years, my mother stayed closely connected with Maija's three children. My mother was the one who sponsored the emigration from Finland of her younger sister Aili and her family, as well as the three children of her oldest sister, Lydia. Her loss of family when she emigrated fueled her commitment to keep family connected.

I am certain that both my mother and father wanted very much for David to farm. How could they not? But when he left, first for college in 1965 and then to Canada to protest the draft in 1968, they had no knowledge he would return. They could not have known that he would meet William Sloane Coffin, the American Christian clergyman and peace activist who convinced him to stay in the States to follow through with his resistance to the draft. They could not have known that David would meet Sally Anne, and that the two of them would return to Minnesota to make their life on the farm, a better future for it than my parents could have imagined.

When I think about my mother, I often think about how girls and women everywhere over time have tried to shape their lives. I have come to understand more fully her shame and pain about my divorce. I had made a choice that not only went against her deeply held belief about the value of marriage but had also broken my family and separated my daughter from her father. I had let go of the security of having a man in my life. Her deep distress at my divorce diminished over time. Eventually, she was able to say that she could see my divorcing was a good thing. She saw that I thrived. Over the years, she saw that Maja thrived as well. I know, too, that she was very happy Tim and I had found each other.

I regret I did not tell her often enough that I loved her, that she was brave and smart and generous, that her convincing my father I should go to college changed my life. I took her for granted. I wish that I had been more present to her, especially in the last years of her life. Yes, I had a cancer diagnosis. Yes, I was in the beginning of my relationship with Tim. Yes, my place of work, Samaritan, was falling apart. Still—I wish I had spent more time with her. There were things I did not ask her—about her childhood, her women friends, her spirituality. I wish I had asked her about Punkaharju, that amazing land bridge in eastern Finland we visited when I was nineteen. I remember her words, "It's so beautiful, so beautiful." I cherish those words that reveal her love of the natural world and her longing for her homeland. I never told her what Punkaharju meant to me. I knew that she and my father went back to Sweden and Finland several more times. Did she go to Punkaharju again? I wish I had asked. I want to believe that both of us, those many years ago, experienced the earth itself as the body of God. When I want to go in my imagination to a place in nature, it is either the pink rock in the pasture from my childhood or the pine needle floor of Punkaharju.

In the late 1990s, my mother's thinking became distorted. She believed that Gladys, whom she was visiting, had not been providing food for her. This phenomenon seemed to pass, but then she began to lose language. Her letters became a mix of English and Finnish, then spoken language disappeared almost entirely. Yet, she always recognized family members. When I went to visit her in the nursing home in the last year of her life, she greeted me as she did other family members, clapping her hands, smiling, and saying joyfully, "Mine, mine."

The last Christmas that David drove her to St. Paul we gathered one evening in the living room to visit and sing carols. We sang carol after carol, verse after verse: "Silent Night," "O Come All Ye Faithful," "Joy to the World," "O Little Town of Bethlehem," "Away in a Manger," and more. Within moments of beginning, we realized my mother was singing. In English. All the words. All the carols. All the verses. I was weeping so much I could scarcely play the piano. Her essence was still with us.

My best memory of her in her old age is a 1999 visit when Maja and I brought newborn Eli to her. Her face that day, holding Eli, was alighted with joy. She was beautiful. I wept. In March 2002 David called to say her death was imminent. Tim and I drove immediately to Worthington—but we were too late. She had gone home to God in the presence of David and Sally Anne. She was ninety-three. I am grateful for the time I was able to spend with her body, touching her face, holding her hand, kissing her. She loved her children and her grandchildren. She loved me. I did not doubt that.

In 1990 Maja recorded extensive interviews with my mother and then transcribed them. I love those stories of her life, told in her own words. We shared many of them at her memorial service, children and grandchildren reading sections of the interview. We buried some of her ashes in the church cemetery. The other half we carried to a field at the center of the farm, where we had scattered our father's ashes. Standing in a big circle, we took turns lifting handfuls, letting the ashes settle into the earth. At the memorial service and again at the center of the farm we sang "This Is My Song," a poem set to the music of Finnish composer Jean Sibelius' *Finlandia.*

> This is my song, O God of all the nations,
>   a song of peace for lands afar and mine.
> This is my home, the country where my heart is:
>   here are my hopes, my dreams, my holy shrine;
> But other hearts in other lands are beating
>   with hopes and dreams as true and high as mine.
>
> My country's skies are bluer than the ocean,
>   and sunlight beams on cloverleaf and pine;
> But other lands have sunlight, too, and clover,
>   and skies are everywhere as blue as mine.
> O hear my song, O God of all the nations,
>   a song of peace for their land and for mine.[36]

Whenever I hear the first few bars of the melody, I come to tears, wondering again what it might have been like for my immigrant mother leaving her homeland with her hopes and dreams.

---

36 Lloyd Stone, "This Is My Song," *The New Century Hymnal* (Cleveland: The Pilgrim Press, 1995) 591.

Climate Change: Creating Community

I have been paying attention to climate change for many years. Yet my concern and commitment took big steps forward when, in 2009, my friend Katie called me to read me the poem "hieroglyphic stairway" by Drew Dellinger. It shook me. It begins:

> it's 3:23 in the morning
> and I'm awake
> because my great great grandchildren
> won't let me sleep
> my great great grandchildren
> ask me in dreams
> what did you do while the planet was plundered?
> what did you do when the earth was unraveling?
>
> surely you did something
> when the seasons started failing?
>
> as the mammals, reptiles, birds were all dying?
>
> did you fill the streets with protest
> When democracy was stolen?
>
> what did you do
> once
> you
> knew? . . .[37]

---

37 Drew Dellinger, *love letter to the milky way: book of poems* (Ashland OR: White Cloud Press, 2011) 1.

That year, my grandchildren, Eli, Alistair, and Siri, were ages nine, seven, and three. Katie and her partner Ruthann's grandchildren were similar ages. It was not that I had not thought and read and talked about climate change. But hearing Katie read the poem brought climate change and my grandchildren together with a crash that made me set priorities. Within a few weeks, Katie and I put together a presentation focused on climate change for Sunday morning worship at our church. At the same time, we worked to establish a Green Ministry Committee, although it did not seem to gain much traction.

That same year, 2009, Tim and I, with several neighbors, had already begun to turn our attention and energy toward climate change. We were part of a longstanding group called Neighbors for Peace, active in our community prior to and during the Iraq War. We recognized that we were not influencing foreign policy regarding war, but we thought we might impact climate change on a local level. As a group, we read Pat Murphy's *Plan C* and then moved on to *The Transition Handbook* by Rob Hopkins, the founder of Transition Towns, now an international movement that inspires and supports local communities to respond to the effects of climate change. Our group of a dozen neighbors met regularly to read and discuss what kind of actions we might take in our community. Green on the Screen, a recurring event that featured a range of films and videos about the effects of climate change, was our early attempt to provide information and a format for discussion for our wider community.

We applied for status as a Transition Town, joining hundreds of communities worldwide. Our local group's motto is "Smaller Footprint, Stronger Community."[38] After three community meetings, one of which drew a couple hundred people, we formed working groups focusing on transportation, land use, solar energy, zero waste, food production, and preservation. While acknowledging that direct action was very important, several of us believed that people needed time to meet and talk about the issues, to find support to face a changing climate. So, we formed a reflective circle to meet this need, meeting once a month at the local library or the local Catholic church. The reflective circle clearly worked for several years, and then participation diminished, even as information about the reality of climate change increased.

Tim was absorbed in the solar group that explored ways to put solar

38 Transition Town – All St. Anthony Park, accessed April 12, 2021, https://www.transitionasap.org.

panels on homes and other buildings in our community. And although Tim and I are together in our concerns about climate change, we have different skills and interests. I knew I wanted to focus on the inner work we need to do. Tim has a gift for careful research, for creating tables and charts that communicate data, for investigating how community solar might work and how we can move away from fossil fuels. Tim's response to climate change is practical and energy focused. He was the point person for a thorough energy assessment at our church and arranged for the work that reduced the church's natural gas use by one-third. Tim, the engineer, needs his engineer community. I needed to find a way that suited my own skills and interests.

In 2013, John Wallace, one member of our reflective circle, suggested a series of study circles focused on climate change. I jumped to join him. John has a long history of creating story circles in various settings, including his years as a professor of philosophy at the University of Minnesota. He was a colleague with whom I could help people create meaningful connections about climate change.

John and I shaped a format for our climate study circles, one similar in format to *lectio divina,* where we presented a text and invited participants to respond. TED talks by Hans Rosling[39] were especially effective "texts." After a first viewing, each person in the circle is asked for a single-word response to the question, "What strikes you?" Then we viewed the video a second time. This time the prompt for the circle go-round was, "What is Rosling really saying?" After each person contributed their understanding of the text, we invited crosstalk and discussion. The third prompt was "Does this change anything?" and we concluded with the prompt, "What do you take with you as you leave?"

The conversation moves slowly in stages that unfold, inviting careful listening to both the text and other participants. It invites understanding of the text before opinions are shared. There are no wrong answers. The feedback we have received is that participants leave with a broader perspective, a sense of the complexity of the issues around climate change, ideas for action to be taken, and gratitude for a deepening of connections to other people. Even though climate change is many people's biggest concern, our anxiety is often lessened by participation in these circles; we are building community. We

39 Hans Rosling,"Global health expert; data visionary," TED Talks, accessed April 12, 2021. https://www.ted.com/speakers/hans_rosling.

trust that we are motivating others to consider a smaller footprint. Working with John on climate change convinced me that it is community that will sustain us in the hardships ahead.

I come back often to the four approaches to climate change in Pat Murphy's book *Plan C*. Plan A: Business as usual; Plan B: Technology will save us; Plan C: Curtailment and community; Plan D: Die off. I am aware that, like many others, I readily place my hopes in Plan B: Technology. The "curtailment of our way of life" means losses now, losses we don't want to choose. Somehow, we manage to fend off our awareness of the immense, catastrophic losses that are already happening and are yet to come. Recently I viewed the 2020 film *Once You Know*. The story of Emmanuel Cappellin's journey—physical and spiritual through his awakening fully to the reality of climate change—shows us the physical, political, and economic disruption that is happening, that will happen. We witness the grief and despair of the filmmaker, his search across continents. We meet Richard Heinberg, one of the world's top authorities on climate change. We go to Bangladesh to meet Saleemul Huq, an important figure in the emerging science of climate adaptation. The third interview is with Susanne Moser, a geographer who specializes in climate change adaptation and communication. She suggests that we, humans, have an opportunity, rather like an individual facing death, to face climate change in a similar way—more fully alive, more engaged, more aware of the preciousness of all life.

On a Friday in the spring of 2019, Tim and I caught the #3 bus and joined our granddaughter Siri and seventy-five of her middle school friends at the Minnesota State Capitol in St. Paul to "strike for the climate." The courage of Greta Thunberg, the Swedish teenager and climate activist, and thousands of kids around the world, had inspired Siri and her friend Alice, both seventh graders, to organize their classmates to join a thousand students at the capitol to raise awareness about climate change. The sign I made to carry read, "What will you tell your grandchildren?"

Carrying the reality of climate change is a challenging spiritual practice. Every morning, when I open my refrigerator to make breakfast, I see these words from Wendell Berry that I placed there years ago: "Be joyful though you have considered all the facts." Of the many deepening circles I have been part of—whether overtly spiritual, psychological, or political—climate change will be a major focus in these latter years of my life. There is no doubt that our response to climate change is a deeply spiritual issue. Whatever one's theology or cosmology, the earth and all that is, is God's, or whatever word you use for the Mystery that there is anything at all.

Earth Is Not Ours

Eating apricots he wonders,
    Will there be fruit trees when he grows up?
He's twelve and knows the bees are dying.
Earth will do what it will do.

Not what do I say to my grandchildren,
But what does my life tell them?

My life is telling them

That I like my clothes dryer,
    the soft towels and smooth blouses.
That I drive a Prius, but too fast and too often.
That I wear silk underwear and
    still keep the heat up.
That I flew to Greece last spring,
    Maine and California this summer.
Meager, meager, I tell myself.

It rains on the just and the unjust,
My father said when the hail
    took the oat crop.
Earth will do what it will do.

Jimmy Carter put solar panels on the White House.
Ronald Reagan took them off.
We have known a long time.
Earth will do what it will do.

I pay two dollars and thirty cents for a gallon of gas.
People cry, "No gas tax increase!"
Swedish cousins pay six dollars and fifty cents.

Maple seeds take root in the Boundary Waters.
Evolution too slow for birch, spruce, and tamarack.
California is on fire again.
Earth will do what it will do.

One dark morning I read about survivalists with money
who build bunkers in Oklahoma and Kansas,
With plans to save personal pilots and their families.

Adolescents, we pretend earth sets no limits.
Seduced, we trust technology to save us.
Earth does not promise us that all will be well.

Earth will do what Earth will do.

2018

Gladys and the Geese

In late September 2018, I walked north on Cleveland Avenue to the open fields next to the University of Minnesota's agricultural campus. The wild geese were gleaning, hunting for residue of the harvest in the experimental plots. I stood facing the morning sun, still low in the sky. Suddenly, with a swoosh of wings, the geese rose into the bright cold air. There was no other sound, only the rustling of wings. I let out my breath. Fifteen of them circled into formation and headed south. I watched until they were gone from my sight. The sound of their wings opened me to the sorrow and joy of the last months of Gladys's life.

Gladys's illness had begun a decade earlier with stumbling, a weakness in her left leg. Little by little, her mobility and balance diminished. Many tests and doctors' visits finally determined that her diagnosis was primary lateral sclerosis: a rare disease, difficult to diagnose, and somewhat comparable to what most of us know as Lou Gehrig's disease. It was a disease with an inevitable trajectory.

First, she used a cane, and then, a walker. Ten years older than me, she had been the big sister, capable and mature. Now I cared for her as she had cared for me when I was an infant and toddler. When I was a teenager, she and her husband, Ray, had opened their home to me, a place to live during my high school years when I wanted so much to participate in the school activities that the long bus ride from the farm prevented. She was the constant presence in the months of my treatment and recovery from breast cancer, driving from her home in Wisconsin every three weeks to go with me to my chemotherapy treatments. Now, I accompanied her. Taking her to appointments became half-day events for me and Shirley.

The day we chose the electric wheelchair was an occasion of both relief and loss. Sometimes we cried together. Other times I waited to weep until I was driving home. She fell many times, only some of which she told us about. Two falls resulted in broken bones and weeks in rehabilitation. The therapy staff named her their star pupil. She did all they asked and more. Several of us gathered at the care center to celebrate her eighty-third birthday and eat cake with her between her physical therapy and occupational therapy appointments.

Gladys understood her disease. She was a nurse and a teacher of nursing. And she understood hospice. She was part of a team that began a hospice program at Midway Hospital in St. Paul in the 1980s, and after retirement, she continued to work in a hospice program in northern Wisconsin. She had accompanied many people on this journey that now became hers. She knew that hospice would be the next step. As her illness worsened, we arranged in-home hospice care. Several times a week, the nurse, the social worker, and the chaplain came, and several volunteers as well.

By the time she and Ray moved from their condominium to an assisted living apartment, she was spending her days in a recliner or a motorized wheelchair. Always the teacher, she invited me to see how the Hoyer lift worked, moving her from her recliner to the toilet and back to the recliner. Her disease progressed more rapidly after their move. Within a few weeks, the staff at their assisted living home, the in-home hospice staff, and family members realized that we could no longer manage her care. She moved to Wedum Hospice on April 25, 2013.

During her last nineteen days she was rarely without family or friends at her bedside. Ray, Mark, Shirley, David, Sally Anne, and her nieces sat with her, sang to her, read psalms, and shared stories. Many times, I sang hymns from the old Baptist hymnal. Sometimes she hummed along. One time when I began singing "The King of Love My Shepherd Is," she waved her arms and shouted, "No, no, not that one." I turned a couple of pages and sang something else.

On one visit, I stood at the side of her bed as she held both of my hands in hers. Her grip was fierce. I was weeping; my nose was running. "Gladys," I said, "let go for a bit. I need to get a tissue." She held on even more tightly. Again, I said, "Please, let go." Finally, still hanging on tightly with one hand, she grabbed the hem of her short nightgown, lifted it up toward me, and said clearly in her big sister voice, "Here, use this."

We called the people she wanted to see. One was a man from her nursing school days whom she had dated before she began dating Ray. I told her I was not sure we could locate him after so many years. She was adamant, saying, "Find him." I found him. I was anxious when I called him. He had likely not seen or spoken to her for over fifty years. I spoke directly, telling him who I was, that Gladys was dying and wanted to talk to him. I asked him to call her. He called her the next day.

We wondered aloud whether she wanted to see a couple, once good friends, from whom she and Ray had been painfully estranged for many years. She agreed. We called them. They came the next day, driving two hundred miles to be with her. Walking in with no hesitation they came close to Gladys's bed. I stood in the far corner of the large room mouthing, "Thank you, thank you" as first one and then the other leaned close. Gladys was doing her work of dying.

She was finding a way to say what she needed to say. Wanting to give them privacy, I slipped from the room and walked to the end of the hall, grateful that we had called them and now trusting that healing would happen.

Four days before Gladys died, our brother David spent much of the day with her. Most of the time she slept. Intermittently, she raised her arms, reaching high into the air. Then she awakened and said, "Bird, bird crying." After a time, she said, "Birds fly." David listened and waited several minutes. Then she said, "I want to fly." Again, he waited, wondering. Finally, she said, "Help me fly." It was then that David turned and saw a wild goose outside the sliding glass doors of the suite, making small noises, walking about the patio, pecking the patio stones, and looking through the glass. He said to Gladys, "Yes, yes! There's a goose here. Right outside the door." Holding her hand, he sat quietly, watching, until the goose flew away. That evening, when he told us about the goose, about what Gladys had said, we remembered how our mother had told us the Finnish belief she carried from her childhood, that a bird entering a house is a sign of a death approaching.

At noon on May 13, I received a call from the hospice nurse: "Come. Now." When I arrived, I saw that the staff had hung the stained-glass dragonfly, that symbol of transformation, on the doorpost outside her room. I joined Ray, Shirley, and Sharon around Gladys's bed. Her breathing had changed; sometimes it was very quiet, other times rattling. Her feet were cold to my touch. Her face, although sunken, had a translucent glow. Her son, Mark, came at 5:00 p.m. We waited. We did not wait long.

In her last moments, we circled her bed, the five of us, holding hands. I felt in my body the contradiction of wanting her release, of letting her go to God, and yet holding on. And then, so quietly I could not tell when it happened, she took her last breaths. Suddenly, I needed to breathe deeply. I had been holding my breath as she took her last—as if the oxygen I did not inhale in that moment was hers to use. Such a thin membrane this is, between life and death. So quietly crossed.

Still circling her bed, we began the Lord's Prayer. Without any comment, together we slipped spontaneously into those familiar words. We stood there, this circle of love and sorrow, holding her and us together. Then we sang the old Swedish hymn: "Children of the Heavenly Father, Safely to his bosom gather, / Nestling bird nor star in heaven, Such a refuge ere was given."[40] Then the first verse in Swedish, just as we had sung at the funerals of our mother and father.

Other family members arrived: Tim, Maja, Ken, and his daughter Becca. David and Sally Anne drove from the family farm in southwest Minnesota. After each of us had time with Gladys's body, the nurses came. We stood aside as they wrapped her in white blankets and covered her with a quilt embroidered with dragonflies. Over the quilt we draped the woven ropes of dragonflies that Maja had brought from home.

Then we gathered in an anteroom. There, we sat around a large table and ate an odd assortment of food, some brought from home and some the hospice offered. We told stories about Gladys. We remembered her generosity to so many, especially to Ray's twin brother's three children, who, in turn, during their high school years, left their parents in Japan to live with Gladys and Ray. We told of her professionalism when, in her first years as a surgical nurse, she assisted in a surgical procedure for a friend who had caught his arm in a corn picker. We told of her commitment to the families in rural Wisconsin, especially Native American families. She had spoken many times of driving in the middle of the night to a family whose loved one's dying was imminent. We remembered her sewing projects, the quilts made from silk neckties and the cloth squares from Japan. David told again the story about Gladys and the goose outside her patio door. We cried and laughed. And we breathed.

After the stories, it was time for us to let her body be taken away. Time for Mark to call the mortuary. The nine of us gathered in her room, standing silently as the nurses and the gentleman from the mortuary gently moved Gladys's body, covered with the dragonfly quilt, to the gurney. One of the nurses asked quietly, "Do you want to follow her out? We always do."

---

40 "Children of the Heavenly Father," in *The Book of Hymns* (The United Methodist Publishing House, 1964), 521.

"Oh, yes, yes," we said. And so, family and nurses stepped into this procession, this going home, escorting this wife, mother, sister, aunt, hospice nurse, down the long L-shaped hall, past other doors where dragonflies would soon find a place. Mark, carrying the dragonfly, walked with Ray after her body, the rest of us following. We sang again "Children of the Heavenly Father," weeping, holding hands, and hugging.

We followed her through the double doors and into the evening light. As we walked down the long sidewalk to the van that would take her away, we looked up. Then it happened. From the west two wild geese high above were flying directly toward us. At first, they were calling. Then, gliding silently and gently over our heads, they landed on the edge of the pond on the other side of the sidewalk. Gladys's body was slipped quietly into the hearse. We stood speechless at this blessing.

The rear doors of the van closed. We watched it move slowly away, out of the parking lot and into the street toward the freeway. Embracing one another, we walked slowly back into the hospice building. In the chapel, Mark placed the dragonfly on the tall glass window where it would rest with others until it would be placed outside another door.

We gathered all the things we had brought with us over the nineteen days to help Gladys go to God and to help us let her go. The Bible, hymn book, poetry book, tissue boxes, photos, the granola bars in the back of the drawer of the bedside table, the flowers, the cards. We hugged the nurses, those amazing nurses. And then we went home.

All those icons of our past, the Swedish hymn, the Lord's Prayer, the psalms we had read, the hymns we had sung during those last weeks, I carry with me. But there is another that is fresh every time I think of Gladys's death: the geese. When I hear the geese overhead in spring and fall, I know again the blessing of that evening in May when Gladys went home to God.

Later that month, we drove three hours south to Worthington to place Gladys's ashes in the cemetery at Indian Lake Baptist Church. The family plot is near the west edge of the church property, a few yards from cornfields. Some of my parents' ashes are buried there; the remainder are scattered into the soil of the family farm.

On the morning of the memorial, David borrowed the key from the pastor and opened the door to the cavernous fellowship hall. (When empty of tables, it becomes a basketball court.) David and Tim arranged chairs; thirty were enough for our family and a few friends. We found a small lectern and placed tall vases of prairie flowers on either side. Shirley, Sally Anne, and I put the coffee on, found platters, coffee cups, small plates, and napkins, and arranged the cookies and bars we had brought.

As we waited for guests to arrive, I set my notes on the lectern and walked back through the hall and up the half flight into the foyer toward the sanctuary, where the church's photo directory hung on the wall. There were the names I remembered: Nystrom, Larson, Swanson, Moberg. There were many new faces and new names I was not sure how to pronounce. "Shirley, David, come here," I called.

"Oh yes," David said, looking at the photo board, "I understand the church membership is almost half Karen now. Remember when we were kids, those Baptist missionaries on furlough who came for special meetings? Some of them went to Burma where the Karen live. Probably some of those converts immigrated to the United States and eventually moved to Worthington."

Struck with the evolution of the congregation, we spoke of our childhood, of sitting on folding chairs in the church basement, listening to the missionaries telling stories and showing us slides. Then we spoke about how our parents were immigrants to the United States ninety years ago, and more than seventy years ago, they moved to this farming community. My mother, the lone Finn in a community of Swedes, felt isolated and worked hard to assimilate. I knew that immigrants from many non-European countries had been coming to Worthington in the last twenty years. Each wave of people worked first at the meat-packing plant and later moved to other jobs. The Karen Baptists were now part of this church where I grew up, the congregation I left as a college sophomore.

I found more photos on a wall in the sanctuary of the ministers of the church going back 135 years. They were almost entirely white men. A few photos showed children of the church who went on into Christian ministry. Two among them are women—one of them is a contemporary of my younger brother. I am the other. At some point, quite a few years ago, my sisters said that it was about time that my photo was on that wall. I do not know to whom they talked. I would like to have heard the conversation.

Still in the sanctuary, I sat in a pew. I remembered how in childhood my feet did not touch the floor. I closed my eyes.

I am sitting between my mother and Shirley. My mother is telling me to stop swinging my legs. The Reverend Johnson in his black suit stands in the pulpit. Now he stands at the communion table, flanked by four deacons in suits, white shirts, and ties. He hands each of them a silver tray with little glasses of grape juice. They walk up the aisles, two in the middle and one on each side. The tray is at the end of our pew and coming toward me. I will be careful not to spill on my Sunday dress. I am anxious. Am I forgiven?

Later, when I took my place at the lectern, I looked out at old friends of our family who had come to bury Gladys's ashes. "Thank you, thank you for coming, thank you for being here." As I said these words, I realized that my gratitude was for more than their presence. It was gratitude for this long-lasting, imperfect community of faith that is open to transformation. And gratitude also for this experience that invited me to continue to let go of the echoes of fear and judgment that I carry. I took a big breath and continued: "We are gathered here to commend to God the ashes of Gladys Benson Karhu: wife, mother, sister, friend, beloved child of God."

Burdened

As I sat in silence one morning, an image from the 1986 film *The Mission* came to me: the mercenary and slave trader Mendoza, dragging a bag of his armor and weapons behind him. He is traveling with the Jesuit priest Gabriel to Mission San Carlos high in the mountains of Brazil. Having killed his brother in a fit of rage, Mendoza is offered a means of redemption by Gabriel. The scene imprinted in my memory is Mendoza struggling to climb a rocky cliff, the heavy bag of his sins weighing him down. He is perilously close to falling to his death. Tension continues to build when a villager, knife in hand, reaches down toward Mendoza. To our amazement, the knife cuts the rope, not Mendoza, and his burden drops into the river below. In this act, forgiveness is granted by the villagers he previously sought to sell as slaves.

This scene unfolded in a mere second of time, yet it was followed by my tears and my awareness of the burden I have carried and sometimes still carry. I imagined the sweet release of it dropping. What's in my bag? What makes it so difficult to let it go once and for all? What have I not worked through? Still? Is its essence the same? I recall what we students in chaplaincy training said to one another in 1984, paraphrasing Gertrude Stein, "My issues are my issues are my issues." Is this true? What do I carry so deeply that some mornings when I sit, I soon move to murmur with the out breath, "Fear," and with the in breath, "Grace"?

How do I let go of this residue that is bigger than I can name or even know? A residue of fear, shame, guilt, and despair that I ought to have been different and done it differently. Done what? Achieved salvation? Accepted salvation? Believed rightly? Surrendered to something? Language from the Baptist church comes to me. My frequent fears in childhood were that I had committed the unforgivable sin, the sin against the Holy Spirit. I remember also clinging to the assurance that if you thought you had committed the unforgivable sin, you had not. Where I find myself in the darkness of some mornings at 4:00 a.m. is slipping into that childhood place of fear and abandonment, where proof of being saved was feeling saved. I want to curse this punitive, damning theology residing in my cells. I remember finding some understanding and relief when I read James Fowler's words in *Stages of Faith*. In his summary of Stage 1, Intuitive-Projective Faith, he writes:

> The dangers in this stage arise from the possible "possession" of the child's imagination by unrestrained images of terror and destructiveness, or from the witting or unwitting exploitation of her or his imagination in the reinforcement of taboos and moral or doctrinal expectations.[41]

Yes, yes, I said.

What cuts the rope and releases the burden are the voices of others, from other centuries and other lands. I go to my bookshelves to get *Love Poems from God: Twelve Sacred Voices from the East and West*[42] and page through it slowly, looking for those passages I remember from other times of fear and despair. I find Meister Eckhart, fourteenth century Dominican mystic and priest, who writes, "It is a lie—any talk of God that does not comfort you." And Thomas Aquinas: "I have come to learn that God's compassion and light can never be limited; thus, any God who could condemn is not a god at all." And a favorite from Kabir, the Indian mystic and poet, especially the last lines:

> And what kind of God would He be
> if the vote of millions in this world could sway Him
> to change the divine law of love
> that speaks so clearly with compassion's elegant
> tongue, saying, eternally saying:

---

41 James W. Fowler, *Stages of Faith: The Psychology of Human Development and the Quest for Meaning* (San Francisco: Harper & Row, 1981), 134.
42 Daniel Ladinsky, trans., *Love Poems from God: Twelve Sacred Voices from the East and West* (New York: Penguin Compass, 2002), 118, 148, 213.

> all are forgiven—moreover, dears, no one has ever
> been guilty.

There are Mary Oliver's words, from her poem "Wild Geese," which Tim letterpress-printed for me twenty-five years ago:

> You do not have to be good.
> You do not need to walk on your knees
> for a hundred miles through the desert repenting. . . .[43]

And Kathleen Dowling Singh's words that I read and reread a few weeks ago. I know just where they are in *Unbinding*:

> As we proceed on our path, we come to see that grace is with us every step of the way. Our awakening has very little to do with egoic effort beyond requiring our intention to align with grace's work upon us.[44]

I want to be done with theology, with trying to figure it out, with the work of ego, with trying to understand. Perseverating at age eleven did not get me surety, and in older age it does not bring equanimity. I will trust in Kabir's "divine law of love:" We are loved. And in some amazing paradox of grace, we are forgiven—we have never been guilty.

---

43 Mary Oliver, "Wild Geese," in *Devotions: The Selected Poems of Mary Oliver* (New York: Penguin Press, 2017), 347.
44 Kathleen Dowling Singh, *Unbinding: The Grace Beyond Self* (Sommerville, MA: Wisdom, 2017), 64.

Palm Sunday Tears

On Palm Sunday, I wept. The first tears came while singing the choir anthem "The Ground" in Latin, those words I've sung so many times over the years, "*Pleni sunt caeli et terra gloria tua. Osanna, Osanna in excelsis. . . .*" They really started to flow when we broke into six-part harmony with *Agnus Dei, qui tolis peccata mundi*; I could not see the score. I tried to blink away the tears. I wanted so much to be able to sing those words, to be part of the whole, to hum those last measures where we shifted to the *mmm*. We finished, stood for a few moments, and then recessed off the chancel steps to the pews.

My eyes still swimming, I slipped between my daughter and my husband. The next reading from the Gospel of Mark had begun. Maja put her arm around me. I rummaged for more tissues, blew my nose. There were three more readings, one hymn, and two periods of silence before it was my turn to read. I knew my tears were coming from a deep place, and that I could not stay with them right then.

A few days earlier the pastor had asked me if I wanted to read from Mark on Palm Sunday morning. Mark 14 is the story of Peter's denial of Jesus. I practiced, especially the voice of the servant girl who says, "You also were with Jesus, the man from Nazareth." And Peter's words, "I don't know what you're talking about." Should his tone be perplexed? Indignant? Does his anxiety show strongly? His guilt?

When it was time to read, I took deep breaths, walked slowly in the silence to the pulpit, and began. I could tell I was going to be all right. I entered the story yet was in control. Then I got to the last lines, after the cock has crowed: "And he broke down and wept." My voice almost quavered. The word *wept* seemed to stand out in bold on my sheet of paper. I paused and then walked slowly to the pew.

The remainder of Palm Sunday was busy—choir practice for Easter Sunday, a quick lunch, seeing Siri in the middle school musical, eating dinner with friends. I did not have much time to wonder about my tears.

I awoke before four o'clock on Monday morning with the question: What did my tears yesterday mean? What is it about sacred and liturgical music that makes me cry? I have asked myself this many times before, but not often with a sudden waking out of sleep at four o'clock. Hold this, I told myself and went back to sleep.

After breakfast I said to my husband, "I think there are two reasons why I cry during worship." Then I backed up and said, "Maybe not exactly reasons, but two things going on, contradictory, paradoxically, or something." He waited. He's good at waiting. I blurted out, "I want desperately what I am singing to be true, and at the same time, I am afraid that it is not." I did not say more at the time, but it felt like a breakthrough.

What do I want to be true? What do I want to believe, hope to believe, need to believe? I want to believe that there is more than material life. That life means something. That my life means something. That finally, everything is sacred. And that whatever I or anyone says about God is partial. That I can trust that God, whatever name we use, *is*. That God is revealed in the natural world, in relationship, deep within me and in all that is. That Jesus points us to God. That there is grace and mercy. For me. For all. That the God who sustains me in life will sustain me in suffering, in dying, and in death. That, as Julian of Norwich said, "All will be well. . . ."

And of what am I afraid? That what I want to be true is not. I can slip back and down into fear so readily. So much of what I was taught about God, I found not to be true for me. I could not assent to it intellectually. I did not experience what I was told I should experience. Yet I know that I did experience Presence, the Sacred, growing up, although I could not name it. I hold my doubts and fear in one hand and my hope and longing in the other. Often, I think of that BBC interview with Carl Jung forty years ago when he was asked if he believed in God. He waited a bit, and then said simply, "I don't believe, I know." There are times when I also can claim this knowing. Other times, I cannot.

What I do set my heart on is inclusion, compassion, justice, mercy, forgiveness. And awe. These, I have experienced again and again. I will trust that these are of God. I do not have a better name.

Former evangelical pastor and author Brian McLaren lays out many reasons for abandoning Christianity in his recent book, *Do I Stay Christian?* And then he argues for embracing a radical redefinition of Christianity. So, what might I say if I were asked if I am Christian? To paraphrase Matthew Fox, I say that Christianity is one well to the great underground stream. It is the one I was born into and the one I find I can claim. I also know that others drink deeply from other wells and their explorations and reflections continue to help me. Reading theologian Paul Knitter's book *Without Buddha I Could Not be a Christian* was liberating. Kathleen Dowling Singh's writings in *The Grace in Dying* and *Unbinding* invited me into a contemplative life in ways that Christian writings have not. The source I go back to again and again is Daniel Ladinsky's *Love Poems from God: Twelve Sacred Voices from the East and West,* where I can read Teresa of Avila, Francis, Rumi, Hafiz, Eckhart, Aquinas—all who have gone deep into their respective wells.

I have been trying for a lifetime to untangle myself from fundamentalism and to claim Christianity's core truths. I struggle less now with what has been said and written about Jesus. Jesus points us to God. He does not point to himself. Jesus called us to follow him, not to worship him. It is Jesus's care for the poor, the disenfranchised, the excluded, the marginalized, and his speaking truth to power that calls me. Progressive Christian writers Marcus Borg, John Dominic Crossan, and Walter Wink helped me understand that God did not require Jesus's death to atone for our sins. Jesus's execution instead resulted from his life and ministry and his challenge to the powers of religion and government of his time.

What I claim now is a Christianity that does not make Christ the last name of Jesus. In *The Universal Christ*, Richard Rohr writes about the first two thousand years of Christianity, "We ended up spreading our national cultures under the rubric of Jesus, instead of a universally liberating message under the name of Christ." Rohr's words give me hope. He writes, "Christ is a good and simple metaphor for absolute wholeness, complete incarnation, and the integrity of creation. Jesus is the archetypal human just like us (Hebrews 4:15), who showed us what the Full Human might look like if we could live fully into it (Ephesians 4:12-16)."[45]

---

45 Richard Rohr, *The Universal Christ* (New York: Penguin Random House, 2019), 18, 23.

My inner conversation and dialogue with others about God, the Christ, and Jesus continues even now.

Amends and a Bookend

When my daughter Maja turned fifty, her father flew from California to take her out to lunch. Since I initiated the divorce in 1972, B. and I had had limited contact except in relation to our daughter. After our first grandson, Eli, was born in 1999, we saw one another occasionally, usually once a year at Thanksgiving for amiable visits over pumpkin pie. B.'s coming to Minnesota without his wife to celebrate Maja's birthday presented an opportunity I had been considering for several years.

I had been reading Kathleen Dowling Singh's *The Grace in Aging* for almost two years and meeting with friends every month to write from prompts and talk about our inner work, about aging and dying. It was time to make my amends explicit.

I emailed B. and asked him whether he was interested in going out for coffee with me. His "yes" was encouraging. We went for coffee—and a four-hour conversation. We spoke of our marriage, our divorce, our coparenting, our hopes for Maja and Kermit, our delight in our grandchildren. Our conversation could have come straight from Dr. Ira Byock's book, *The Four Things That Matter Most*.[46] Byock tells many stories about people coming to peace in their dying. Neither B. nor I was about to die, but it was time to say "Thank you. I forgive you. Forgive me. And I love you." Yes, even "I love you," although I don't think we literally said those three words.

Because it is not far from where I live now with Tim, I often drive past the motel where B. and I spent our wedding night. I catch glimpses of that messy mixture of feelings I experienced—fear, anger, confusion, and despair. I feel immense empathy for both of us, caught in the internalized expectations of culture, family, and religion. At that time, neither of us had found ways to shed or even begin to understand those expectations. Years and lots of therapy have brought me to understand that he and I were both too young and unformed to marry, even though I was twenty-six and he was twenty-two. All we could do then was try to fulfill the expectations of our culture, our parents, and

46 Ira Byock, *The Four Things That Matter Most* (New York: Free Press, 2004).

the religion we thought we had rejected. I told B. I had come to understand that my projections on him were damaging to him as well as to me. I had unconsciously wrapped my own spiritual yearnings into a package that I had handed over to him. When he dropped out of seminary during the first year of our marriage, he gave the package back to me without knowing he had ever carried it. It took me years to unwrap it, this gift, this box of darkness. Many times, in many life situations, I have repeated a therapist's statement to me that nothing is wasted. His refusing my projections was a gift.

In our conversation, B. and I both made amends and affirmed that amazing new life had come from our marriage and divorce. For both of us. Even I, who has fantasized all sorts of alternate versions of my life, cannot imagine a world without Maja, Kermit, Eli, Alistair, and Siri. They are the living, breathing fruits of our short time together. The other is the paradoxical grace that has come, and continues to come, through not getting what I want, but what I need.

Maja: Sacred Text

Has Maja influenced my spirituality? How could she not? Her presence is embedded in me. It has been with me and in me since she was born.

I met Maja several hours after her birth by emergency caesarean in the small Quonset hut public hospital in Bethel, Alaska. I remember waking up to the voice of a nurse who was bringing Maja to me. I looked in the bassinet. There she was. She was alive. I was alive. I was flooded with gratitude and awe that here was this tiny human being, this person. Here was someone I could love fully, wholeheartedly, someone for whom I was enough. I remember the one time during the early years of my separation from Maja's father when I experienced a moment of deep despair and imagined crashing my car. In that moment I chose life, mine and hers.

Recently, after I had reread Paul Tillich's sermon, You Are Accepted, I realized that in some paradoxical way, Maja's coming into the world meant that I was accepted. I could not love her father. But, I could love *her*. I experienced Maja's trust in me to care for her through childhood and into adulthood as a gift. I do not think I ever doubted that I would love her and care for her. Maja has given me the opportunity to learn to accept the other. This has been true for fifty-six years, and it undergirds everything else. I cannot imagine whom I might have been had Maja not come into my life.

When I offered retreats about spirituality, I often spoke of how our human relationships and our relationship with the Mystery that is God have similarities, such as showing up, being present, paying full attention, setting an intention, making commitments. I remember what Roy Fairchild, professor of religion and psychology at San Francisco Seminary, said about prayer—that it is paying full and fervent attention to all you know of God with all you know of yourself.

I did not attend to Maja with all of myself, with the full attention and experience that I have brought to my grandchildren. If anyone had said to me in those early years in San Francisco that Maja was my sacred text, as I say about my grandchildren, I would have looked at them and thought, "Hmmm

. . . a bit too New Age for me." But my hindsight tells me that she is sacred text, and that parenting and grandparenting are profound spiritual practices that are lifelong.

In Maja's childhood, I trusted her intuitive awareness that there is more than the material world. There are specific moments I have written about when I was startled and changed by her spirituality. Her words to me, "Shh . . . God is walking down the aisle," sent me to the Unitarian church and my mentor Katharine. Her love of Aslan, the Christ archetype in C. S. Lewis' The Chronicles of Narnia, invited me to see Jesus in a fresh way. Her imaginary world of colored pencils with their names Peace, Happiness, and Love was a sign that she experienced original blessing. I had grown up with original sin, but her childhood imagination was not highjacked by fundamentalist theology.

I realize that I gave her the experiences in childhood that influenced her. I had chosen the city and the culture in which we lived. I brought her to Quaker Meeting and to Pendle Hill and ARC. I trusted that the rope I was giving her to hold onto was very different from the one I had grasped. I wanted to honor her path, her own experience of the Mystery that is God.

I was happy when Maja moved to Minnesota to take a job as a religion reporter at the *St. Paul Pioneer Press* in 1996—happy about her living in the same city and about her presence in my life. Later, she began attending my church. She was the one who saw the power of the Godly Play curriculum, the telling of the stories and the wondering. As she considered participating more in church and explored her identity as a Christian, she was baptized and asked her Uncle Ken to teach a series of classes he called The Bible as a Whole. She said something about needing to know more about what she was considering.

The conversation fifty-plus years ago when my friend Gina said, "Marilyn, if you don't want to give her a choice, why did you ask her?" helped shape my relationship with Maja. It called me to respect Maja and invited me to talk with her about anything and everything ever since. We both know that I am not her therapist. And we both know that much of the time if one of us is in the middle of something sticky or painful, what we need from the other is a trustworthy, accepting listener. At times of conflict between us, we affirm clearly that we can work through it. We know that our respect and love for one another is solid.

Maybe a result of having grown up on a family farm motivates me to find many ways to work side by side with Maja. We garden and cook together.

And I welcome her invitations on Saturdays to come to her house and help her clean. Our working together provides many intermittent conversations about both the mundane and the profound. Our work is a third thing, Parker Palmer's apt phrase.

Little more than a year ago Maja joined our church choir. I have sung in our choir for thirty years, first as a soprano and more recently as an alto. There is something fresh and lovely about singing next to her at rehearsal on Wednesday evenings and in worship on Sunday mornings. We have chosen an activity where together we are learners, and we are participating in something larger than we are—something deeply meaningful.

Maja and I rarely talk directly about theology. I have never asked her, "Do you believe in God?" That is not a question I would ask her or anyone else. Rather, I would notice how a person lives—wonder what and whom they set their heart on. How do they live out justice, love mercy, and walk humbly? In her work as a journalist for over thirty years and her current work as a producer at Minnesota Public Radio, I see Maja's desire to understand, her curiosity, her commitment to fairness and truth. And her compassion. I see these also in her parenting and other relationships. She inspires and invites me. I am deeply grateful that she is in the world and that I am part of her life.

Surrendering to Love

Resolve to be tender with the young,
compassionate with the aged,
sympathetic with the striving,
and tolerant with the weak and wrong. . . .
because sometime in your life you
will have been all of these.

Anonymous, posted on my refrigerator

On the second Sunday of Advent in 2019, I slipped on the ice. I was in a rush after worship, walking too quickly across our icy driveway. *Whomp!* Down on my left side. I crawled upright, grasping the side of the car. Staggering into the house, I sat and put my head between my knees. Tim, who had stayed home from Sunday worship with a noisy cough, called from our bedroom, "Are you all right?"

All I could say was, "I fell." After fifteen minutes I took two Advil and made it back to the car on Tim's arm. I was not going to miss Alistair's piano recital.

That evening, I silently wondered whether my falling had begun the trajectory downward. Was this pain the injury, the broken hip, that I had read about? "She fell and broke her hip, and it was all downhill after that." My imagination got going. I was frightened. Maja drove me to urgent care the next morning. While nothing was broken or even fractured, over the next several days my lower back continued to scream. Could I have this much pain from muscle damage? Would I need to throw out all my Christmas plans?

In two weeks, extended family members were coming for the afternoon and evening for our annual Christmas gathering, and I had planned to sing with the choir for Lessons and Carols. Maja, Kermit, and the grandchildren were coming Christmas Eve and staying the night, our traditional plan. And we had plans for the six of us to spend five days on the North Shore of Lake Superior at Lutsen, to Nordic ski, snowshoe, walk, read, play games, and eat good food. I didn't want to miss those things. I didn't want our plans to change. I was in pain, frightened, and struggling to be hopeful.

When I was in my forties and fifties, I led many retreats. The theme of one retreat I led several times was The Gift of Finitude. Sitting on the sofa that first week after falling, with a hot pack on my lower back and buttocks, it occurred to me how presumptuous I must have been to field such a thought in that young and healthy season of life. I also wondered about the other times of physical pain and disability: being pregnant and having an emergency cesarean in the Alaskan bush, breast cancer, two broken arms, and a broken foot. I could not remember feeling this vulnerable before. Was this to be my new reality?

I was not in control. The bodily security I had experienced most of the time for almost eighty years was gone. I could scarcely walk. Both waking and sleeping, I was in intense pain. My niece Sharon, an occupational therapist, came and taught me several ways to mitigate the pain. She showed me how to get into bed by falling face first into the mattress, an appropriate posture of humility. For two weeks, I could not put on my socks or my pants without Tim's help or stand on my left foot without collapsing. I could not stand in the shower. Then the sciatica pain started, shooting down my left leg, keeping me awake at night. The chiropractor was out of town and then ill. The sports medicine doctor was ill. Finally, in the second week of January, I saw the chiropractor and the acupuncturist. Slowly, relief.

During those five weeks, I was irritated at my limitations and struggled to accept my vulnerability and need for help. And I was such a grump. But intermittently, I was in touch with my gratitude for Tim's constant presence. From the sofa, I'd ask, "Tim, would you bring me a glass of water and an Advil?" "Tim, will you put the gel pack in the microwave?" In bed, I'd say, "Tim, could you tuck the covers over my back?" Hanging laundry on the drying rack, I'd call, "Tim, can you put these on the lower rungs?" After a while, I even stopped apologizing when I asked for help.

For the next three weeks, with my vulnerability ever before me, I left the house only with another person and my walking stick. The spiritual practice of those weeks (and the rest of my life) is to accept loss of control and loss of bodily security, to accept help, to embrace this moment as it is. I did sing with the choir for Lessons and Carols; I gratefully accepted the offer of a chair during rehearsals. We celebrated Christmas with more than enough help from family members. A few times I took the opportunity to sit on a chair and point regally with my walking stick, “Yes, that’s where the wine glasses go.” We went to the North Shore.

Six weeks later—after many appointments, scans, saunas, hot gel packs, chiropractic adjustments, and acupuncture—I felt gratitude for the gifts of my experience, especially for the love of so many. Being lovingly cared for diminished the defenses that I did not even realize I still had. And when I let go of control and let myself be loved, I stopped being grumpy. I am grateful, not only for the healing of my body, but for being able more fully to receive love. My compassion for all of us who are vulnerable, who will be vulnerable, has deepened. I have come to understand that the power of this experience ultimately has to do with my death, the big letting go. Dying will probably not be graceful for me. I hope that it can be grace-filled. May I let go of my need for control, for security, for approval. May I let go into love again and again. This, too, is spiritual practice, perhaps the most difficult of all.

Time to Let Go

The Avowal

As swimmers dare
to lie face to the sky
and water bears them,
as hawks rest upon air
and air sustains them,
so would I learn to attain
freefall, and float
into Creator Spirit's deep embrace,
knowing no effort earns
that all-surrounding grace.[47]

Denise Levertov

It is time to let this memoir go. Life will always give me another experience to wonder about. But while I have not given away all those books of theology, psychology, philosophy, spirituality, and Biblical study, more and more I surrender instead to grace, accepting that I am accepted, accepting that I do not need to figure it out. In fact, I *cannot* figure it out.

Gone is the intense fear and resentment of the ten-year-old girl who spent so much of her energy trying to figure it out—the *it* being salvation—and along the way feeling neither safe nor saved. I have come to understand that my childhood questions and doubts were the beginnings of working out my salvation. I remember with gratitude finding Thomas Merton's words: "To work out our own identity in God, which the Bible calls 'working out our salvation,' is a labor that requires sacrifice and anguish." Merton was writing about my life! It was—and is—all right to push the boundaries of family, culture, and church. It was not only all right, but it was existential and universal.

47 Denise Levertov, "The Avowal," in *Oblique Prayers: Oblique Prayers: New Poems with 14 Translations from Jean Joubert* (New York: New Directions Books, 1984), 76.

That rope that I was given in childhood did have the core strands that I needed. But I could not access them. They were smothered by the dominant strands of God's judgment and my sinfulness. In my twenties I tried to let go of the rope. I wandered around blindly in the blizzard until little by little, I found other ways to think about God and more importantly, ways to experience the Mystery. My memoir is a story of my living through the fears of my childhood into discovering my own experience of God, and my own voice and authority.

Like the farmer who goes to the barn and back to the house again and again, the journey is never over. The rope that I needed has been beside me all along. I claim these core strands: God, the Mystery, is, and is beyond my understanding; there are many wells to the underground stream, and Christianity is one of them; Jesus points us to God and shows us what God is like; I am called to follow the path Jesus shows us—of inclusion, compassion, forgiveness, and justice; God is present here, now, everywhere, and always; the earth, the universe, and all that is reveals God.

I circle back to Carl Jung, to ego and self. Richard Rohr reminds us that the ego, what he calls the false self, is not bad.[48] It is necessary, but we are called to let it go, again and again, so that our true self, our self in God, becomes more and more the place from which we live. This is the task of the second half of life.[49] It is learning to attain freefall, so, in the words of Denise Levertov, we can "float into Creator Spirit's deep embrace, knowing no effort earns that all-surrounding grace."

Finally, I come back to Auden's "A Christmas Oratorio," an enduring touchstone:

> For the garden is the only place there is, but you will not find it
> Until you have looked for it everywhere and found nowhere that is not
>   a desert;
> The miracle is the only thing that happens, but to you it will not be
>   apparent,
> Until all events have been studied and nothing happens that you can
>   not explain;

---

48 Richard Rohr, *Immortal Diamond: The Search for Our True Self* (San Francisco: Jossey-Bass, 2013), 27.

49 C. G. Jung, The Structure and Dynamics of the Psyche, (*The Collected Works of C. G. Jung, Volume 8)* (London: Routledge & Kegan Paul, 1969), 398.

> And life is the destiny you are bound to refuse until you have
> consented to die.[50]

I looked for the garden. I looked for it desperately in the religion of my childhood. I looked in the books I read. I looked at the lives of my peers. I looked for it in my first marriage and subsequent relationships. I tried. I once told a therapist that the epitaph on my gravestone should read, "She tried, she really tried."

I lived in the desert, especially in those years of young adulthood and my first marriage. But paradoxically, living in my inner desert brought me courage and the capacity to recognize the miracle. That Sunday morning when I read the advertisement for Katharine's class on the bulletin board of the Unitarian church in San Francisco, I was ready for the miracle of Katharine's full acceptance of me and what she pointed me toward.

Through these many years I have consented to die, with much struggle to the plans I was making, to the relationships I wanted, to the way I wanted the world to be, to my ego. But my life has been more amazing, more deeply meaningful, more joyful than I could possibly have imagined when I was that teenage girl in the upstairs west bedroom on the farm, wondering, longing, and imagining.

---

50 W. H. Auden, "For the Time Being: A Christmas Oratorio," in *Collected Poems* (New York: Vintage Books, 1991), 353.

Afterword

Dear Reader, as you have read this memoir, I hope you wondered about the rope you were given. If you have wandered in the desert, may you have found your way to the garden. And may you claim your experience of the Mystery—whatever name you use. And know that grace accompanies you all the way.

Acknowledgements

First, my thanks to Katharine Whiteside Taylor, who never knew how her wise wonderings over tea shaped so much of my early adult life, and to my spiritual director, Kay Vander Vort, who companioned me for over thirty-five years. She wept, laughed, and rejoiced with me, and encouraged me to write and to publish, reminding me that we find the universal in the singular. And thank you to Scott McRae, my current spiritual director, especially for his wise interpretation of the Enneagram. Deep gratitude for my peer supervision group, for over forty years of companionship and friendship: for John Ackerman, who died in 2013, leaving us too soon; for Joanne Dehmer, Virginia Matter, and Joel Wiberg, with whom life continues to deepen.

Thank you to Gina Clewley and our sixty years of friendship. You were the first to encourage my writing.

Thank you seems too small a gesture to my family, these dear ones who have supported and loved me. I do not have the right words, so these words will need to suffice. Thank you, thank you, to my sister Gladys and brother-in-law Ray, whose hospitality and generosity shaped my teen and young adult years. To my sister Shirley and brother-in-law Ken, especially for your readiness to live together at ARC and the triplex where we had many conversations about theology, Biblical studies, and community. To my brother, David, and sister-in-law Sally Anne, who have shared my pain and my joy so fully, and certainly longer than anyone else. And for always reminding me that if all else fails, I can come and live with you on the farm and plant potatoes.

Maja, daughter and dear friend, you came into my life at a dark time to invite me to love and to grow for these fifty-plus years. Recently, your conversations and wise editing have been an extra gift. To Kermit for your support, for loving Maja and sharing your family so fully. And to our grandchildren—Eli, Alistair, and Siri. You three continue to be the occasion of surprise, delight, and joy. Finally, my thanks to my husband, Tim, who never doubted I would finish this manuscript, who was always ready to listen and comment, whose solid editing, tech support, and wise responses to content helped bring it into being, and whose love sustained me in my attempt to say something meaningful about the Mystery.

Thank you to Walter Brueggemann whose writings about the Hebrew Psalms—orientation, disorientation, and reorientation—gave me a framework to understand the unfolding of my journey.

I thank many people who have helped me get this memoir into print. My thanks to Elizabeth Andrew whose early prompts and suggestions got me started, to my writing group members—Ranae Hanson, Regula Russelle, Sandra Olson, and Audrey Murray—who traveled with me, reading and commenting on one or two chapters every other month. Thank you to first-draft manuscript readers for their affirmation and recommendations: Joan Wells, Katie Herman, Ted Bowman, Doug Federhart, and Geena Mitchell. Thank you to Becca Emmons and Don Breneman who helped who helped with photos.

Amelia Boulware, friend and editor, your guidance and affirmation were invaluable. My memoir would probably be a series of files in my computer except for your initial encouragement at coffee one morning and your ongoing vision of what my memoir could be.

Thanks to all at Beaver's Pond Press who have brought my memoir into being: thank you to Lily Coyle who welcomed me, and deepest gratitude to my project manager, Alicia Ester, my editor, Kerry Stapley, and book designer, Dan Pitts.

Bibliography

Adams, Ansel, and Nancy Newhall. *This Is the American Earth.* San Francisco: Sierra Club, 1960.

Auden, W. H. *Collected Poems,* edited by Edward Mendelson. New York: Vintage Books, 1991.

Becker, Ernest. *The Birth and Death of Meaning: An Interdisciplinary Perspective on the Problem of Man.* 2nd ed. New York: The Free Press, 1971.

Becker, Ernest. *The Denial of Death.* New York: The Free Press, 1973.

Berry, Wendell. *The Unsettling of America.* San Francisco: Sierra Club, 1986.

Berry, Wendell. *Hannah Coulter.* Washington, DC: Shoemaker Hoard, 2004.

Berry Wendell. *Jayber Crow.* New York: Counterpoint, 2000.

Berryman, Jerome W. *The Complete Guide to Godly Play.* USA: National Council of Churches of Christ [Division of Christian Education], 1971.

Borg, Marcus. *The Heart of Christianity.* New York: HarperOne, 2003.

Borg, Marcus. *Meeting Jesus Again for the First Time.* New York: HarperSanFrancisco, 1994.

Borg, Marcus and N. T. Wright. *The Meaning of Jesus: Two Visions.* New York: HarperCollins, 1999.

Brandenburg, Jim, photography, text by Paul Gruchow. *Minnesota: Images of Home.* Blandin Foundation, 1990.

Brower, David, ed. *Not Man Apart: Lines from Robinson Jeffers.* San Francisco: Sierra Club, 1965.

Buechner, Frederick. *Wishful Thinking: A Theological ABC.* New York: Harper & Row, 1973.

Byock, Ira. *The Four Things That Matter Most.* New York: Simon & Schuster [Free Press division], 2004.

Campbell, Joseph. *The Hero with a Thousand Faces.* 2nd ed. Princeton: Princeton University Press, 1968.

Coffin, William Sloane. *Credo.* Louisville: Westminster John Knox Press, 2004.

Daly, Mary. *Beyond God the Father: Toward a Philosophy of Women's Liberation.* Boston: Beacon Press, 1973.

Dellinger, Drew. *love letter to the milky way: a book of poems.* Ashland, OR: White Cloud Press, 2011.

Dove, Rita, ed. *The Penguin Anthology of Twentieth-Century American Poetry.* New York: Penguin Books, 2011.

de Mello, Anthony. *Sadhana: a Way to God: Christian Exercises in Eastern Form.* St. Louis: The Institute of Jesuit Sources, 1980.

Egan, Timothy. *The Worst Hard Time: The Untold Story of Those Who Survived the Great American Dust Bowl.* Boston: Houghton Mifflin, 2006.

Eisler, Riane. *The Chalice and the Blade: Our History, Our Future.* San Francisco: Harper & Row, 1987.

Eliot, T.S. *Four Quartets.* New York: HarperCollins, 1971.

Fowler, James W. *Stages of Faith: The Psychology of Human Development and the Quest for Meaning.* San Francisco: Harper & Row, 1981.

Matthew Fox, *Meditations With Meister Eckhart*. Santa Fe: Bear & Company, Inc., 1983.

Fox, Matthew. *One River, Many Wells: Wisdom Springing from Global Faiths.* New York: Jeremy P. Tarcher/Putnam, 2000. o Frankl, Viktor. *Man's Search for Meaning.* Boston: Beacon Press, 2017.

Gilligan, Carol. *In a Different Voice: Psychology Theory and Women's Development.* Cambridge, MA: Harvard University Press, 1982.

Gray, Elizabeth Dodson, ed. *Sacred Dimensions of Women's Experience.* Wellesley MA: Roundtable Press, 1988.

Greenblatt, Stephen. *The Rise and Fall of Adam and Eve: The Story That Created Us.* New York: W.W. Norton and Company, 2017.

Gruchow, Paul. *Grass Roots: The Universe of Home.* Minneapolis: Milkweed Editions, 1995.

Hawken, Paul, ed. *Drawdown: The Most Comprehensive Plan Ever Proposed to Reverse Global Warming.* New York: Penguin Books, 2017.

Hopkins, Rob. *The Transition Handbook: From Oil Dependency to Local Resilience.* White River Junction, VT: Chelsea Green Publishing, 2008.

Housden, Roger, ed. *Ten Poems to Change Your Life.* New York: Harmony Books, 2001.

Johnson, Elizabeth A. *She Who Is: The Mystery of God in Feminist Theological Discourse.* New York: Crossroads, 1994.

Johnson, Robert A. *He: Understanding Masculine Psychology.* New York: Harper & Row, 1974.

Johnson, Robert A. *She: Understanding Feminine Psychology.* New York: Harper & Row, 1976.

Johnson, Robert A. *We: Understanding the Psychology of Romantic Love.* San Francisco: Harper & Row, 1983.

Jung, C. G. *The Structure and Dynamics of the Psyche* (*The Collected Works of C. G. Jung, Volume 8*). Translated by R. F. C. Hull. London: Routledge & Kegan Paul, 1969.

Jung, C. G. *Memories, Dreams and Reflections.* New York: Random House, 1965.

Keating, Thomas. *The Human Condition: Contemplation and Transformation.* New York: Paulist Press, 1999.

Keating, Thomas. *Open Mind, Open Heart: The Contemplative Dimension of the Gospel.* New York: Continuum, 1992.

Kelsey, Morton. *The Other Side of Silence: A Guide to Christian Meditation.* New York: Paulist Press, 1976.

Knitter, Paul F. *Without Buddha I Could Not Be a Christian.* Oxford: One World, 2009.

Ladinsky, Daniel, trans. *Love Poems from God: Twelve Sacred Voices from the East and West.* New York: Penguin Compass, 2002.

Levertov, Denise. "The Avowal," *Oblique Prayers: New Poems with 14 Translations from Jean Joubert.* New York: New Directions, 1984.

Marshall, George. *Don't Even Think About It: Why Our Brains Are Wired To Ignore Climate Change.* New York: Bloomsbury, 2015.

McLaren, Brian D. *Do I Stay Christian?* New York: St. Martin's Essentials, 2022.

Merton, Thomas. *New Seeds of Contemplation.* New York: New Directions Publishing, 1972.

Metzger, Bruce M., and Roland E. Murphy, eds. *The New Oxford Annotated Bible.* New York, Oxford University Press, 1994.

Miller, Alice. *The Drama of the Gifted Child: The Search for the True Self.* New York: Basic Books, 1997.

Murphy, Pat. *Plan C: Community Survival Strategies for Peak Oil and Climate Change.* Gabriola Island, BC: New Society Publishers, 2008.

Myers, Isabel Briggs. *Gifts Differing.* Palo Alto, CA: Consulting Psychologists Press, 1980.

Niebuhr, H. Richard. *Christ and Culture.* New York: Harper & Row, 1951.

O'Connor, Elizabeth. *Eighth Day of Creation: Gifts and Creativity.* Waco, TX: Word Books, 1979.

Oliver, Mary. *Thirst.* Boston: Beacon Press, 2006.

Oliver, Mary. *Devotions: The Selected Poems of Mary Oliver.* New York: Penguin Press, 2017.

Palmer, Parker. *Let Your Life Speak: Listening for the Voice of Vocation.* San Francisco: Jossey-Bass, 2000.

Palmer, Parker. *A Hidden Wholeness: The Journey Toward an Undivided Life.* San Francisco: Jossey-Bass, 2004.

Peck, M. Scott. *The Road Less Traveled: A New Psychology of Love, Traditional Values, and Spiritual Growth.* New York: Simon & Schuster, 1978.

Phillips, Dorothy Berkley, ed. *The Choice Is Always Ours: An Anthology on the Religious Way.* Wheaton, IL: Re-Quest Books, 1975.

Plotkin, Bill. *Nature and the Human Soul: Cultivating Wholeness and Community in a Fragmented World.* Novato, CA: New World Library, 2008.

Riso, Don Richard, and Russ Hudson. *The Wisdom of the Enneagram: The Complete Guide to Psychological and Spiritual Growth for the Nine Personality Types.* New York: Bantam Books,1999.

Rohr, Richard. *Immortal Diamond: The Search for Our True Self.* San Francisco: Jossey-Bass, 2013.

Rohr, Richard. *The Universal Christ: How a Forgotten Reality Can Change Everything We See, Hope For, and Believe.* New York: Penguin Random House,2019.

Rosling, Hans. "Global health expert; data visionary," TED Talks, accessed April 12, 2021, https://www.ted.com/speakers/hans_rosling.

Rumi. *The Essential Rumi: New Expanded Edition,* trans. Colman Barks. New York: HarperOne, 2004.

Singh, Kathleen Dowling. *Unbinding: The Grace Beyond Self.* Sommerville, MA: Wisdom, 2017.

Singh, Kathleen Dowling. *The Grace in Aging: Awaken as You Grow Older.* Sommerville ,MA: Wisdom Publications, 2014.

Steere, Douglas V. *Gleanings: A Random Harvest.* Nashville: Upper Room, 1986.

Swimme, Brian and Thomas Berry. *The Universe Story: From the Primordial Flaring Forth to the Ecozoic Age – A Celebration of the Unfolding of the Cosmos.* New York: HarperSanFrancisco , 1994.

Tillich, Paul. *The Shaking of the Foundations,* New York: Charles Scribner's Sons, 1948.

Transition Town – All St. Anthony Park. Accessed October 21, 2023. https://www.transitionasap.org.

Vander Vort, Kay, Joan H. Timmerman, Eleanor Lincoln, eds. *Walking in Two Worlds: Women's Spiritual Paths,* St. Cloud, MN: North Star Press, 1992.

Wickes, Frances G. *The Inner World of Choice.* Englewood Cliffs, NJ: Prentice-Hall, 1976.

Wink, Walter. *Transforming Bible Study: A Leader's Guide.* Nashville: Abingdon Press, 1980.

Wink, Walter. *Engaging the Powers: Discernment and Resistance in a World of Dominance.* Minneapolis: Augsburg Fortress, 1992.

Wohlleben, Peter. *The Hidden Life of Trees: What They Feel, How They Communicate.* Vancouver: Greystone Books, 2015.